Reading Engagement for Tweens and Teens

Reading Engagement for Tweens and Teens

What Would Make Them Read More?

Margaret K. Merga

LIBRARIES
UNLIMITED™
An Imprint of ABC-CLIO, LLC
Santa Barbara, California • Denver, Colorado

Library of Congress Cataloging-in-Publication Data

Names: Merga, Margaret K., author.
Title: Reading engagement for tweens and teens : what would make them read
   more? / Margaret K. Merga.
Description: Santa Barbara, California : Libraries Unlimited, [2019] |
   Includes bibliographical references and index.
Identifiers: LCCN 2018028656 (print) | LCCN 2018044249 (ebook) |
   ISBN 9781440867996 (ebook) | ISBN 9781440867989 (hard copy : alk. paper)
Subjects: LCSH: Reading promotion. | Preteens—Books and reading. |
   Teenagers—Books and reading. | Reading (Middle school) | Reading
   (Secondary)
Classification: LCC Z1003 (ebook) | LCC Z1003 .M547 2019 (print) |
   DDC 028.5/5—dc23
LC record available at https://lccn.loc.gov/2018028656

ISBN: 978-1-4408-6798-9 (paperback)
      978-1-4408-6799-6 (ebook)

23 22 21 20 19   1 2 3 4 5

This book is also available as an eBook.

Libraries Unlimited
An Imprint of ABC-CLIO, LLC

ABC-CLIO, LLC
130 Cremona Drive, P.O. Box 1911
Santa Barbara, California 93116-1911
www.abc-clio.com

This book is printed on acid-free paper ∞

Manufactured in the United States of America

Contents

Acknowledgments

I was strongly motivated to write this book after presenting my talks as a volunteer Older Reader judge for the Children's Book Council of Australia Awards. I cannot describe how amazing it was to discover that my research could be so valued, so I would like to thank the enthusiastic teachers and librarians who were so keenly interested in my research in this area. It's always nice to discover the things that obsess you are of interest to other people in the real world. I would also like to thank the attendees at my presentation at the International Literacy Association in Florida in 2017 for the selfies and for asking me if I was writing a book—it motivated me to write faster.

I would like to thank my children, Sam and Gabe, for being patient with me, for dragging me out of my nerd state back into humanity, and for respecting the "no spoilers" decree (most of the time!). Thanks to my husband Marián for always supporting me and making *excellent* food. Thanks to my parents for making books available to me as a child, for taking me to the library a lot, and for giving me time and space to read. Extra thanks must go to my mum, who provided great feedback on the early drafts of this book.

Thanks to Curtin, Murdoch, and Edith Cowan Universities who have supported my research. Thanks to my mate and colleague Dr. Saiyidi Mat Roni for being both a highly valued collaborator and an inspiration (bro', your genius is unnatural). Thanks to Dr. Susan Ledger, collaborator on the RAS project and generous former neighbor in the Murdoch Education building. Thanks to Dr. Leonie Rutherford, Michelle McRae, Associate Professor Katya Johanson, and the rest of the Deakin team for fun times in Melbourne and for sharing the challenge of engaging young people in reading. I would also like to thank my former doctoral supervisor and coauthor Associate Professor Brian Moon, who allowed me free reign on my PhD and who built my sense of confidence in my research by allowing me high autonomy. Your enabling attitude gave me the confidence and space to find my passion for research. Thanks to Dr. Julia Morris for being a great colleague, friend, and inspiration and to Associate Professor Laura Perry for the supportive mentoring.

I also thank Professor Daniel Callison for approaching me to express his interest in my work and for recommending my work to the publisher. I am grateful for the amazing support that I received from Sharon Coatney at ABC-CLIO. I would also like to thank the editorial team at ABC-CLIO for their hard work in polishing my book.

I need to thank all of the schools, teachers, teacher librarians, and parents who have been involved in my research, and each child who took the time to answer my questions and share ideas with me. This book really is for you.

Introduction

If you are reading this book, you are probably already an engaged reader. If this is the case, you have experienced firsthand the benefits that being a reader confers upon you. You probably have a wide vocabulary and a strong command of grammar. It is likely that you can string together an effective sentence without breaking a sweat. As a reader, you have the luxury of taking for granted a range of literacy skills that may pose a significant challenge for those who do not read regularly.

However, I doubt that many of you approach reading with one goal—to improve your literacy outcomes—though this may be a factor in your engagement. Few of us would sit down with a book with the isolated purpose of improving our communicative capacity. We typically read for recreation because we enjoy it. This joy can come from many diverse factors, as I explore in this book, but the pleasure afforded by reading would be the primary motivation for most of us to engage in the practice.

As you have selected this book, I imagine that you have a keen desire to awaken this level of reading engagement in others, to justify your role as a literacy educator or advocate, and to look for new and novel ways to shape the attitudes of the young people in your life toward reading books. As a teacher, parent, librarian, or other literacy advocate, you are no doubt aware that reading—book reading in particular—is known to confer a range of benefits upon the reader. However, you may also have questioned whether books and reading have continued relevance in the so-called Digital Age. Blaring media headlines announce that the book is dead, that libraries are obsolete, and that the future is digital. These dire announcements and prognostications may give us pause; while these proclamations are usually debunked in a timely manner (e.g., Darnton, 2011), we retain a sense of unease. We want to provide learning that is relevant, engaging, and important for our children and students, but what if we are fighting for a lost cause?

In addition, the amount of time our young people spend engaged in alternative recreational pursuits may make us wonder whether, realistically, we can anything do to ensure the transmission of a love of reading. We note that books compete against a range of pursuits that can give more immediate gratification, that may be more highly valued in the peer and home communities, and that may be more readily accessible. It is likely that you may, at some time, have wondered how much of a difference you can make when it comes to instilling a love of books and reading in young people, particularly teenagers, who are constructed as highly autonomous and potentially immune to some forms of adult influence. As adults, we hope that surely there is much we can do to get them reading more, especially when we may note the negative effects of some of the activities that occupy their recreational time, such as the popular pursuit of online computer gaming (King et al., 2018). But can we shape or even change young people's attitudes toward books and reading? And if we can, how can we best act to effectively support the fostering of a lifelong love of reading?

A number of interesting and useful books have been written in this area, offering practical suggestions for fostering a love of reading in young people. While many of them are excellent and highly valuable contributions to an educator's or advocate's tool kit, what some of these books may lack is a strong, robust, and current research base, upon which these recommendations are based. While anecdote and personal experience can be invaluable resources for building best practice knowledge, there are risks in solely or strongly relying on this information base. As you will discover in this book, a number of myths about children and reading have such traction in society that they dictate policy and practice, despite a lack of sound supporting evidence. The idea that all young people prefer to read on screens is one such myth that I address in this book. When we drill down into the genesis of these myths and explore the stereotypes they perpetuate, their continued proliferation is concerning. This book is directly responsive to the current research in this field, and it seeks to tackle some of the myths that inexplicably thrive in the advocacy environment.

As I explore in my final chapter, research is not perfect, and all methods and approaches are burdened with inherent and emergent limitations. Nonetheless, a research base remains the most important foundation for best practice if we want to avoid the errors of subjectivity, and if we want to mount a strong argument for reading engagement with school administrators and the broader community. From the numerous e-mails in my university inbox and messages on my ResearchGate account, I know that literacy educators and advocates actually need access to empirical data to keep afloat and to justify maintaining their advocacy role and resourcing allocation. Sometimes when we ask for money to buy fresh new books or try to put aside regular time for reading in the school day, we are asked by an administrator or our employers to "show me the benefit." This response may frustrate us, particularly when the same administrators and employers do not necessarily insist on seeing the research benefit of the latest shiny new educational fashions and toys on which the budget is spent.

Those of us who work in this space know that literacy is so important, but, at present, it is not that fashionable. In our urgent need to meet the needs of 21st-century learners, somehow it is easy for some to forget that literacy is still crucial. For instance, in present times, we are consuming written information in massive quantities on a daily basis, and, without strong literacy skills, we lack the power conferred by communicative competence. We need the research so that when literacy advocates need to fight for book supply funds or for time in the crowded curriculum for school-based silent reading, success is more likely. We may also need the research to justify our very existence as the unique and powerful contributions of some literacy educators, such as teacher librarians, are not always well understood, as I explore further in this volume. Our own communicative power is enhanced when we can put forward a cogent, research-supported argument.

It is particularly important that the research body being drawn upon includes recent findings, as young people's ideas and preferences in relation to reading tend to evolve over time. For this reason, much of the research cited in this book is less than a decade old. Though some far older, seminal works are also referenced, this has been kept to a minimum to serve the purposes of this book.

In what may feel like an ever increasing number of barriers to facilitating reading, we need current, high-quality, and reputable weaponry in our arsenal. So, while I am aware that books without a sound research base can be really helpful and will often reflect similar conclusions, you will not find them frequently cited here, as I need to privilege evidence-based research in this book so that it is fit for our purpose. In addition, while this book will focus on tweens (aged 8–12) and teens (aged 13–19), it also draws on relevant research from younger children and adults, typically where what happens before and after these years is relevant.

My role as an academic researcher focuses on book reading as an educational and social practice, a research area I moved into after I left teaching English (known in the U.S. as English Language Arts) to focus on chasing answers to some of the questions that I had previously pondered as an educator in schools. When I am not teaching at university, conducting research in schools, speaking at events, or performing the other diverse roles that are part of academic life, I spend my days closely reading the existing research in this area and publishing peer-reviewed papers to report on my recent research findings. My work has been published in a wide range of peer-reviewed international literacy, education, and librarianship journals. I have spoken at an array of research and education events both in Australia and internationally, and my research has recently been well received by the media.

I am really passionate about research translation. My findings must be useful to someone, somewhere, or my research is not worth conducting, and I should get back into the classroom full-time where I know I can make a concrete difference every day. While I know that librarians, teachers, and parents are making use of my findings because you have told me so, sometimes my research papers, which are typically written in a rather dry academic voice, are not the most interesting and accessible pieces of communication. I thought I would try to bring it all together (so far) in a book that can be used by literacy educators and advocates as a reference point for key issues or that can simply be read from cover to cover by someone seeking an overview of the recent issues in this area.

My background as an energetic and active researcher means that I have personally collected some of the data that informs this book. As mentioned previously, I have been involved in several reading studies in recent times, and these projects have continued to flesh out my understanding of what would make young people read more. Not all of the reading research has immediate practical relevance, perhaps instead making a contribution to the formulation of a theory or some other important function. However, most of my papers do have immediate practical implications for teachers, librarians, and/or parents. For instance, I have *literally* asked teens and tweens what would make them read more and published their views (see Merga, 2016a; Merga, 2017c). These findings can guide our interventions to increase young people's reading engagement. While I will report on a wide range of research studies in this book, I will draw heavily on the recent quantitative, qualitative, and mixed-methods research in this area with which I have been involved.

Table I.1   Brief Summary of My Recent Reading Research

Study	Years	Sample and Size	Co-researchers and/or Coauthors	Funder
Western Australian Study in Adolescent Book Reading (WASABR)	2012–2014	520 adolescents at 20 schools	Brian Moon	Australian Postgraduate Award
International Study of Avid Book Readers (ISABR)	2015–2016	1,136 avid readers from 84 countries	Saiyidi Mat Roni	Murdoch University School of Education Strategic Funding
Western Australian Study in Children's Book Reading (WASCBR)	2015–2017	997 children at 24 schools	Saiyidi Mat Roni	Ian Potter Foundation
Teen Reading in the Digital Era	2015–2017	555 adolescents at 13 schools	Leonie Rutherford, Michelle McRae, Katya Johanson, Lisa Waller, Elizabeth Bullen, and Andrew Singleton	Deakin University Central Research Grants Scheme and Copyright Agency Cultural Fund
Western Australian Study in Reading Aloud (WASRA) (also known as For the Love of Reading project)	2016–2017	624 respondents involved with 21 schools 220 children (7 schools) 303 parents, 101 teachers (14 schools)	Susan Ledger	Collier Charitable Foundation
*Teacher Librarians as Literature and Literacy Advocates in Schools (TLLLAS)	2018–2019	30 teacher librarians in Western Australian schools	None at this stage	Copyright Agency Cultural Fund

*Project in progress; results are anticipated in 2019–2020.

A brief overview of these studies is available in Table I.1; for greater detail, you are advised to visit the appendices at the back of this book, though researchers seeking further depth will need to refer to the academic papers cited in this book for a more fulsome description of the research.

These studies were a great opportunity to place children's views at the center of my research. As adult researchers, we often make assumptions that tend to lump all young children together, while as adults, we insist on having our diversity recognized. If I have learned anything from my research, it is that while there are certain very interesting and important general trends in the findings, at the end of the day, to influence young people to read more, we need to understand their individual preferences and desires, as well as account for the wide range of influential factors that I also explore in this book.

The good news is that both my research and the work of many others suggest that books are not dead and that social influences like you can play a powerful role as advocates for book reading. Young people can be inspired to read more by the powerful social influences in their lives. I hope you find this edition both a useful tool and an interesting read.

I

Why Is Book Reading (Still) Important?

This chapter will explore the range of benefits of recreational reading for numerous literacy outcomes. It also touches on emerging research linking reading to benefits for cognitive stamina as well as empathy and pleasure. In addition, I argue that there is insufficient evidence to suggest other text types can offer benefits equal to those of books, with fiction books particularly associated with benefit. The impact of socioeconomic factors is also introduced here.

As adults, we typically have busy lives, and most tweens and teens do too. Just as book reading can struggle to compete with other required and recreational activities in our lives, the same occurs in young people's everyday lives. Book reading does not give the instant dopamine rewards of first-person shooter gaming (Weinstein, 2010), and, with some notable exceptions, books are not often promoted through advertisement on the same level as the latest toys, technological devices, movies, or television shows.

For example, for the teenager speaking next, as for many others, reading simply could not compete with other recreational possibilities at this stage of his life. For this student, playing online games was a fun and socially rewarding pastime.

I: So, tell me how you feel about reading books in your free time.

T: Well, it's fun, but I don't do it much because, I'm normally playing sport or playing games.

I: So, what do you do more, play sport or play games?

T: Mostly games.

I: What kinds of games do you play?

T: Usually online games where I play with my friends, and you know, I play the ones where you run around [laughs] and you know, stab each other and stuff like that.

Recreational reading is not necessarily promoted as a valuable pastime at school and at home. Book reading does not immediately align with the needs of high-stakes testing at school; though book reading can play a very important role in helping young people to achieve their required literacy outcomes, we tend not to test engagement in recreational reading. While that is a good thing, because we do not test it, contemporary schools may not necessarily value it. In addition, many parents and teachers do not fully understand the importance of reading beyond the early years, so their ability to share a valuing of the practice with their children and students can be limited. In many contexts, the school curriculum is so heavily laden with competing demands and priorities, finding time at school for what may be seen as an optional extra may be challenge, even for teachers with the best intentions.

We also know that young people appear to be reading books less frequently in general. International research suggests that young people's engagement in reading for pleasure is in decline (Common Sense Media, 2014; Organisation for Economic Co-operation and Development [OECD], 2011a; Scholastic, 2015). We need to communicate the value of reading so that it is seen as a pastime worth the investment of young people's valuable and often scant time. Despite the dire statistics showing reading declines, young people *can* be keen readers. We should not be disheartened; rather, we should continue to actively encourage our young people to both establish and maintain a lifelong love of reading. Promoting positive attitudes toward reading is an essential starting point, as I further explain in this chapter.

ATTITUDES AND ACHIEVEMENT

Keen readers read more often. Unsurprisingly, young people's attitudes toward reading influence their willingness to engage in the practice, as well as their ultimate literacy attainment. Regular readers experience the literacy benefits of reading that lower the skill barriers to further reading and to reading more complex texts. This is why reading "will" is so important; motivation to read is an essential starting point, a neglected but essential factor in successful reading (De Naeghel et al., 2014). To become effective readers, young people must have both the skill and the will to read (Gambrell, 1996), and the mutually reinforcing relationship between these two aspects needs to be recognized.

The focus in literacy education in the United States, Australia, and worldwide is heavily concentrated on skill acquisition and particularly targeted toward the skills that children typically develop in the early years of schooling. However, the role of pleasure and reading will should also be an essential consideration, primarily due to the relationship between reading skill and reading will. Understanding how to effectively foster positive attitudes in young people toward reading is essential to form and build reading skills. As enjoyment of reading is positively associated with literacy achievement (Lupo, Jang, & McKenna, 2017; OECD, 2011a), encouraging children to be lifelong readers is an educational imperative.

However, fostering a love of reading is not always the curricular priority that it should be. For example, I recently conducted a content analysis of Australian whole-school literacy policies and plans with my colleague Veronica Gardiner. We found that both lower and upper schools did not typically promote reading engagement as part of a whole-school approach to literacy (Merga & Gardiner, under review). Until our curriculum documents are strongly supportive of the fostering of reading engagement, it is not a great surprise that schools do not prioritize it.

There are many ways to address this issue of fostering reading engagement in tweens and teens, and this book does not argue for the use of one "right" way. It does not suggest that pedagogical strategies such as sustained silent reading or reading aloud can address these concerns in isolation, though they are powerful tools in addressing the issue. While I will discuss the importance of approaches such as these, my work aims to increase recognition of the social nature of reading and the power of social influences in shaping young people's attitudes toward reading.

Here again, I do not claim that one source of social influence will make all the difference. Parents and teachers alone may achieve much, but literacy advocates can also be very effective when they work together. As I will explain, social influences can be effectively expressed across a great range of approaches, and many different people can exert a positive influence on a young person, shaping their attitudes toward reading.

The kinds of influences that have been deemed effective are wide and varied. For instance, while one child might see being extrinsically rewarded for his reading with points toward a book voucher as not very motivating, for another it might be a valued starting point that, when combined with other supportive approaches, helps the student transition into a lifelong reader. One child may become a reader after years of shared reading aloud with her father before bed, the dog warming her feet, while another may be inspired by a teacher librarian who is extremely enthusiastic about dragons and who knows where all of the *good* dragon books are. The English teacher (also known as an English Language Arts teacher in the United States) who finds the perfect series for a disengaged teen and who really understands what he likes after taking the time to get to know him may support a complete attitude change. All of these avenues and influences and more are explored in various forms in this book. We can begin increasing the desire to develop reading will in our schools by increasing the understanding of the relationship between regular reading and the potential benefits that it confers in the influential adults in our students' lives, recognizing that our motivation to perform a particular task can be related to how we view its importance or value (Wigfield & Eccles, 2000).

As educators, parents, and literacy advocates seeking to improve young people's engagement in reading, we understand that it does not matter how much we personally love reading behind closed doors if this attitude is not translated. We need to be seen as models, but we also need to try to amass as many allies as possible. As I will explain, not all children recognize that regular reading is important, but, then again, not all teachers and parents understand and/or demonstrate an understanding of the importance of regular recreational reading, so how should tweens and teens gain this knowledge if we confine the project of attitudinal intervention to young people only? As such, fostering this valuing of reading to increase motivation is not just about improving young people's attitudes toward reading; we also need to increase the valuing of the activity within the homes and schools in our communities. While we may assume that all teachers strongly value recreational reading, and we may hope that parents share these sentiments, research, which I will explore in this book, suggests that these are not assumptions we can confidently make, and thus the project of increasing the valuing of recreational reading extends to all potential literacy advocates, not just the young people with whom we are concerned.

While I will touch on the range of *literacy* benefits conferred though reading engagement to support this starting point, I think it is also important to highlight new and broader directions in the research around reading benefit, which suggest that the range of benefits on offer when delving deeply and regularly into reading is substantial. I will also highlight the research support for the relative literacy benefit of written text types, in response to the broad understanding of what constitutes a written text in the contemporary world and curriculum. As such, if you have ever wondered whether the reading of text messages and e-mails stacks up against the reading of books in terms of literacy outcomes, this chapter will give you some current insights into this area.

READING AND LITERACY BENEFITS

It is pretty much a given that if we want to get better at something, we need to practice it. Whether this involves getting into a regular running program to take on a half marathon or learning another language, there is no way to get around it (though I am looking forward to the day that we really can learn French in our sleep). While we generally associate reading with benefit, the range of benefits has expanded in recent times to encompass a broader range of literacy benefits and also to offer benefits that extend beyond literacy. When I touch on these areas while delivering seminars and professional development sessions, parents, students, and teachers are often surprised by the power of reading. We need to share these benefits so that they are less of a surprise and are instead common knowledge that can subsequently influence how our young people allocate the leisure time that they have at their disposal.

While much of the research on the benefits of regular reading focuses on the early years, in recent times there has been greater research interest in this area, so that reading can be better understood as a valuable practice beyond this time of life. Time spent reading is closely related to reading achievement on a broad range of literacy indicators (Anderson, Wilson, & Fielding, 1988; Moore, Bean, Birdyshaw, & Rycik, 1999; OECD, 2010; Taylor, Frye, & Maruyama, 1990). Specifically, the cognitive advantages conferred by regular reading lead to improved syntactic knowledge, word recognition, and vocabulary (Cunningham & Stanovich, 1998; Stanovich, 1986; Sullivan & Brown, 2013), as well as benefits for reading comprehension, spelling, and oral language skills (Mol & Bus, 2011). Berns, Blaine, Prietula, and Pye (2013) found that reading in adulthood may offer immediate benefits in brain connectivity "which persisted for several days" after the reading experience (p. 590). Exposure to new words through reading during the school years is felt to account for a substantial proportion of vocabulary acquisition during that period (Nagy, Herman, & Anderson, 1985). Krashen (2012) contends that "there is good reason to hypothesize that academic vocabulary is acquired gradually through genuine academic reading for the readers' own purposes and that this path is more effective and efficient than even rich instruction" (p. 233), though further research comparing the efficacy of the two approaches is desirable. Recent research suggests that while tweens tend to show rapid orthographic learning from incidental exposure to language, this "fast learning is only partial learning" (Tamura, Castles, & Nation, 2017, p. 101); more exposure is needed for meaning to be fully constructed. This underscores the importance of regular reading frequency, which can both expedite and enhance this meaning-making process.

Benefits are related to reading frequency and volume, with research suggesting that the more time young people spend engaged in recreational reading, the greater the benefits for their reading comprehension and vocabulary (Samuels & Wu, 2001). Allington's (2014) review of the related research also found that the volume of reading was important, leading him to suggest that "if educators hope to improve either the oral reading fluency or the reading comprehension of struggling readers then expanding reading volume, it seems, must necessarily be considered" (p. 17). Stanovich et al. (1996) challenged the idea that only struggling students stand to benefit from increasing their reading engagement, finding that reading is beneficial regardless of cognitive and comprehension abilities; as long as the individuals in question have basic reading skills, regular reading practice will develop reading abilities. Spichtig and colleagues (2016) found that "present-day students are less efficient readers than their 1960 counterparts," observing a likely "decline in word recognition automaticity" (p. 252). While they suggest that further research is needed to explain why current U.S. students struggle with reading compared with their 1960s counterparts, Spichtig et al. (2016) suggest that "insufficient silent reading practice" could be one of the "plausible contributing factors" (p. 253). Spichtig, Pascoe, Ferrara, & Vorstius (2017) recently discussed the low reading rates of graduating high school students in the United States, where "nearly two-thirds (63%) of U.S. 12th grade students are not proficient in reading and 28% fail to demonstrate even a basic level of reading achievement" (p. 12). They put this disadvantage of poor silent reading efficiency into perspective, showing how it can be a significant impediment to reading comprehension:

> When reading is this slow and arduous, it is likely to be difficult for the reader to sustain the level of attention that close reading requires. Moreover, students who read this slowly are likely to be devoting a considerable portion of their cognitive resources to decoding and sounding out words or trying to figure out what words mean, and will therefore find it difficult to focus on the broader meaning of what they are reading. (p. 12)

In this way, infrequent reading can lead to more slowly developing reading skills, which in turn inhibit the reading of more complex texts. I explore the impact of this Matthew effect in more detail in Chapter 2.

These benefits uncovered in the research must translate into plain language so that we can explain them to young people and their parents. Simply, the more we read, the better we will be at reading. The research also means that reading can help us to recognize words so that we can read them again more easily in the future, and it can also expand the range of words that we feel confident using in order to communicate. It can help us to spell difficult words, it can make us better speakers, and it can improve our ability to understand writing, so that we can find the meaning in what is written. We will not have to work as hard to make sense of complex texts, and we will be able to read more in less time. It is easy to see the practical advantages of these research findings when we translate them into more accessible language: Most young people and their parents would be able to look at their own lives and their unique literacy needs and find areas in which improving these skills could be highly beneficial.

We also need to discuss the overarching benefits of enhanced literacy skills. We need to make it clear that communication is powerful and that literacy skills enhance our power as communicators. It can be argued that literacy is more important in our contemporary world than ever before; our young people need high-order literacy skills to succeed (Moje, Young, Readence, & Moore, 2000). The ability to understand what we learn through reading a variety of different written texts— from addressing selection criteria for our first jobs, to accurately reading exam questions, to decoding e-mails from our romantic partners (is she really that into me?)—is at times crucial to our academic, vocational, and social success. The fact that our literacy level can impact all three of these dimensions is not always well understood by young people, who may be quick to dismiss literacy as a learning or testing "thing" and not see its broader importance and implications. As parents and literacy educators, we may tend to stress the benefits for academic attainment. The reality is that not all children necessarily care that much about that, particularly if they have already lost confidence in their ability to achieve in literacy, which often occurs if they have compared their ability to peers in terms of literacy testing scores. The importance of literacy extends far beyond the immediate, though young people do not necessarily grasp this (Merga & Mat Roni, 2018c).

As a result, I think that it is really important to point out that, while literacy skills will be very useful for performing well at school, we also need to be aware that they can help us in our jobs, and, perhaps more importantly to some, it can also help us socially, as it can help us to communicate more effectively with others (and make better arguments). So much of our social interaction is mediated through written, auditory, and oral exchanges that are commonly facilitated through technology in the current times. Reading is not just for school; it is about work beyond school, and it is about our everyday texts, social media posts, negotiations of train timetables, and the backs of our cereal boxes. Young people who understand the broad importance of reading and who enjoy it are more likely to be readers, as I explain in this book.

Some tweens, such as Louise, understand this importance, at least to some extent. Others do not.

> I think that it is extremely important to read in . . . school. It helps you to prepare for later experiences in life that include reading. Also, reading is just naturally fun! I love imagining characters and different settings described in the book. I also like to think thoroughly about the book I'm reading. I also enjoy collecting different sets of books. I don't mind what type or genre of the book. I also don't mind if the book has pictures or not. In fact, most books I read don't have any pictures at all.

Reading is also potentially good for our brains and well-being. Regular reading has been associated with resistance to cognitive issues into old age, as it may offer a protective effect to resist dementia (e.g., Lopes, Ferrioli, Nakano, Litvoc, & Bottino, 2011; Vemuri & Mormino 2013; Verghese et al., 2003; Wilson et al., 2002; Wilson et al., 2013), so encouraging our young people to become lifelong readers can offer extended benefits for health. Vemuri and colleagues (2014) found that reading books in mid- and late life may offer more than three years of protection for at-risk individuals, and more than seven years for those not at risk. Regular reading is also associated with benefits beyond literacy, such as improved performance in mathematics (Sullivan & Brown, 2013), and even longevity (Bavishi, Slade, & Levy, 2016). While we need to learn more about these potential benefits through further research, at this stage they are worth noting.

IS THERE A TARGET?

I am often asked how frequently young people should read in order to experience literacy benefit. I totally understand this need for a target, as in our lives we are consistently trying to find balance between all of the competing requirements that we juggle. We know how many fruits and vegetables we need to consume for good physical health, and likewise it is handy to know how many books we need to consume in order to experience optimal literacy benefit. While obviously, we would encourage young people to read as often as possible, the research suggests that daily reading is associated with higher performance on literacy assessments (Institute of Education Sciences [IES], 2011; OECD, 2011c).

Reading regularly is arguably more important than doing homework every day. An analysis of diminishing returns for time invested in homework and recreational reading in early adolescence found a positive association between reading frequency and achievement, and it also found that returns for time invested in homework diminished far sooner than those spent on reading, which exhibited "far more gradual diminishing returns extending to six or seven times per week" (Walberg & Tsai, 1984, p. 449). This is why we should encourage our children and students to be daily recreational book readers (Merga, 2014c).

However, some of the young people who participated in my research were reprimanded for reading when they were supposed to be doing their homework. For instance, Samuel, a student in Year 4, explained that "sometimes I get in trouble for doing it, because I do it at the wrong time," "basically when I'm getting dressed, and sometimes when I'm doing my homework," "and maybe even when it's dinner time, I will probably keep reading for a couple of seconds." I would argue that the message that homework is more important than reading for a boy of 9 may need rethinking in light of the research. Homework was also identified as a barrier to reading by teens in the WASABR, such as by this student:

> Due to the amount of homework given to us at the school, it is very hard to try and fit reading in, and even if you end up having a little bit of time, you are generally so exhausted you don't feel like sitting down and reading, you just want to stop thinking.

As such, educators could consider moderating the amount of homework issued and communicate an expectation that some of the spare time be used for reading, which is of educative benefit.

I am also often asked how many books we should read, but when I look at the variability in size, font, and width of the books on my shelf, I admittedly shrug at this, as I do not think it is the most useful target. Suggestions around the number of books that should be read are less helpful due to the variation in book size and complexity; "read every day" is a simpler message.

I might recommend reading for an hour a day where possible, though this suggestion can be met with incredulity, as though an hour is a really long time. When we compare this suggestion with the amount of time young people typically spend on online recreational pursuits such as watching videos, chatting on social networking forums, and playing games online, which are not strongly associated with educative benefit (and may even pose health risks) (Merga, 2015b), it is not actually that unreasonable a suggestion. However, we want reading to be associated with pleasure and enjoyment, so simply demanding that children or students read for recreation an hour a day is unlikely to yield a positive result in terms of fostering a lifelong reader, unless this expectation is balanced with consideration of how to support the child to both find and access books that are enjoyable and at an accessible skill level.

LITERACY, OPPORTUNITY, AND TESTING

I would like to return to the advantages of regular reading and its links to achievement. Literacy is strongly related to academic performance beyond lower school (Daggett & Hasselbring, 2007; Marks, McMillan, & Hillman, 2001). While literacy has always been important for academic achievement, for better or for worse, increasing emphasis on international literacy testing and benchmarking has increased the visibility of current literacy levels. Literacy is also increasingly recognized as an essential skill for achievement in other subjects beyond English (or English Language Arts). In the United States, the Common Core State Standards recognize the importance of literacy skills for achievement in subjects beyond the English Language Arts, positioning literacy as a cross-disciplinary responsibility:

> The Standards insist that instruction in reading, writing, speaking, listening, and language be a shared responsibility within the school. The K–5 standards include expectations for reading, writing, speaking, listening, and language applicable to a range of subjects, including but not limited to ELA. The grades 6–12 standards are divided into two sections, one for ELA and the other for history/social studies, science, and technical subjects. This division reflects the unique, time-honored place of ELA teachers in developing students' literacy skills while at the same time recognizing that teachers in other areas must have a role in this development as well. (Council of Chief State School Officers [CCSSO], 2010, p. 4)

U.S. research has increasingly focused on developing literacy skills across core areas other than English (as explored in Heller & Greenleaf, 2007). Similarly, in Australia, the relatively new Australian Curriculum positions literacy as a General Capability, to be demonstrated across all learning areas, including everything from math and science to sport. This recognition gives credence to the role that literacy has always played in other areas; for instance, a child who fails a math test based on word problems may fail due to poor reading comprehension rather than low numeracy skills. This is one of the reasons that literacy skills are not just about performance in the English classroom or even in writing. Literacy skills are absolutely foundational, gateway skills to achievement across the subjects.

Since 2003, U.S. children in grades 4 and 8 have participated in reading assessments that test a range of literacy skills, such as reading comprehension and vocabulary (NAEP, 2016). In Australia, literacy skills are something that are subject to national assessment even earlier (Year 3) as well as more often (Years 3, 5, 7, and 9). Children commonly participate in high-stakes testing from the point of expected independent reading skill acquisition as part of the National Assessment Program–Literacy and Numeracy (NAPLAN). In the UK, testing begins even earlier, in Year 2, when children are typically only six or seven years old. The rationale for this test is as follows:

> The tests are a tool for teachers to help them measure your child's performance and identify their needs as they move into key stage 2. They also allow teachers to see how your child is performing against national expected standards. (Standards and Testing Agency, 2018, p. 2)

Testing is also done in the UK in Year 6 to "help measure the progress pupils have made and identify if they need additional support in a certain area" and "to assess schools' performance and to produce national performance data" (p. 3).

While high-stakes national testing can play a role in the early identification of learning issues and can help identify areas where schools need to build capacity and support, research suggests that high-stakes testing changes the way that students are taught (see Polesel, Dulfer, & Turnbull, 2012 for a review). These issues are common in contemporary schooling; for instance, in the UK, the Office for Standards in Education, Children's Services and Skills (Ofsted) (2012) continues to observe "inappropriate attention at too early a stage to the skills needed for external tests and examinations" (p. 15). There is also a strong assessment orientation in the United States. School reforms "can be best summed up in three words: standards, accountability, and testing" (Wamba, 2010, p. 190).

However, we are currently at an interesting position. There is a growing acceptance that high-stakes testing has failed to yield any educative benefit, leading to calls for a review or overhaul of these high-stakes testing regimes (e.g., Perelman, 2018). Perhaps we will no longer expect that relentlessly weighing the pig will make it fatter, and I am heartened by the manner in which inauthentic literacy experiences associated with assessment that have been privileged in the classroom are being soundly critiqued (Perelman, 2018). Most parents and literacy educators who have been involved with preparing students for high-stakes literacy testing are frustrated with the kind of teaching and learning environments and experiences that these mechanisms typically foster. The sacrifice of the volume of learning time involved in testing preparation would be worth it only if we saw some kind of educative benefit. To date, this is simply not the case. Some might argue that it is the emperor's new clothes moment that we had to have, and perhaps we can now all stop pretending that subjecting students to poorly designed high-stakes testing is in any way a beneficial educative experience, as we have the stagnant literacy scores to prove this (Hinz & O'Connell, 2016).

In the United States, "despite innumerable efforts to reinvent and reform education," student performance in reading is actually worsening, with the SES (socioeconomic status) achievement gap growing (Neuman & Knapczyk, 2018, p. 2). We know that "half of all students in the U.S. complete high school with reading rates that are far below or at best comparable to typical conversational speaking rates in

English" (Spichtig et al., 2017, p. 12). Spichtig and colleagues (2016) describe how educational reform initiatives in the United States have "placed a considerable emphasis on improving reading performance, recognising that reading volume and content play a key role" in skills development (p. 254). It is well accepted that increasing reading volume confers literacy benefits; however, how can we increase the reading volume of our young people is less well recognized. We know that it is unlikely to magically just happen.

In Australia, low literacy can prevent students from attaining their secondary education certificate. For example, the Online Literacy and Numeracy Assessment (OLNA) is an additional high-stakes test recently added in Western Australia. The OLNA is taken by students who do not attain Band 8 in Year 9. This means that students who are typically aged 13 to 15 need to demonstrate an adult level of literacy proficiency in order to avoid the OLNA, as Band 8 aligns with Australian Core Skills Framework (ACSF) Level 3 (School Curriculum and Standards Authority (SCSA), 2015), as the ACSF is principally concerned with adult learning and adult skill acquisition (Philippa McLean Consulting, 2012). Little consideration is given to the impact of failure to attain Band 8 while still in the middle of the upper schooling experience, trying to reach a standard deemed functional for adults; this framework was not designed for the assessment of children. A similar assessment will commence in New South Wales in 2020 for students who do not achieve Band 8 in Year 9, and, again, these students must pass this test in order to graduate. As upper school English is a time when teachers need to explicitly unteach some of the devices and structures that students have learned (such as overuse of the personal pronoun in persuasive arguments) in order to do well on the NAPLAN, adding the need to pass the OLNA beyond Year 9, which has a similar but not identical marking rubric to the NAPLAN, can potentially stymy teachers' efforts to further their students' abilities to write for a context other than that encountered in high-stakes testing.

Literacy skills continue to be highly valuable beyond the school-based learning context, as higher literacy skills are linked to a higher range of vocational possibilities as well as other benefits. At an international level, literacy skills have been associated with vocational prospects beyond school (Kirsch et al., 2002; OECD & Statistics Canada, 2000), and Australian research shows a significant relationship between the likelihood of employment and literacy levels for both young people and adults (ABS, 2013). Therefore, it is not surprising that literacy skills are also generally associated with higher earnings more generally. For example, a study using UK data, some of which were longitudinal, found that, even when controlling for socioeconomic background, higher literacy skills are associated with higher earning potential (McIntosh & Vignoles, 2001); thus, unsurprisingly, recent international research suggests that the literacy proficiency of a country "influences its level of productivity and hence its future economic potential" (Keslair, 2017, p. 2). Literacy skills are also related to social participation and health (Keslair, 2017). In order to encourage our students to read more, it is essential to help them understand that literacy is not just a "school thing" to be tested but instead a skill that can offer lifelong benefits both in the classroom and beyond.

In the past, when I have taught first-year teacher education units to young people primarily enrolled in a range of teaching majors, from early childhood education to high school mathematics, I have not simply relied on tapping into their desire to pass the unit or to be well equipped to support literacy in their teaching role. I have also tried to show my students how literacy relates to our successful communication in our daily work and social lives. The threat of negative consequences from communication "fails" in the online work and social spaces is ever present and explored with a degree of vitriolic energy in the media. For example, last year we discussed a White House gaff, where a piece of satire critiquing Trump's budget is mistaken as an endorsement of it, perhaps due to poor reading comprehension and a lack of understanding of satire. The hilarious *Washington Post* article, titled "Trump's Budget Makes Perfect Sense and Will Fix America, and I Will Tell You Why," was clearly not given close consideration by Trump's staff, as it was not particularly subtle, including text such as this:

> This budget will make America a lean, mean fighting machine with bulging, rippling muscles and not an ounce of fat. America has been weak and soft for too long. BUT HOW WILL I SURVIVE ON THIS BUDGET? you may be wondering. I AM A HUMAN CHILD, NOT A COSTLY FIGHTER JET. *You* may not survive, but that is because you are SOFT and WEAK, something this budget is designed to eliminate. (Petri, 2017)

I wonder how many of us who chuckled over this reading comprehension failure were guilty of the same sorts of error in our daily lives, whether it be misunderstanding an e-mail or accidentally mistaking a source of Internet news as legitimate, when it was in fact anything but truthful in its account. The sheer volume of written material that many of us consume as part of our daily lives can be staggering; I consider myself to be quite highly skilled in reading comprehension, as well as critical literacy, and I know that it is only a matter of time before lax attention to my reading or poor understanding of the contexts in which a text is created—or any other reading comprehension blunder—will lead to my promoting fake news as fact. The need to be a discerning and close-reading individual has arguably never been so high.

As previously mentioned, young people who are not highly academically motivated, or not focused on attaining a particular vocational role, may not necessarily see the value in developing their literacy skills. They may even dismiss literacy and reading as school things with limited relevance to them. However, considering how strongly our contemporary society relies on literacy for effective communication, even though research is comparatively lagging in this area, it is easy to make a cogent argument that establishes the importance of literacy for academic, vocational, and social successes. The ability to effectively persuade and negotiate are transferrable skills that are not limited to meeting the needs of assessments. Being able to mount a convincing argument will not only help you get a good job; it can also help you to win friends, be influential within your peer group, and negotiate your way out of getting grounded when you accidentally dent a fender in the drive-through. More research is needed in this area to link literacy performance with social opportunities so that it can be better understood.

THE PROBLEM WITH "READ ANYTHING"

While later in this book I will question whether young people really do think that books are uncool, there is little question that some *researchers* and *school administrators* certainly feel that books are no longer relevant for young people. Before I explore this, I would like to start by pointing out that I am not against the multiliteracies movement, which positions a wide range of texts and modes as valuable for young people. It is responsive to a vision of education taken to facilitate young people's participation in economic, public, and social life (New London Group, 1996). I agree that multiliteracies are very important; young people need to be equipped to use, create, understand, and critically engage with a very wide variety of texts applicable to a burgeoning degree of contexts. In my role as an educator of future teachers, I ensure that my students understand the value of these text types. However, I do not suggest that the reading of all text types offers equal literacy benefit because the current research in this area does not support this contention. Academic discussion of texts and reading tends to focus more on these "new developments," with far fewer articles about the reading of books (Cliff Hodges, 2010, p. 60), though in recent times I have been working somewhat feverishly to address this imbalance. As books were the privileged text for so long, I feel that now we have gone to the opposite extreme in some areas of research.

It may be tempting to put a comic book in the hands of young Sammy, who has been lurking purposefully among the shelves, pretending to read during silent reading, so that we can have him sitting and absorbed and thus managed for the remainder of the silent reading period. We can tell ourselves that it does not matter, as we are being responsive to his interests, and that all reading counts. After all, the popular notion of "read anything" in schools positions all reading as the same. But are all types of reading equally beneficial? The issue with this is that while comic books are associated with minimal literacy benefit, books are (OECD, 2010). If we consistently furnish our students with comic books rather than support them to find books that are both appealing and at an accessible reading level, because it is easier and more immediate, we are potentially limiting their literacy achievement. In some countries, the reading of comic books is actually associated with lower overall reading performance (OECD, 2010). Not all text types offer equal literacy benefit for readers (Spear-Swerling, Brucker, & Alfano, 2010), and it is struggling readers that we tend to give the comics to, potentially compounding their unequal literacy outcomes.

Can we count chuckling our way through our social networking pages as comparable to book reading in terms of literacy benefit? While traditional book reading has been found to benefit reading comprehension and vocabulary development, reading e-mails and social networking posts has not been found to offer the same benefits (Pfost, Dörfler, & Artelt, 2013). Books, particularly fiction books, tend to be most closely associated with literacy benefit in the limited number of comparative studies in this area. International research found that while reading newspapers, magazines, and nonfiction books can offer some literacy benefit, "the effect of these materials on reading performance is not as much pronounced as the effect of fiction books" (OECD, 2011b, p. 100). In addition, a U.S. study found that reading for information in nonfiction texts (including Internet-based reading) offered less benefit than fiction reading (Baer, Baldi, Ayotte, & Green, 2007). While we may hope that time spent text-messaging and reading online is offering equal literacy benefit to book reading, this is contested by recent research (Zebroff & Kaufman, 2016).

One day we may have a robust body of research that suggests that some text forms offer benefit equal to or greater than that of book reading and particularly the reading of fiction books, but we are not yet at that stage. The research in this field suggests that books are superior in this regard. As such, I would be very cautious about adopting a wide "read anything" approach. Again, I am not suggesting that other text types are therefore somehow "bad"; as I have established earlier, the benefit of exposure to diverse test types can relate to areas other than literacy skill development. For instance, young people need to know how to compose a work e-mail using appropriate language, and while the range of books celebrating diverse characters has grown substantially in recent times, it can be argued that many books still privilege a white middle-class viewpoint, and I certainly don't wish to diminish this argument. However, I am concerned that the well-intentioned "read anything" idea is part of a broader movement that now positions books as irrelevant and comparatively worthless, and this is not the case. Students like Sammy who are actually "reading anything" other than a book, who are often directed to the comic books or magazines or graphic novels, are often students who are lower literacy and who are struggling with reading. While in the short term this can keep these children busy during silent reading and expose them to small snatches of text, I wonder about the effects of this easy-way-out approach over time on these struggling readers.

FICTION AND EMPATHY

When we read fiction, many of us go on a journey with our characters. Batson, Early, & Salvarani (1997) explain that "imagining how a person in need feels evokes relatively pure empathic emotion, which has been found to evoke altruistic motivation." Some of us may almost dissolve our own sense of self when we read, inserting ourselves wholly into the worlds and perspectives of our admired protagonists, and this also affects us, as "imagining how you would feel in that person's situation evokes a more complex mix of other-oriented empathy and self-oriented personal distress" (p. 757). Like many people, when I read, I am closely concerned with the well-being of the characters that I care about; this is why books can make me laugh, cry, and get pretty frustrated at times too. I've even noticed that I have a weird tendency to crave whatever the main characters in my book are eating. My sons are also readers, and they both like to talk about what they are reading and how they feel about their protagonists' growth (or irritating lack thereof). Recently, my eldest son was still in front of the fire, laughing his way through a humorous supernatural series, while my younger son looked tense as he read the first installment of a postapocalyptic series. Sitting in the middle, it was interesting to notice the range of emotions passing over their faces; my eldest son occasionally read some of the funny parts out loud because they were too funny not to share, but my younger son was on a journey, and that kind of interaction would have disrupted his engagement.

My research in adult reading motivation suggests that this emotional engagement is one of the reasons that avid readers like to read:

> Readers may desire to access a broad emotion experience; for example, an avid book reader stated "it brings me joy, excitement, love, peace, anxiety, sorrow, happiness and anticipation for what's to come," and another stated that they "get attached easily to characters and locations so I laugh and cry along with the characters." (Merga, 2017b, p. 152)

As such, the kinds of emotional connections that we form with the characters in fiction texts can increase the enjoyment of reading.

Storytelling has long been a core aspect of human interpersonal interactions. Anthropologist Wiessner (2014) contends that storytelling was common to almost all hunter-gatherer societies and that "together with gifts, they were the original social media" (p. 14032). As such, research that suggests that the books and characters we read can shape our attitudes and values is unsurprising. For instance, Appel & Mara (2013) found that, generally, people are more likely to adopt the values of a fictional character who is perceived to be trustworthy than one who is not. Thus, while we may acquire a wealth of valuable information from the reading of nonfiction, the notion of fiction as a noneducative, soft alternative may not be legitimate. This is interesting in the context of the relative positioning of the genres, with works of nonfiction typically seen as "improving works" when compared with popular fiction, which has been historically viewed as inferior and even "mind-weakening," as explored by Ross (2009).

It seems that we do also learn from fiction reading experiences, with recent research suggesting that fiction may actually literally change our minds. While it is premature to say that there is a sound understanding of the influence of fiction reading on the brain (Jacobs & Willems, 2018) and that further research is needed in this area (Panero et al., 2017), the reading of fictional narratives has been found to offer the potential for an intensively immersive experience (Alderson-Day, Bernini, & Fernyhough, 2017). In addition to my adult research respondents, this emotional immersive experience was clear in some of the young interview responses in the WASCBR. For example, when I asked Samara what she thought was the best thing about reading, she described the emotional impact of reading:

> It's probably when the author expresses the character's feelings, and it just makes you feel how they feel, and it just makes you feel happy or sad depending on how the author's put it into words, and how they express all the feelings in the book.

The link between reading, emotions, and behaviors is being increasingly established in the consideration of how reading fiction can foster prosocial skills, such as empathy. The reading of literary fiction may have a more powerful impact than genre fiction on *theory of mind*, known as the capacity to understand other people's mental states and to make inferences about them (Kidd, Ongis, & Castano, 2016; Mar, Oatley, & Peterson, 2009). My research with avid adult readers found that, in addition to enjoying the emotional aspects of reading, adopting the point of view of others can be what some readers find most engaging about the reading experience. For example, one reader described their enjoyment of book reading as follows:

To look at one situation from different points of view. What books have taught me is that what you think is "real" and "true" might not be for another person. By reading, you learn how people may live and experience the same situation; you learn to accept that several attitudes and behaviors of people DO exist. People are different, and they will always behave different[ly] from you, but it is not for this reason they may be wrong. People should read to become open minded. And to try to understand others. (Merga, 2017b, p. 150)

This attitude is known perspective-taking, which can be characterized as imagining how characters feel and/or imagining how the reader would feel in a similar situation (Batson et al., 1997). Interestingly, the impact on readers may be different depending on which kind of relationship they develop with the characters. Those who imagine how a character feels experience empathy, and those who actually imagine *themselves* in the situation of the character may go even further, feeling both empathy and "self-oriented personal distress" (Batson et al., 1997, p. 757).

Books can also help us by imparting more than just knowledge. The emotional response that readers can experience while reading can also support emotional regulation and healing, which is why they have been used as part of bibliotherapy practices to illuminate strategies for dealing with a range of issues from a safe distance (Heath et al., 2005). Lenkowsky (1987) explains that "bibliotherapy arose from the concept that reading could affect an individual's attitude and behavior and is this an important influence in shaping, molding and altering values" (p. 123). Both children and adults may informally use books and reading to deal with difficult emotions or to avoid feeling them. For example, Sadie, a tween, explained, "I like to read books when I am stressed or alone, and sometimes scared or worried; it makes me feel calm, because sometimes books tell me a story about other people's life." This was similar to the adults who described reading as a valuable escape and as an activity that benefited their overall mental health, such as the adult who explained that "if I don't read, I feel empty, lack confidence, become uneasy and world weary. Reading makes me forget about my troubles while it lasts. Reading is a sort of super getaway for me" (Merga, 2017b, p. 152). It was also reflected in some of the teenagers' responses in the WASABR:

There wasn't a question on why I love reading. If there was I would've said: I love reading because it doesn't matter what is happening in your real life, it only matters what is happening in the characters. The author's writings whisk you away into a world which may or not be real. You can often feel the author's pain or feelings in the writings. And that makes the books special.

Clearly, reading fiction can play an important role in fostering social skills and empathy, as well as the ability to consider the perspectives of others, enabling us to better understand the attitudes, values, and lived experiences of those from cultures and identifications that might otherwise be entirely foreign and unimaginable. These altruistic and empathetic skills can support our young people to grow into well-rounded, active citizens who do not mistake their worldview as homogeneous, no matter what their social position. Building these capacities is increasingly an educational priority. For example, the Australian Curriculum includes seven General Capabilities, which are to be explored across all areas of the curriculum. As previously mentioned, literacy is one of these capabilities, but the reading of fiction can also support the fostering of "personal and social capability," "ethical understanding," intercultural understanding," and "personal and social capability."

With reading situated as one practice that has the capacity to foster positive characteristics and capabilities, it is surprising that regular time for independent self-selected fiction reading is not a uniform requirement across all schools. Instead, many literacy advocates literally fight with their superiors to justify this time and space in the crowded curriculum. In addition, considering these possible benefits, there are clearly implications for steering children toward nonfiction due to an imagined gender-based preference. I explore this issue in further detail in Chapter 4.

This does not mean that the reading of non-fiction is not valuable. Indeed, there are many kinds of nonfiction that may potentially offer benefit in diverse areas, and narrative nonfiction is very close in form to fiction. As a group, avid nonfiction readers have tended to be under-researched, though recent findings from the ISABR study suggest that they may be more likely to be male and older than avid fiction readers and that they may read less frequently, though they may read more books. When we analyzed the motivation of nonfiction book readers, it tended to challenge the idea that all readers of nonfiction read purely to learn. While knowledge was a strong and recurring motivation for reading in this group, nonfiction readers also often read for inspiration and self-improvement, enjoyment, relaxation and comfort, identity and habit, and to escape everyday life (Merga & Mat Roni, 2018a). The diversity in motivation may be reflective of the diversity of subgenres within the body of nonfiction—it could be surmised that a regular reader of self-help books may differ from a regular reader of military history. It certainly may be the case that reading a narrative nonfiction biography may offer equal or even greater benefits for fostering empathy and perspective taking than the reading of fiction, but further research needs to be done in this area.

WHY DO READERS READ, AND HOW CAN THIS KNOWLEDGE SHAPE OUR READING SUPPORT ROLE?

We need to understand what makes readers read. Some people read regularly and have a positive attitude toward reading into adulthood, and it is useful to attempt to understand the forces that have shaped this ideation in the hope that they can be identified and replicated. While it is likely that no two readers have arrived at this habit via the same path, understanding why readers read in general can help us to further our knowledge around how these attitudes are fostered. This is why, in addition to examining the social influences on self-identified avid readers, I also sought to identity their self-prescribed reasons for reading, which I will now explore further.

It is also important to note that reading is important not just in childhood; adults should also be regularly reading in order to maintain and further their literacy skills. As previously mentioned, reading beyond the early years offers benefits beyond literacy maintenance and development, as reading is increasingly being found to offer a protective effect against cognitive decline and dementia into old age (Vemuri et al., 2014; Wilson et al., 2013). Findings from the 2015 ISABR study of avid readers from 89 countries around the world suggest that avid adult readers are motivated to read by a diverse range of possible factors and that many readers identified more than one of these factors as a driving force in their reading. Which of the following relate to your own reading motivations?

Social, Psychological, and Emotional Characteristics

- **Perspective taking:** Reading to experience the point of view and experiences of characters
- **Personal development:** Reading for self-improvement
- **Escapism and mental health:** Reading to temporarily withdraw from reality into an engaging space
- **Books as friends:** Reading to enjoy time with a source of comfort and support
- **Imagination and creative inspiration:** Reading to stimulate creativity

Intellectual Pursuits and Skill Development

- **Mental stimulation:** Reading to activate critical inquiry and deep thought
- **Knowledge:** Reading to expand the scope and depth of knowledge, both generally and/or in key areas of interest
- **Writing, language, and vocabulary:** Reading for the enjoyment of language and to foster language skills

Recreation and Identity

- **Habit, entertainment, and pleasure:** Reading as integral, something you just do, and enjoy. (Adapted from Merga, 2017b)

As apparent from this list, the reasons for reading are diverse, and this broad scope also suggests a range of points for possible engagement. While I hope to soon generate a similar model for younger people in order to determine the extent to which they are comparable, this model can be a useful starting point for linking reasons for reading with books. It also highlights the importance that we find out what (if anything) the young people in our sphere of influence enjoy about reading. For example, children who enjoy perspective taking could be recommended books that facilitate this, with engaging and strong central characters. Young people who read to distract themselves from feelings of worthlessness could ideally be guided to choose books that can enhance their optimism and self-efficacy. Young people who read for mental stimulation and challenge will need to be given books that make them feel as though they are learning. Thus, a model such as this serves as a reminder of the diversity in motivation that we may experience when engaging in reading, as well as raising possibilities about how these differences can be understood to increase engagement.

When examining why readers read, it is also important to look at the role that social influences can play. While I was careful not to assume that all of my survey respondents had experienced a key shaping social influence, the ISABR found that nearly two-thirds of my mostly adult respondents believed that there was a significant social influence in their life who had influenced their positive attitude toward books and reading. As such, the vast majority of avid readers may not have attained this ideation and practice without the influence of others. The results suggest that, while parents were very strongly featured as influences, the total range of possible positive influences was really broad, suggesting that pretty much anyone can constitute a significant social influence. So if you are reading this book as an interested grandparent or aunt, for instance, do not doubt your ability to be a profound influence in the lives of your granddaughter or nephew (Merga, 2017f). While I accept that, to some extent, the young persons themselves will determine who will be a successful social influence, we can all at least try to exert a positive social influence through the varied mechanisms detailed in the subsequent chapters.

I would like to point out that the "how" of making a difference is also surprisingly diverse, so if you are a parent who is not a confident reader and would rather make a difference by talking about books with your tween or teen, this is also one of many supportive avenues of encouragement. In the ISABR, the types of influences that made a difference widely varied, including (but not limited to) the following:

- **Indirect avid reader influence:** The reader observed an avid reading model and desired to emulate that person. This model did not even need to necessarily know the recipient of their influence.
- **Author influence:** The reader connected with an author who seemed to understand her and her interests. Again, the author did not necessarily interact with the reader.
- **Fostering access:** Someone helped the reader to get books, for example by giving books to him or by taking him to the library. Gifts were particularly powerful as they also communicated valuing.
- **Shared social habit:** Reading was an important part of socializing with another person or people. These could be family members or members of a social group.
- **Reading for approval:** The reader was seen to be reading in order to receive praise or positive feedback. This highlighted the importance of reading as it was situated as a praiseworthy practice.
- **Recommendations and supporting choice:** A key social influence guided the reader's choice by suggesting books to her. This could also involve showing her how to independently select engaging material.
- **Exposure to reading aloud:** The social influence is reading to the reader. This often led to the respondent seeking out similar books or other books in the series or rereading the book independently. (adapted from Merga, 2017f)

In many cases, these social influences were described as transformative. For example, a young Malaysian respondent made the following comment, which shows how an American woman was a powerful model without even being related to the subject of influence.

> I went on a student exchange program to the United States of America in the year of 2014. My host mother was constantly on her Kindle when she wasn't too busy running errands. My host mother seemed so engrossed with her Kindle and that sparked

my curiosity. She seemed so wise for her age and perhaps it was from reading count-less books. I'd like to be just as wise if not wiser.

In subsequent chapters, I will also explore in further depth and detail other relevant findings that investigate how key influences can shape young people's attitudes, but I wanted to foreground this subsequent investigation by establish-ing at the outset that those who feel they have become lifelong readers clearly often do so as a result of the support of others, and for a range of their own per-sonal motives. Our efforts to foster a love of reading can bear fruit, and it is never too late to add some extra possible approaches to our tool kit for supporting read-ing engagement. Also, it is not a hopeless task to attempt to engage young people in reading, as some tweens can and do prefer it to other forms of entertainment, such as Cissy who explained that "reading books makes me feel like I've turned right through the planet Earth, and to a completely different planet. I much prefer books than television [sic], because they can have more story and a lot more information."

READING FOR PLEASURE AND LEVELING THE PLAYING FIELD

Research suggests that a number of factors shape the literacy outcomes of young people and that not all children are equally positioned by their circumstances to build their literacy skills.

I explore the gender gap in further detail in Chapter 4, but I also wanted to draw attention to the effects of socioeconomic status (SES). Poverty is felt to be the factor most strongly associated with constrained literacy achievement (Cunningham, 2006; Kellett, 2009). Thus, literacy education at school is positioned as crucial to closing the achievement gap, which limits children's engagement across the breadth of the curriculum as well as beyond school (Wamba, 2010).

Literacy education at home is also positioned as a key contributor to the achieve-ment gap. Indeed, it can be contended that school reforms that attempt to resolve the issue of the SES-related literacy gap by addressing only what occurs in the school environment may obscure "the reality that factors outside of school heavily constrain school reform" (Wamba, 2010, p. 190). It is not sufficient to focus solely on school-based initiatives; "efforts focused solely on classrooms and schools could well be reversed by what takes place outside the school setting" (Wamba, 2010, p. 190). Research suggests that a range of factors, such as "home literacy environ-ment, number of books owned, parent distress, and receipt of center-based care" may be "significantly related to reading outcomes" (Aikens & Barbarin, 2008, p. 248). Some of these factors that may contribute to this inequity can be influenced by external literacy advocates. For instance, "lower reading achievement is not nec-essarily due to household poverty but rather is often due to a paucity of in-home literacy experiences" (Bhattacharya, 2010, p. 135); if advocates can promote liter-acy in the home and, crucially, provide resources to support these initiatives, this effect can be mitigated. This contention is supported by findings suggesting that students from low socioeconomic contexts who are exposed to strong "in-home literacy experiences" typically show higher reading achievement than those who do not have exposure to these experiences (Bhattacharya, 2010, p. 135). Interventions can be powerful, with research finding that:

> the relation between SES and children's initial reading competence is mediated by home literacy environment, number of books available within the home to the child, parental involvement in the school, parental role strain and warmth, and provision of center-based care prior to kindergarten. This is a useful finding. Although it may be difficult to alter family SES quickly enough to make a difference for young children, interventions can reduce the adverse effects of family mediators. (Aikens & Barbarin, 2008, p. 248).

As such, literacy advocacy and interventions that support home literacy experiences and resources can be highly effective.

However, while this book offers suggestions around how to improve access to books in the home and how to support home literacy that can support children from diverse backgrounds to attain literacy growth, it accepts that not all families will have the time and resources to implement home support strategies. Parents face so many challenges, such as health problems, low literacy, long working hours, and a range of other issues that school-based literacy educators may have limited powers to mitigate. As such, while I urge educators to support at-home learning, schools must also accept and maintain responsibility for support reading engagement and growth beyond the early years of schooling.

As such, we need a strong understanding of how to support students from low-SES contexts using best practice. We should avoid reinforcing deficit notions, as many of these students may have rich literate backgrounds in languages other than English. Li (2010) contends that literacy educators:

> must extend their efforts beyond the four walls of classrooms and schools to address the limit situations outside schools that constantly impede students' learning inside the classroom. This can be achieved through improving students' social environments and implementing pedagogical practices that link students' learning inside school with their lived realities outside school. For example, . . . they can design reading and writing activities that involve more interaction and dialogue among students of different cultural, ethnic, or social class backgrounds. They can also involve students in writing commentaries or opinion papers about their ideas to solve these problems and improve the social environment. (p. 160)

In addition to framing literacy in a way that draws on the experiences and cultural capital of students, recent researchers urge that reading for pleasure should remain in focus in low-SES contexts, avoiding the adopting of a *pedagogy of poverty*. As reviewed by Hempel-Jorgensen, Cremin, Harris, & Chamberlain (2018), the pedagogy of poverty (referred to as PoP) may typically entail "particularly strong teacher control, where their role is to transmit knowledge to children who are positioned very passively" (p. 1). There is a focus on basic skills that denies the opportunity to develop critical thinking, creativity, and problem solving, as well as a focus on improving high-stakes testing performance. This approach bears a strong resemblance to teacher-centered performative pedagogy, and it is reflected in low-SES schools' approach toward reading for pleasure:

This pedagogy was underpinned by the teachers' and thereby the children's understanding of reading as primarily a matter of proficiency. This was despite the discourse of head teachers, reading coordinators and the teachers who indicated that they aimed to foster children's desire to read. (Hempel-Jorgensen, Cremin, Harris, & Chamberlain, 2018, p. 7)

The traditional teacher-centered approach may be a well-meaning back-to-basics response to SES constraints. However, in the context of the rich research supporting the relationship between reading engagement and reading achievement, if schools in low-SES contexts do not prioritize reading for pleasure and encourage it as a social and enjoyable practice within schools through approaches and practices that I describe in great detail throughout this book, we run the risk of compounding inequity for students who are already vulnerable to comparative underperformance in literacy. If anything, these schools and students need an even greater focus on reading for pleasure than their higher-SES counterparts, certainly not the reverse.

2

From Learning to Read to Reading to Learn

Why Does Reading for Pleasure Fall by the Wayside?

This chapter will highlight possible reasons for increasing aliteracy as students move through schooling. This involves understanding the infrequent reader.

Perhaps the young people in your life do not read as often as they ideally should. If this is the case, take dubious pleasure in the fact that you are not alone. In the previous chapter, I suggested that an hour a day was a good target; however, research suggests that most young people are not reaching this target and that students read less often as they move through the years of schooling. Recent U.S. research noted upper school students' lower motivation to read, and lower value for reading, when compared with younger students (Parsons et al., 2018). While this research was not longitudinal, we know that research suggests that young people generally show a tendency to read for pleasure with decreasing frequency over time. Sometimes this transformation from reader to nonreader has been associated with the move from lower school to high school, though it has also been located just past the expected period of independent reading skill acquisition, characterized as a "fourth-grade slump" (Brozo, 2005), suggesting that reading engagement may commonly falter once children can read. Australian research found that while 45% of Australian primary students enjoyed reading for pleasure, less than a quarter of high school students do (Nieuwenhuizen, 2001). Findings from the WASABR suggest that only 23% of girls and 15% of boys in high school are daily readers (Merga, 2014c), and PISA (Programme for International Student Assessment) data suggest that 37% of Australian 15-year-olds do not read for pleasure at all (Thomson et al., 2011).

The research around children's reading frequency suggests that this is an issue of broader international significance (Scholastic, 2010). The recent Scholastic reports from the United States, the UK, and Australia (Scholastic 2015; Scholastic 2016a; Scholastic 2016b) also suggest that young people in later years of schooling read less than students in earlier years and that this decline begins quite early in schooling. This decline is known as *aliteracy*, where young people have learned independent reading skill, but they choose not to read (Nathanson, Pruslow, &

Levitt 2008), but to characterize this decline as simply a *choice* can be a bit misleading, as I will subsequently explore.

Unfortunately, just because a child enjoys reading in the early years of schooling, this does not necessarily mean that he or she will become a regular reader by choice beyond this point. Sometimes tweens and teens describe reading as though it is something they grew out of. For example, tween Paulo noticed that he read less over time, sharing the following on the open field of the WASCBR survey. While I have typically provided quotes in edited verbatim form in this book where there have been minor issues with spelling or grammar (so that you can read them easily), I have kept Paulo's comment exactly as he typed it into the open field of the survey in order to highlight the current issues with his literacy, which could be improved by greater reading. Paulo stated: "i use to read alout when i was nine and ten but now that im 11 and neally 12 i dont read as much as i us to."

I also present the following teenager's written response without editing it; you will see why once you read the comment:

> I was tought to read from a very young age and was influenced alot by my father. At age 7 I read the Tomorrow When the War Began series. At age 9 I was reading multiple adult books at one time. As I got older I found reading less interesting a began socializing and playing sport more. By age 13 when I started high school I had almost completely stopped reading. I believe my reading of adult books at a young age contributed to my extensive vocabulary and high english competency. It would be ironic if I spelt anything wrong in this however.

Each time I reread this quote, this clever student makes me smile, but the irony was ultimately apparent in this instance. This quote provides really interesting insight into how, while some students do see the benefit in reading during the early years, they do not necessarily understand the continuing benefit conferred if they continue to read beyond that point. It also highlights the importance for young people that they engage in socially relevant and socially sanctioned leisure practices.

Despite these dire statistics of reading decline related to age, it is perfectly possible for young people to love reading, and losing a love of reading is not an inevitable aspect of the human condition, no matter what you read elsewhere. All of you will know at least a handful of avid readers from both male and female genders who keenly enjoy reading beyond the early years of schooling. As such, we cannot say that all young people dislike reading, and we cannot say that it is impossible to influence young people to read in contemporary times. While there are tweens such as Anna, who explained that "sometimes I get a little bored when I'm reading . . . but to be honest I prefer playing on my iPad," there are also tweens such as Neil, who found reading "really fun" for the following reasons:

> There's lots of interesting things in the book, and also it takes a lot of time, and some of the books I read, they really capture me in the book, so I don't want to stop. I think it's just very fun, it captures you in the book and it takes up a lot of time instead of just sitting around.

As such, attempting to improve students' attitudes toward reading is not an impossible cause, no matter how resistant a child or a group of young readers may seem to be at the outset.

EXPIRED EXPECTATIONS

So why do some children seem to cease reading once they have achieved the skill to read by themselves? While interviewing teens as part of my doctoral research in 2012, I first came across what can be characterized as *expired expectations*, where young people believed that reading was no longer important for them after independent reading skill acquisition because important social influences in their lives, namely parents and/or teachers, had stopped transmitting its importance. When these social influences stopped expecting them to read, they stopped viewing the practice as important, and other recreational pursuits were selected instead. Where young people who had enjoyed reading while younger had parents and teachers who inadvertently transmitted the idea that reading for pleasure was no longer important for them, this was often felt by them to be a significant contributing factor to their decreased reading engagement. Students such as Cal explained. In this instance, Cal is describing his parents' attitude toward his reading and how it changed over time:

> They do think reading's important, but they're not exactly worried about it as much anymore. Because, they know that I know a lot of stuff now, and I did it for such a long time. But they definitely think it's important at a younger age. (Merga, 2014a, p. 153)

Cal's comments highlight a serious issue that is supported by a growing body of research: dwindling expectations are associated with a corresponding notion that reading is no longer a valuable practice. Similarly, Max explained that "his parents encouraged him 'less,' as, 'I had to learn how to read then, and now I know how to read, so, yeah, don't need to keep learning that'" (p. 153), and Tony explained that "I kind of just fell away from the reading, when it came optional. But when it was . . . compulsory, I used to do it" (p. 154).

Teenage students also often felt that they had received far more encouragement to read from their lower school teachers. For instance, Zara explained that "back in lower school, a lot of the teachers were like, 'Reading's fun' [laughs]. So, we got to—we got encouraged a lot back then, but not so much now." In high school, Leon read less than he had in lower school, and he felt that he received less encouragement to read from his teachers, as reading of school texts rather than self-selected reading was expected, explaining that "we were probably encouraged to read more in lower schools, kind of read 20 minutes every night or whatever, but—now it's more just like, read—it's just something you should be doing." Similarly, Hans experienced far more encouragement to read in lower school, where he "tended to read more books for the fun of it, and I sometimes had discussions with my teachers about what I had read, they'd explain some things to me if I didn't understand." These comments show how expectations and their cessation or withdrawal can influence young people's engagement in recreational reading and that these expired expectations are occurring both at home and at school.

As I have mentioned, reading should not be seen as optional, as independent reading skill acquisition is not the end destination; this research also highlights the fact that the will to continue reading has not been fostered in many young people. To build on my previous interview findings in this area, I decided to try to find out more about younger people's understanding of the continued importance of reading beyond skill acquisition. Considering what I found out from the interview data on the WASABR, I thought it would be useful to be able to quantify how many tweens understood that reading remains important over time. As part of the WASCBR survey, children aged 8–12 were asked, "Once you know how to read, do you still need to read?" Nearly a fifth of respondents did not agree with this statement, suggesting that we cannot assume that young people necessarily understand and value the ongoing importance of reading (Merga & Mat Roni, 2018c). As this knowledge is something that I feel that we can easily take for granted, I think it is important to use these findings to consider how effectively we transmit ongoing expectations that young people read for pleasure. Stacy (age 9) specifically asked me about this:

> I think that reading books is a good way to learn to spell and learn about comprehension. The question I would put for it is: Do you think reading is helpful for learning and if so what does it help with?

There is clearly room for further intervention in this area to improve young people's understanding of the ongoing importance of reading.

I would also like to draw attention to what we are learning about periods of underuse, as these findings suggest that young people may tend to view their literacy skills as immutable once gained. However, we face a use-it-or-lose-it situation with literacy and reading, at least to some extent. Research increasingly suggests that children who do not frequently read for enjoyment may experience dilatory improvement across literacy outcomes, and their literacy skills may actually decrease during periods without educational exposure, such as school holidays, with children from low socioeconomic backgrounds particularly affected (McGill-Franzen, Ward, & Cahill, 2016; Shin & Krashen, 2008). This suggests that if we do not continue to develop our literacy skills though supportive practices such as regular recreational reading, we run the risk of these skills stagnating or even regressing to some extent. However, this use-it-or-lose-it situation is not necessarily well understood by children and, indeed, by their educational supporters.

We need to greatly improve young people's understanding of the importance of reading. The reason this matters is because we know that research into young people's motivation to read suggests that the way we value the importance of an activity can influence willingness to engage in it, as recognized by expectancy value theory (Wigfield, 1997). This all sounds very intuitive and sensible, but when we consider that we, as influential social agents, play a potentially vital role in children's attribution of this valuing, we can be inspired to be explicit about the often taken-for-granted value of reading. Our research has found that children who believed that reading was important were almost twice as likely to read every day, highlighting the need to teach children about the ongoing benefits of regular reading (Merga & Mat Roni, 2018c). Hannah, a tween, described her reasons for reading as follows:

> I usually read books more often at night, and most of them are diary books from people, but their story is fake. I find that reading books is important, and that's why I read, but I also read it because I am either bored or am interested in the book.

Children such as Hannah can be motivated by the importance they attribute to books and reading, among other factors.

BALANCING EXPECTATIONS AND ENCOURAGEMENT

I would like to be careful here to make clear that I do not think that expectations alone are necessarily enough to foster keen reading. While expectations are clearly important and they communicate an ongoing valuing of reading, as I mentioned previously, my research does not offer a single silver bullet approach to solving the issue of young people's infrequent engagement in reading as they age. As I will explain herein, expectations need to be coupled with other supportive practices to make a real difference in encouraging young people to read.

When I first found expired expectations emerging as a real issue in the research, I wondered about the role that expectations might play in influencing young people's behavioral decisions in general. While various motivational theories touch on this, I wound up returning to previous reading that I had done in the area of parenting psychology, Baumrind's configural approach to parental authority (CAPA). This relatively simple but powerful construct considers how parental authority and responsiveness impact upon adolescents (Baumrind, 2005). You have probably heard others talking about it when discussing the "authoritative parent" or the "authoritarian parent." While the CAPA focusses on parental influence, this model could have implications for teacher approaches to the issue.

The CAPA is interested in the balance of two aspects characterizing the parenting styles defined by Baumrind (2005): demandingness and responsiveness. *Demandingness* is essentially concerned with behavior management, compliance, and monitoring, as well as high expectations for academic and behavioral performance. As such, expectations that young people continue to read can be seen as typically a form of demandingness. *Responsiveness* is the mechanism by which parents demonstrate "warmth, autonomy support, and reasoned communication" (Baumrind, 2005, pp. 61–62). While the two approaches can be viewed as really different, as I will explain, where they are used together, such as in the authoritative parenting style, they are most effective.

When we think about which kinds of parenting approach might work best, most of us probably will not imagine extremes. Baumrind categorizes four parenting styles—authoritarian, authoritative, permissive and rejecting-neglecting (1971)—and looks at how these styles typically use demandingness and responsiveness. The simple diagram in Figure 2.1 helps to illustrate how this works in relation to their support of demandingness and responsiveness.

Authoritarian parents have a high degree of demandingness (D) and low degree of responsiveness (R); at the extreme, I imagine them as a kind of prison guard parent, in a uniform with a whistle around their necks and a clipboard with a list of requirements (and perhaps a big stick).

The permissive approach is characterized by a high degree of responsiveness and low degree of demandingness; at the extreme, I imagine them as a kind of placid parent, perhaps wearing a daisy chain. This parent allows the child to walk all over them, providing plenty of hugs but no structure or discipline.

A rejecting/neglecting approach lacks both factors and has not been applied to teaching models to date.

The balance is the authoritative parent, who provides both demandingness and responsiveness, who places expectations while at the same time giving emotional

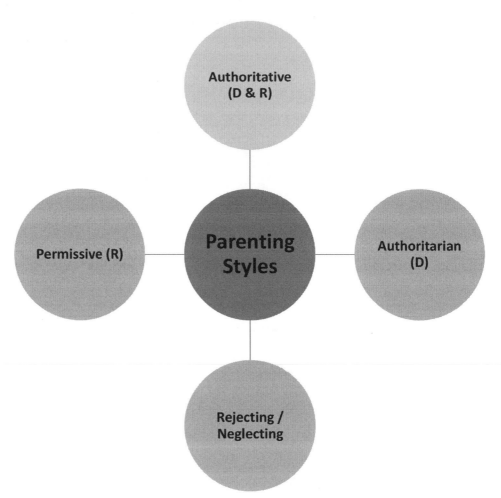

Figure 2.1 Baumrind's CAPA—Parenting Styles and Demandingness/Responsiveness

support. These parents exhibit "high control and positive encouragement of the child's autonomous and independent strivings" (Baumrind 1971, p. 1), which are beneficial beyond childhood years into adolescence (Baumrind 1978; Baumrind, 1991). Research has linked authoritative parenting practices to academic achievement across cultures (Gray & Steinberg, 1999; Dai, 1998).

It would seem that a degree of demandingness, or expectations, could be important when we are seeking to foster certain behaviors in young people, but these expectations need to be balanced with responsiveness. I do not suggest that expectations alone are likely to shape young people's behavior; indeed, in my research where parents demanded that their children read but did not support this expectation with other more responsive forms of encouragement, this tended to be not a very successful approach, as I will illustrate further.

For example, Rob, a teenage participant in the WASABR whose parents had high expectations that he read but little knowledge of his reading preferences, was not a keen reader, describing his recreational reading as follows:

It's kind of a forced reading though 'cause I—I don't really enjoy it as much as I probably like did *Harry Potter*, or something, but it's good for reading, it's a good book I've kind of found, so. I'm kind of enjoying it, but I'd rather be doing like sport or something in my spare time than reading it. My parents still have a hard time trying to make me read it.

Rob's parents made him read nonfiction, which was not a preferred genre, so this demandingness without responsiveness did not inspire Rob to read for pleasure. His parents wanted him to read to improve his grades, but they did not understand what he liked and meet those preferences. It would seem that we may be able to extrapolate aspects of the CAPA to the context of encouraging children to read, suggesting that sustained expectations can be important for fostering continued engagement in reading, though they should not be exerted without responsive strategies such as knowing children's interests. This means that, at the end of the day, while it is very important to keep demonstrating clear expectations that our children and students read, we will also need to include a range of other supportive strategies if we want them to become enthusiastic recreational readers. If we feel that we may just be demanding and expecting that students read but not balancing this with responsive behaviors, we can adjust our approach accordingly.

THE ORPHANED RESPONSIBILITY

So whose job is it to keep young people reading beyond the early years? As parents, our role is relatively straightforward in the early years, as the school typically tells us what it wants from us as literacy supports. For example, we might get a journal to sign to show that we have read a book with our child. In Australia, we know that, as parents, we need to equip our child with the relevant wands or bows and arrows as part of their Book Week costume, and we are typically expected to provide our children with a library bag, which they will dutifully fill with a self-selected book once a fortnight or so, if they are fortunate enough to attend a school with a library. Other than defending that book from the other horrible things that may lurk at the bottom of a school bag—an odd assortment of rejected fruits and sports socks—our expectations are relatively low and clear. However, what we are supposed to do when the journal is no longer sent home, once our children can read, and when the library bag comes home full infrequently if at all is not necessarily effectively communicated.

From a teacher's perspective, it is also a little more complicated than you might expect. We cannot just park the car of reading responsibility in the teachers' parking lot and expect them to drive it off into the sunset. While the extensive literacy, literature, and language skills that children learn at school are typically clearly outlined in the curriculum, building or maintaining a love of reading in our students is not always foregrounded. As teachers, we face arguably relentless pressures to prepare our children for testing, we may have to argue for time and space for supportive practices such as sustained silent reading, and we may struggle with what may seem to be stronger competing demands on our students' time. In addition, some teachers do not fully understand the benefits conferred by regular reading for pleasure. Some would argue that fostering a love of reading is more typically a focus of teachers in the early years of schooling. For example, as teen Krysta reflected on who the most encouraging teachers had been for her:

> I guess it was probably one of my Year One teachers, because it was very early on in reading, they got you to take home your little books and read them, so I guess, yeah, so the younger primary school teachers encouraged us more.

These are some of the reasons why that, in addition to expired expectations, young people may also find that the educational agents supporting their will to read may experience role confusion, as well as role relinquishing as per expired expectations, leading to reading support becoming an orphaned responsibility.

As teachers, when we talk about roles in supporting reading, we are usually talking about roles in skill development. We think about what teachers and parents need to do in order to teach children to read, we argue about the relative merits of a phonological or whole-word approach to reading (even though we should know by now that there is no reason at all that these should be mutually exclusive), and we discuss measures of skill acquisition through testing of frequency or prosody. While these conversations are usually valuable, the motivational dimension of reading, which is so crucial to support frequency of continued engagement in the practice, can be neglected. Particularly as we move past the period of skill acquisition, it is little surprise that the role of motivational support can become an orphaned responsibility, where both teachers and parents may perceive it as the role of the other party.

In addition, simply reading more frequently can help students achieve many of the skill goals that inhibit their progress in areas such as reading comprehension. For example, I recently presented a professional development session for the English Teachers' Association of Western Australia, focusing on reading comprehension. While I drew on the research around specific strategies that expert readers use when they read (e.g., Dole, Duffy, Roehler, & Pearson, 1991) and a range of in-class strategies to support the development of reading comprehension, such as literary discussions (e.g., Anderson, 2016), I also needed to draw the audience's attention to the research evidence linking independent reading to reading comprehension skill development (e.g., Pfost, Dorfler, & Artelt, 2013). Our students benefit from metacognitive strategies to enhance their reading comprehension, but simply increasing reading volume is also a powerful strategy, as is reading books aloud as students read along (e.g., Westbrook, Sutherland, Oakhill, & Sullivan, 2018).

While it has been relatively under-researched, there is support for the idea of the orphaned responsibility in the available literature. As I will discuss further in Chapter 5, parents may often cease to read aloud to their child once independent reading skill has been acquired, seeing their job as done. In earlier Australian research, Bunbury (1995) has suggested that while parents may view encouraging reading as the responsibility of the school, teachers may view it as a parental responsibility. Parents may dramatically reduce their support for reading once their children have shown mastery of the skill, assuming their job has been done, with parents far more likely to read to primary-aged children than older children (Clark & Foster, 2005). Similarly, U.S. research exploring parents' role in their early adolescent children's literacy experiences suggests that "it is not that they don't want to be involved, but somehow they feel they are not supposed to be" (Morris & Kaplan, 1994, p. 130). I would suggest that it is the responsibility of both parties, though teachers should know that not all parents are necessarily aware, able, or willing to shoulder this responsibility, and as a result, fostering and maintaining a love of reading should always be part of the teaching requirements. Teachers should also take some responsibility for educating parents about their continued importance as both models and supports of reading where possible.

I previously mentioned the overall international trend toward young people reading less in general over time. In addition, research consistently suggests that as children age, they are less inclined to read for pleasure and that *expired expectations* and the *orphaned responsibility* of reading can be two potential causes of this decline, where we inadvertently socially transmit a diminished importance of reading. While I am not suggesting that the phenomena of expired expectations and the orphaned responsibility are the only factors that lead to this decline, I do suggest that these factors warrant closer consideration.

REASONS FOR TEENS' READING INFREQUENCY

You know these students; they are the usual suspects. During silent reading, they may spend the entire period browsing the shelves, looking at covers, flicking through books, and shooting surreptitious glances at the clock. While many of these students would be categorized as struggling readers, these students typically know how to read, but they seem to actively avoid it, even when we may deem that they are presented with ample opportunity to engage in the practice. They are a source of teacher frustration and parental confusion because we know that the reluctance they show toward reading can further compound the delays we may note in their literacy development. In many cases, they are tested, as we suspect other issues may be at play, but the testing often draws a blank on dyslexia and other related issues. They seem to be simply allergic to reading. However, not all infrequent readers are reluctant readers, as I will discuss further, and the cause for reading infrequency is infrequently simply an aversion to reading.

Why do some young people read more frequently than others? While there is quite a lot of speculation in the available literature on reasons for reading infrequency beyond the early years, bringing to light an array of possible reasons (Sanacore & Palumbo, 2009), comparatively little research looks at why infrequent readers who have the skill to read do not engage in the practice with greater frequency. I reviewed the available research in this area and used the research to inform parts of my subsequent surveys. The key reasons that young people who have achieved the skill to read choose not to read, as explored in the literature, included the following:

- **Time availability:** When young people said that they did not have time to read, this usually related to either time availability or time allocation. While time allocation involved choice, time availability was a different issue, as some students had significant extracurricular demands that were to a considerable extent beyond their control, such as employment, sibling care, and homework. These activities restricted their recreational time (Gordon, 2010; Hughes-Hassel, 2008; Merga, 2013).

- **Preference:** Also termed time allocation, this related to the choice to spend time on other recreational pursuits. Research suggests that for some children, recreational book reading holds comparatively low appeal, with other recreational pursuits deemed more attractive (Gordon, 2010; Hofferth & Jankuniene, 2010; Manuel, 2012). Only students who solely subscribed to this choice could be deemed truly alliterate.

- **Skill deficit:** Even if teens can read, they may not be able to read well (Gordon, 2010). Many teens are not competent readers for a range of skill-related reasons that can be compounded by a "Matthew Effect, by which the 'rich get richer' and the 'poor, poorer': 'children with inadequate vocabularies—who read slowly and without enjoyment—read less, and as a result have slower development of vocabulary knowledge, which inhibits further growth in reading ability" (Stanovich, 1986, pp. 381).

- **Access and choice:** Poor access to books and a lack of book choice were presented together due to their close relationship, as "access and choice issues can arise from a paucity of books or a dearth in the quality and breadth of options available" (Merga, 2014b). Providing access to books alone is not enough; if these books are not interesting, relevant, and current, young people are less likely to read them (Hopper, 2005; Hughes-Hassel, 2008). In addition, students' book choosing skills (or lack thereof) could have influence in this area. Access to books in the home is related to higher educational outcomes, even when socioeconomic factors are taken into account (Evans, Kelley, Sikora, & Treiman, 2010).

- **Physical and cognitive factors:** Issues in these areas "include all bodily or cognitive limitations to reading, whether they are reliant on attention elements (such as issues with concentration), visual language processing, optical issues or any other physical or cognitive impediment" (Merga, 2014b). Cognitive issues could lead to physical ones. For example, attentional issues could lead to an inability to sit still for the amount of time required for reading.

While these reasons are all potentially powerful and compelling, I wanted to know how prevalent each of them was in a population of teens who could read but who did not typically read for pleasure. One of my key interests in conducting this investigation lay in the fact that I think that we may be somewhat quick to assume that young people with the skill to read, do not do so purely because of their choice not to; this is implied in the definition of aliteracy. However, both anecdotally and in the literature, it seemed that preference for other leisure pursuits was part but not all of the issue. I also noted that some of the students who said that they preferred to do other things, such as playing computer games, also had issues with other areas, such as sustained attention, making me wonder to what extent this preference was really a choice.

I was able to investigate this area of interest further in the WASABR, as all of the teens who reported reading books for pleasure *less than once a month* or *never* were characterized as infrequent readers, and the survey redirected them to an extra question to gain further data around the reasons for their reading infrequency. A total of 185 respondents fell into the category of infrequent readers and were thus referred to this question.

The data seemed to confirm my suspicions. What became clear as a result of this survey was that, for many teens, preference was a controlling factor (as shown in Table 2.1, 78 percent of students agreed with the statement, "I would rather do other things with my free time"). However, students were permitted multiple responses, and for many, choice was not the only reason, as you can see from Table 2.1.

I was particularly interested to see that nearly a third of teenage infrequent readers struggled to sit for the period required for reading and that nearly two-fifths found it difficult to locate interesting books to read.

As such, I wonder if most so-called aliterate students are being correctly classified. While for most students, preference was a factor, a noteworthy number of respondents also indicated that they were affected by physical and cognitive factors, a skill barrier, issues with access and choice, and limited time availability. There is rarely just one reason. For instance, one teenage WASBAR respondent explained the range of barriers faced when attempting to read:

> I find that when I am reading a book and I find it not interesting, I just stop reading and don't continue. I also don't get enough time to read a book continuously because I prefer not to get interrupted. I get interrupted at home by chores and homework. I also get distracted by social networking sites like Facebook and Tumblr. However, if I do get enough free time to read books that I like, which are most likely to be a book on romance or about personal experiences, I would most likely get hooked on the book and not put it down.

Table 2.1   Reasons for Infrequent Book Reading

Reasons for Infrequent Recreational Book Reading	%	Reason Identified from Previous Research
I don't have time to read.	28%	Time availability
Reading books is boring.	45%	Preference
I would rather do other things with my free time.	78%	Preference
I am not good at reading.	14%	Skill
I would rather read something else (e.g., magazines, Web pages, Facebook).	44%	Preference
I can't find interesting books to read.	39%	Access and choice
I can't sit still for that long.	31%	Physical/cognitive
I can't get any books to read.	2%	Access
Reading gives me a headache.	8%	Physical/cognitive
Reading makes me sleepy.	15%	Physical/cognitive
I find reading hard.	8%	Skill
None of these reasons/other reasons (Please give your own reason.)	8%	Various

Source: Adapted from Merga, 2014b.

This suggests that it is appropriate to view reading infrequency as being caused by a number of factors, many of which are under our control as parents, teachers, and literacy advocates. If there is more than one reason not to read, we will need more than one solution to the problem of reading infrequency. The decision not to read is not always a straightforward choice, and other factors are involved that we, as social agents, may hope to mitigate. We can potentially have the most immediate effect on supporting these reluctant readers to find books that are of interest to them. Once we accept that the reason infrequent adolescent readers do not read is not solely related to preference for other activities, we can stop viewing them as a uniform group of aliterates and rather focus on what we can due to mitigate each of these identified barriers. That less than half of these infrequent teen readers agreed that reading books is boring is a very positive finding, suggesting that the attitudinal barriers toward reading may be smaller than we may anticipate. I explore these ideas further in the following chapter.

3

Are Books Really Uncool?

This chapter explores the current social status of books and reading for young people, challenging the notion that books are seen as "uncool" by most young people.

When we imagine an avid book reader, we contend with a cultural stereotype. Traditionally, this tends to be a bespectacled older woman, reading in a comfortable chair with a cat on her lap or even multiple cats, all purring in perfect harmony with one another. However, in reality, the social status of books in contemporary society may be potentially higher; books might not be uncool.

It can be suggested that the opposite of the cat-lady stereotype would be the rugged, young male football player. In 2016, the coach of the premiership-winning Australian Football League (AFL) team, Luke Beveridge, made the news for using literature as a motivational tool. He read his players, an team of young, extremely athletic Australian men, a children's book in order to motivate them to victory, and his plan was successful: His team won the AFL premiership, which some would argue is the nation's highest (and coolest) honor (Olle, 2016).

Books may have also come out of the shadow of the nerdy stereotype for young people. When I was a young person, intelligence was associated with an undesirable nerd identity, but in the current generation, intelligent people are often presented as cool in films and books. The cross-media promotion of young adult books made into games and films, such as the *Harry Potter* and *Hunger Games* series, has also potentially increased the social status of the original books. It might be time to rethink the position of books in young people's lives. If we persist in a stereotypical conceptualization of books as outdated or even dead, as uncool (Ipsos MORI, 2003), we ignore contemporary movements that have done much to position books at the center of the youth culture, which may actually encourage reading for its potential for social engagement (Scharber, 2009). These movements do make a difference; for example, teen student Julio explained, "I've always enjoyed *Harry Potter* as a kid, that's what got me into reading more." *Harry Potter* also helped a tween, Karen, to change her perception of reading:

> Well, at first I did it because I had to learn, and then once I started reading, I started reading small books, and I kind of thought, that's pretty cool. And one day mum

asked me, "Do you want to read *Harry Potter*?" I'm like, "No, I don't want to read *Harry Potter*." And then I read it, and then that's how I started reading thicker books.

It was also interesting to note how Karen's initial negative response to her mother's encouragement to read was readily overcome; though we do not know how, it is a clear illustration of how young people's initial position on reading can shift with the right books or influences.

Reading is well understood to be a social practice (Allington & Swann, 2009), with reading and writing both closely linked to social purpose (Monaghan & Hamann, 1998). Despite the fact that it is something we often undertake independently, we learn about books and reading from the world around us. We are not born with books in our hands; they are supplied in our school and home environments where resourcing permits, just as we are not born with the ability to read but acquire it through ongoing educational experiences. Our attitudes toward reading are likewise shaped by these social exchanges.

Young people who enjoy reading are more likely to read. We know that young people who value reading and who find it interesting are more likely to read regularly (Wigfield, 1997), and the way young people perceive the social value of books and reading can influence their overall impression of reading and their level of engagement in the practice. For instance, having friends who enjoy reading and who discuss reading is related to the development and retention of positive attitudes toward reading (Bintz, 1993; Partin & Gillespie, 2002), and recommendations from friends are generally highly appreciated by teens (McKool, 2007; Rinehart, Gerlach, Wisell, & Welker, 1998). Getting recommendations mitigates some of the risk involved in choosing an unknown book and investing time in reading it, as explained by Nat, a teen who did not read for pleasure often, apart from during silent reading at school.

I: And when you go to choose a book, how do you do that? What's your technique?

N: First I'd probably just ask if anyone knows any good books. And then if I just had to go and pick one, I'd just . . . look at the cover, look at the title, and then just read the blurb or the first couple of lines of the book. But usually I don't pick a book without knowing someone else has read it.

I: And why is that?

N: I don't know, just 'cause that's like that hardest part is getting into it, but then so far already I know the story, I know what I'm like at reading and then I'm like, "Oh, I've got to keep reading, I've gotta get a good one," if that makes sense. Like I'm not just gonna start it and hope that it's good, I need to know that someone else has liked it.

The risk of an unknown book actually emerged as quite a substantial concern for some young people. For instance, tween Leah explained, "I think everyone should read, because some people tend to hate books just because they read a book they did not like." With friends powerfully situated to mitigate this risk, it is unsurprising that research suggests that friends can typically influence reading choices (Howard & Jin, 2007; Mansor, Rasul, Rauf, & Koh, 2012) and that readers are more likely to have friends who also read (Hughes-Hassell, 2008). This could be because young people are more likely to gravitate toward friends with the same or similar interests, but it could also be due to the transformative influence that one friend with a positive attitude toward reading can exert among their friends. For example, Krysta, a teen student, used recommendations to try to exert a kind of positive peer pressure on her friends who did not read as often, explaining, "I'm trying to get them to read a bit more 'cause I personally love reading, and I guess I'm trying to get them to experience what I experience when I read." Her enthusiasm to share the experience led her to become a reading advocate within her group of friends.

So why might the coolness of books matter? We know that most people care about the social image they project and how others perceive them (Bursztyn, Egorov, & Jensen, 2016), so the desire to adhere to socially acceptable behaviors, at least in public, is typical of most people. My research suggests that young people's perception of the social acceptability of book reading is important. Unsurprisingly, those who deemed books to be socially unacceptable were less likely to read books in their free time and to enjoy recreational book reading; attention needs to be given to raising the social profile of books and reading (Merga, 2014e). This was the case for both boys and girls. Previous research also found that the perceived coolness of reading could be a factor in students' reading engagement (Scholes, 2010).

As much as we might care about what society thinks about us, we may be more influenced by our friends. While research often fails to differentiate between friends' and the peer group's values, which are instead constructed as interchangeable (as explored in Merga, 2014e), it is important to understand that, just as we as adults may be more influenced by what our close friends think, rather than our peers more generally, children may understandably share this orientation. This means that, while keeping our finger on the pulse of the general attitude of young people toward the social acceptability of books is important, we also ideally need to consider how to increase the social status of books and how to increase young people's exposure to new friends with shared book interests through classroom initiatives such as book clubs or online communities like Goodreads.

We also need to provide more opportunities for friend recommendations and encouragement. Less than a fifth of teen respondents in the WASABR reported receiving encouragement to read from their friends, and while girls (25 percent) were far more likely than boys to receive encouragement from their friends (11 percent), it could not be said that either gender was being strongly encouraged by their friends to read (Merga, 2014e). In the WASABR, how young people perceived their friends' attitudes was more significant an influence than the perceived peer group's attitudes, and this influence was stronger for boys than for girls (Merga, 2014e). We need to make talking about books in the context of pleasure a norm, as I will explore in further detail later in this book. If every child we encounter in our capacity as a teacher or librarian recommends just *one* good book to friends through activities that we facilitate, we could make headway toward addressing this issue.

One way I might manage this in a classroom is by letting my students know that, by the end of the term, they need to recommend a book to the class. They can have a choice about how they do this. It could be on a blog post on the shared internal learning management system, a short oral pitch, a poster celebrating the best aspects of the book, or a book "trailer" made in the garage with their mates (imagining it as a film)—whatever method suits the student. I would also let them know that it is first-come, first-served, so no one can recommend a book already recommended by another class member. Getting these positive recommendations out in the public domain can not only boost reading and help young people choose books that can be appealing to them, it can also help to raise their social status. Here are some other ways to achieve this:

1. Encourage students to read for pleasure and to talk about the books they read. Provide a safe environment for them to express their ideas and opinions. Students need to know about good books to be attracted to reading them; strategies such as book clubs, brainstorms of good books, and book swaps can give books more exposure in your classroom and thus, hopefully, raise their appeal.

2. If your students participate in self-selected silent reading at school, consider allowing discussion about books before and after the silent reading session. Students should lead the discussion as much as possible, and they should be encouraged to be tolerant and open-minded about one another's genre preferences. No student should be forced to participate in this discussion.

3. Have students describe the successful strategies they use to choose good books. A library can pose a daunting prospect for students who have little idea where to begin looking.

4. Draw student attention to upcoming films based on young adult texts, and encourage reading them. You may also need to facilitate access to these texts, and you should familiarize yourself with both the films and the books.

5. Connect your students to online book forums that present reading in a positive light, and enable them to connect with readers who have similar interests. You will need to familiarize yourself with these forums and develop an understanding of how they work.

6. Connect your students with books they will enjoy. To do this, you need to have students identify their own reading preferences so that you can provide welcome guidance. Talk to them. (Adapted from Merga, 2014e, p. 480)

EVOLVING COOLNESS?

If you happen to be working in a school where books are deemed uncool, do not despair. While reading may be typically and traditionally associated with being uncool, which may lead to teenaged readers feeling reticent to speak about their reading, readers and reading do not remain static over time. The social status of reading, like all leisure pursuits, is subject to change with regard to its popularity and social acceptability. As a result, it is reasonable to surmise that the perceived social status of books is likely to be subject to significant change over time and within context, so we should probably stop referring to research over 10 years old when talking about the social status of books. You can also play an active role in changing the culture of your school or home to be more supportive of reading as a positive and culturally acceptable pastime. My research discovered that reading books for recreation is seen as a relatively socially acceptable pastime by most contemporary teens, with very few boys (11 percent) and girls (7 percent) agreeing that "it is not cool to read books" (Merga, 2014e, p. 479). This perception was more positive than I anticipated, suggesting that we should avoid generalization and negative assumptions, particularly in light of how swiftly attitudes toward recreational pursuits can change in these evolving times.

Of course, the dominant social construction of the coolness (or otherwise) of reading is not the only determinant influencing young people's attitudes toward reading; individual attitudes also come into play. Here it becomes a little more complicated. While only 49 percent of teens agreed or strongly agreed that they like reading books in their free time, only 27 percent disagreed or strongly disagreed, with a number holding quite a neutral attitude (Merga, 2014c). These results were considerably more positive than Nieuwenhuizen's earlier attitudinal findings in Australia in 2001, suggesting that there may have been improvement in the social status of books over this period, perhaps reflective of the greater promotion of books in current media and film. With efforts to improve the social status of books, hopefully we can at least shift the neutral students into positive territory and maybe even capture some of the negative students as well, especially if we can start to match their unique interests with engaging books in these areas. As I have mentioned previously, there is much you can do to support the shift toward increasing the social status of books and reading.

MORE ON TALKING ABOUT BOOKS

If you have ever taken part in a book club, you will be aware of how influential listening to a discussion about books can be. It is hard not to listen to people discuss books that they have enjoyed without being inspired to read the book, particularly if it is in your area of interest. To raise the social appeal of a practice, it helps if books can become the focus of social interaction. As previously explored, avid readers talked about the significance of shared social habit on fostering lifelong reading attitudes in them, and with my research collaborators at Deakin, we recently explored how the status of reading as a social practice can be enhanced in relation to teens' attitudes toward discussing books and examined implications for practice (Merga, McRae, & Rutherford, 2017). We explored teens' attitudes toward discussing books to investigate reasons for engagement in discussions about books, while seeking to determine which factors inhibited such discussions, in order to try to come up with further ideas about how literacy advocates can best facilitate discussion.

When talking about books for pleasure, we found that teens tended to enjoy discussions where the discussants shared similar interests. Tweens shared similar observations in the WASCBR, such as Zac; when asked if he liked talking about books, he explained that "my friends do sometimes, and at recess we just stop and talk about our books, and then in library we're just telling jokes about the different parts of the books." Whether youngsters are bonding through recounting the humor in a book or discussing whether the second book in a horror series is as scary as the original, when books are discussed in the context of shared interests, enthusiasm can be generated. This is why in addition to a more general discussion about books, we suggest considering the creation of special-interest book discussion groups in classrooms and in libraries or literature circles, with perhaps a stronger focus on preferred genres than the typical book club (Merga, McRae, & Rutherford, 2017). Such groups can inspire young people to read more often.

While talking about books in the context of pleasure can be seen as something that would happen separately from or parallel to the fostering of the technical literacy skills outlined in the Australian curriculum, these opportunities can both introduce and reinforce critical reading skills without being overtly teacherly. By this, I mean that discussions about books in the context of pleasure can be a great chance to begin to critically unpack aspects of the book, such as character construction, without appearing to be a didactic learning experience. Unfortunately, the WASCBR research suggests that tweens may be exposed to limited opportunities to discuss reading books for pleasure in contemporary classrooms (Merga, 2018). Similarly, recent research suggests that some teens have never experienced book discussions (Merga, McRae, & Rutherford, 2017).

Discussion was appreciated for the opportunities it raised for critical exploration, such as through debates about the merits of different characters and plot twists. For example, older teen Chris enjoyed having "small arguments" with his friends about the characters in his favorite book series, and he laughed as he explained his perspective:

> We're talking about favorite characters, and I prefer the evil characters as I find them quite interesting. Like we were just, yeah, talking about the interesting characters, and you know the stereotypical good person is always going to win and that, I can sometimes find it quite boring, so I quite enjoyed the evil character, so that's what we were arguing about. (Merga, McRae, & Rutherford, 2017, p. 8)

Chris raises concepts of stereotyping, audience response, and the values projected by certain characters. Learning about these concepts through enthusiastic debate would arguably be more engaging than completing a character chart or listening to a PowerPoint presentation, and it provides an opportunity for students to explore their own personal responses, enabling them to "construct meaning with their peers, and to question whether meaning is inherent in text," which can help to induct students "into the community of readers" (Raphael & McMahon, 1994, p. 103).

Such discussions are also good for struggling students. While students such as Chris might enjoy discussions about books and use them to build his higher-order skills, for students who are perhaps at the lower end of their understanding of a text, listening to this kind of debate and exchange around character and plot can be really useful. Research suggests that "reading comprehension is enhanced by the classroom interaction of students with their teachers and peers, including both small-group work and whole-class discussion" (Nystrand, 2006, p. 398). We also know that "discussions about and around text" can be "highly effective at promoting students' literal and inferential comprehension" (Murphy et al., 2009, p. 759), though not all approaches were found to be equally effective. Struggling students may benefit more than their higher-achieving peers, with research finding that "use of these discussion approaches appears to be more potent for students of below-average ability than for students of average or above-average ability, possibly due to the fact that students of higher ability levels already possess the skills needed to comprehend narrative text" (p. 760).

Our research found that some struggling teen readers found discussions about books really useful in developing and consolidating their own comprehension, as explained by Spencer:

> Yeah, sometimes I do like to talk about the books that I'm reading. Sometimes I like to talk about the plot of what's going on in it, but I do like to talk about the plot and what's going on in a certain section in the book as well. So, that kind of helps me to understand it, 'cause if I can talk about it to somebody else then that helps me understand it a bit better, and that way I know what I'm reading. (Merga, McRae, & Rutherford, 2017, p. 9)

For students struggling with reading comprehension, book discussion enables them to check and consolidate understanding in a safe space. Students such as Spencer wouldn't be forced to reveal their lack of understanding unless they were comfortable doing so, as book discussions should ideally be structured to avoid "two norms of classroom literacy that may hinder authentic conversations about books: turn taking and the emphasis on individual work" (Raphael & McMahon, 1994, p. 105). Allowing a few students to dominate the conversation for a time is not necessarily a bad thing in this context, as it can further the understanding of struggling students, and students can collaboratively venture to build understanding about the text rather than have a meaning imposed by the teacher for replication. This encourages higher-order thinking, shifting away from a spoon-feeding reading comprehension approach, and also allows for creativity and subjectivity in interpretation.

Choosing a good book can be hard, especially if you are not already a regular reader, with some knowledge and experience of genres and authors. While I will explore the issues that young people experience with choice and a range of ways to support the development of choosing strategies later on in this book, I would like to highlight that book discussions are also valued as an opportunity to make recommendations for further reading. They can also help books compete with other leisure pursuits, as outlined in this teenager's comment:

> I spend most of my time gaming, but when I find a good book, I usually read it fanatically until I finish it. If a friend is reading a book and recommends it, I would get it out of the library and read it. I would usually play cricket 3 times a week, but I am giving this year a miss. I do find reading incredibly enjoyable.

While our research respondents tended to have a positive attitude toward book discussions, opportunities to engage in discussion were not always frequently available in class and at home. This suggests that more can be done to provide contexts where young people can talk about books with interested others, thereby raising the social status of books and reading, at the same time offering benefits for critical reading and comprehension (Merga, McRae, & Rutherford, 2017). Opportunities for book clubs in class, such as special-interest groups, have been associated with improving reading comprehension, attitudes toward reading for pleasure, and social and emotional competences (Tijms, Stoop, & Polleck, 2017). It is easy to mount a strong argument for the educational importance of book clubs in class; a meta-analysis of multiple studies of the comprehension benefits of book clubs found that "Book Club discussions were highly effective at promoting students' metacognition in single-group design studies" (Murphy et al., 2009, p. 760). Book clubs can also enable young people whose friends are nonreaders to socialize about books with a broader potential group of peers, opening the possibility for them to find new friends with positive attitudes toward books, which can be influential (Merga, 2014e).

USING FILM ADAPTATIONS TO INCREASE THE COOLNESS AND ACCESSIBILITY OF BOOKS

These days, multiple films based on popular young adult novels are released each year, and few people in the Western countries will not have heard of Harry Potter or Katniss Everdeen. As such, students may encounter movie adaptations with great frequency, as many of the films marketed to young adult viewers are based on best-selling books also aimed at that demographic. Rather than simply competing with reading, movies based on books may significantly increase the popularity of the related books, as evidenced by the *Harry Potter* record-breaking movies and books (Knapp, 2003), among numerous others. What students make of these textual intersections and how they can be exploited for their literacy benefits have received limited attention from researchers. Letting students know that there will be a movie coming out based on a book in the not too distant future can pique the interest of young people; whether that leads to the increased likelihood that they will read the book is not necessarily a given.

Linking the movie and the book in the minds of young people can be problematic because reading a book for pleasure is a choice, and where other choices such as video games and movie viewing appear to offer more immediate rewards, book reading may easily fall by the wayside. As such, it is unsurprising that movies are often situated as the enemy of literacy and book reading. We have also been quite slow to accept movies as a text in their own right in the English classroom. Even now, in the early weeks of my English teaching courses, when I ask my students to juxtapose two texts, they almost invariably select two written texts, and I have to consistently reiterate that visual and multimedia texts are also texts. Traditionally, print-based texts have been viewed more favorably than non-print-based texts such as movies (Alvermann, 2011), and the study of films as part of an English curriculum has been positioned as part of a "dumbing down" of English (Jetnikoff, 2007). When a book studied in class has an existing movie adaptation, students are usually encouraged to limit their engagement with it, as, generally, "teens are assigned a book, and expressly told by various adults not to watch the movie before reading the book, or not to watch the movie at all" (Flowers, 2011, p. 23). The possibility that movies might act as a friend of literacy and encourage and support some students to read is worth consideration, as is the possibility that, in some cases, watching the movie first might offer significant benefit. However, before we can suggest this, we need a better understanding of what happens when young people view adaptations and of young people's attitudes toward book/film and film/book exposures.

Beyond the novelty of the screen, movie adaptations may act as a device to connect the books upon which they are based to the socially influential media and popular culture domains, thus enhancing the books' appeal and cultural relevance—their overall coolness. As I have mentioned previously, the trend of aliteracy, the condition in which those who can read choose not to, is growing among students in the majority of Organisation for Economic Co-operation and Development (OECD) countries, with the researchers contending that "the challenge for parents and educators is to instill a sense of pleasure in reading by providing reading materials that students find interesting and relevant" (OECD, 2011c). Connecting a book to a movie potentially responds to this challenge. Attention to the intersection between popular culture and in-class instruction has been a key consideration of an increasing body of research in education since the last decade of the 20th century, though notions of the educational value of literary practices that involve student engagement with popular culture texts widely vary (Alvermann, 2011).

We also know that using a movie to support the study of a written text can help struggling students, as long as the plots are sufficiently similar. Students who struggle with reading skills can be excluded from complex analysis of a text due to their effort being focused on essential but lower-order skills, such as comprehension. Cutchins (2003) contends that "watching a movie as part of the study of a written text can help move students of literature beyond understanding a novel or story simplistically, only in terms of its plot or characterization" and that "film can actually teach them some of the more delicate qualities of literature" (p. 296), including aspects of literature that would be otherwise inaccessible. There will, of course, be a trade-off in these instances that needs to be taken into account, as students can easily become confused between the two texts, so this needs to be managed with care. For example, perhaps a teacher is trying to support struggling students to understand how a female protagonist is being marginalized by a powerful male character in a complex book, introducing complex ideas such as oppression, patriarchy, and misogyny. This may be more readily achieved through viewing, where the book is not as easily accessible for some members of the class. In this instance, just parts of the film would need to be shown, reducing some of the risks of the texts blending to the point of confusion in students' minds or of students choosing not to try to read the book because they have seen the movie.

At this stage, limited consideration has been given to exploring a potential positive influence that viewing the movie adaptation could have on reading outcomes for the partner book. There is also limited understanding of how movie adaptations that students may watch in class or in their own leisure time may influence students' understandings of the books, and the reverse. As part of the WASABR, I wanted to consider how viewing movie adaptations of books influences the reading experience of teens. I wanted to ask students how they felt about seeing the movie and then reading the book and about the converse scenario, where possible, in order to examine the advantages and disadvantages of this textual partnership, as well as to illuminate the areas of interest that the students raised. I did not limit the consideration to the books and movies engaged in as part of classroom learning, as I was more interested in reading and viewing for recreational purposes, though these findings clearly also have implications for classroom practice.

WHERE IT WORKS

My WASABR findings suggest that for some students, it appears that viewing the movie first is essential for motivation to read for recreation. A number of students spontaneously chose to address this issue in the qualitative field. One reluctant reader stated, "I only read books that are hell funny, or have become, or are becoming a movie," with another only reading when "inspired by a movie." Another reluctant reader described the current or future existence of a film based on a book being central to the reading practices of her friends, stating that "many of my friends read books which have or will be turned into a film."

The reasons for some students preferring viewing before reading were located around a few key themes, which are now explored.

Reliable Quality Sample

If the movie is found to be enjoyable, some students are motivated to seek out the source book, with the movie felt to be a reliable quality sample, which, of course, is problematic, considering how widely some movies divert from their original source texts. Nonetheless, viewing a movie was a powerful motivator to read for some teens. Sevgi explained why viewing often motivated her to read, stating, "If I see the movie, I really want to read the book, 'cause books are always better than the movie I think." Leona read occasionally for pleasure and was often motivated by movies, stating that "there's a few where I've watched the movie, and then it's been, 'Oh yeah, it's a book too', and I've read it. *Marley and Me*, I've watched that movie and then I've read that book and really enjoyed it." Many teens agreed that books were typically better than the movies, so if the movie is enjoyed, the book is expected to be good. Before committing to a book series, which can involve a considerable time commitment, the movie provides a quality sample for some students; Fatima stated that she would "see one movie first, like the first movie, see if it, like I enjoy it, and then I would go on to the books."

Another advantage of using the movie adaptation as a quality indicator lies in the overall reluctance of the cohort to waste time in books that ultimately fail to engage them. Previous analysis from the WASABR research indicated that, for many students, time spent reading is an investment and a risk, as I explore further later in this chapter. Pre-viewing removes some of the uncertainty, potentially increasing the likelihood that expectations will be satisfied.

Increasing the Appeal of Classics

Movies can provide an entry point to texts that might be otherwise relatively inaccessible to contemporary young people, highlighting their relevance to this audience. For instance, Ciara described her decision to read the classic text *Wuthering Heights* as a product of her attraction to the actor playing the character in the film. When asked why she selected this particular novel, she explained her attraction:

To be honest, it was because I watched the movie, which had a really hot actor in it. And I liked the movie, so I thought, "Hey, may as well read the book, that'll be interesting." And I know the song, the song is good, so . . . I kind of do a trio [book, movie, song] of *Wuthering Heights*.

Enjoying the movie, the song, and the physical appearance of the actor who played the central male character, Heathcliff, motivated this student to persist with a text that she admitted finding challenging to read. Melania, an occasional reader in Year 8, was similarly struggling through *The Hobbit* after watching Peter Jackson's *The Lord of the Rings* trilogy; when I asked her if she was enjoying it, she assented, though qualifying this with the statement, "[I]t's a bit confusing though." She was trying the read the book before the Peter Jackson film *The Hobbit: An Unexpected Journey* was released at the end of 2012; at the time of the interview, she had managed to read the first 50 pages and was mildly optimistic about her chances of finishing before seeing the movie. She was motivated to progress through the book so that she could finish it before the release of the movie, a book that she may not have considered without the refreshing impact of the new franchise.

Imagining It Right

One of the odd and unexpected things that emerged from this research was young people's relinquishing of the right to imagine characters freely. Some students described the value of viewing the movie first in that it prevented them from being disappointed when their imagined characters were not identical to the actors cast in the films. Ciara explained this concern in detail; she preferred to see at least the first movie in a series before reading the subsequent books:

It's easier to read a book after at least seeing, say, the first movie or something, so you have a picture of characters, and it's easier to understand, instead of . . . like when I read a book first before the movie, you picture someone completely different, and it's kind of a letdown when you watch the movie, it's like, "Oh, well that's not how I pictured it." So, a lot of the time, first movie, and then I'll read the whole lot of it.

It is significant that having the job of imagining characters done for her makes the movie "easier to understand"; there is limited research on the impact on student comprehension and cognition when reading this kind of prefabrication of characters and plots through earlier exposure to films.

Ibtesam did not really enjoy reading, preferring screen-based leisure pursuits such as social networking online, though she did choose to read for pleasure occasionally. She found viewing an important precursor to reading, as, "[S]ometimes when I read books, I don't read them before the movie. I watch the movie so I have a—picture in my head, so it makes it interesting." When asked if she had any difficulty imagining the characters based on description alone, the student said, "Yeah, I actually have, 'cause some of—the books explain what they look like, and then, when I watch the movie, it's totally different." For this student also, the incongruence between what their imagination constructed as a consequence of reading descriptions and the appearance of the actors in the film was disappointing.

For these students, it appears that the film version was viewed as the more authentic or real of the two character constructions—the one they imagined and the one appearing on film—and, rather than being unhappy with the casting choices, they tended to speak as though they had imagined it wrong, which was unexpected. O'Toole (1982) suggested that "if a movie tells us that Hardy's Tess looks and moves the way Natassja Kinski does, there's not a damn thing we can do about it other than apply instant criticism" (p. 34), but the students cited here are not inclined to do this. The incongruence almost seemed to be perceived as a failure, in that students almost seem to believe that they imagined characters incorrectly, resulting in a "letdown." I am a little worried by this, as I feel it could potentially lead students to be reluctant to read books if they know a movie is coming out based on the book in order to avoid this perceived incorrect imagining.

Students who use movies to support their imagination to conceive characters and improve comprehension are adopting a distinct reading practice. The extent to which the experience with the movie shapes the understanding of the book is worth consideration, particularly as some students appear to have naturalized a literary reading that places the authenticity of characterization in the movie as more valid than characterization derived from the original book. We do not really know whether this is a good thing. Concentration is already a limitation for some students, as I explore further in Chapter 7. Viewing before reading clearly helped a number of students by providing an imagery scaffold while reading the book, leading to repeated adherence to a reading practice that requires viewing before reading. The dependence some students appear to have developed to viewing before reading suggests that it easier for students to concentrate on a book if they have already viewed the movie, perhaps due to the reduced cognitive imaginative process required.

While this appears to be a helpful and supportive scaffold, a need for future research to determine how dependent these students are on this scaffold is warranted. Ideally, students should still be able to imagine characters without the scaffold; otherwise, an important skill is being unutilized. In addition, if students are already regarding the film as the valid construct of characters rather than the book where the characters originated, students may not be willing to invest the effort to imagine characters if their imagination will not furnish them with the correct actor's features and mannerisms, even if these depart from the book's description.

However, recent research suggests that in an estimated 2 percent of the population (Zeman, Dewar, & Della Salla, 2015), some of our students could lack a capacity to imagine, which involves producing visual imagery. While it has been suggested that this condition of cognitive aphantasia is an inborn trait, further research is needed in this area (e.g., Keogh & Pearson, 2017).

Textual Blending and Juxtaposition

Students' critical understandings of film study can be expected to advance as they progress along the educational continuum, receiving increasing exposure to media studies. Whether students apply this critical awareness to films they are not explicitly studying, such as movie adaptations that are not being subject to examination, is worth consideration, particularly as skills transfer can be indicative of deeper learning. While films are studied in the contemporary English class as texts in their own right, some students seem to easily confuse novel and movie attributes, blending them, in some cases, in their descriptions into a kind of united text, such as the "trio of *Wuthering Heights*," rather than showing an awareness that each text "is a different genre, open to multiple readings and that each one needs to be seen or read in its own right" (Jetnikoff, 2005).

Other students were more discerning and enjoyed juxtaposing the related texts for their enjoyment. Shiva described how he did this:

> **S:** I like reading books and then, perhaps if they have movies made out of them, watching those as well, it compliments them both, yeah.
>
> **I:** So, does that make you want to watch a movie after you've read the book?
>
> **S:** Yes, yes—or perhaps if I see the movie, first, I'd like to read the book, and get to see how the author put it. Yeah.
>
> **I:** So, do you look at the different ways . . . ?
>
> **S:** Yeah, just perhaps how the characters made the movie, and perhaps what things he didn't include, like that's how I started reading the Harry Potter series, I actually saw the movies first.

A keen reader, Shiva liked to compare "complimentary" texts to enhance his experience and understanding of the texts. Zara also described enjoyment from juxtaposition and commented that her friends were usually better equipped than she is to enjoy this experience.

> And then there's a new movie coming out, *Beautiful Creatures*, and that was a book that I got when I was 13, and I really want to read the book before the movie comes out, so I can make the comparisons, so I'll actually be able to do that, and I always get [other] people mak[ing] the comparisons and I don't know.

For Zara, the ability to perform critical juxtaposition is part of the context of the viewing experience. She talks of previously having other friends "make the comparisons" that she cannot make if she has not read the book. By reading the book, she positions herself to be able to contribute to this critique, which is part of her friends' social practice.

WHERE IT DOES NOT WORK

While a number of students were motivated to read by viewing, others firmly defended the importance of reading the book first, and the textual issues raised by plot compression and alteration required by script adaptation were often resented. These recurring themes are highlighted here.

Deficiency of Detail and Losing the Plot

A number of students felt that the book was typically superior to the movie adaptation due to the greater detail possible. All of these students were keen readers who seemed to value these details. For Sevgi, the deficiency of detail significantly impacted upon her ability to enjoy the movie. When asked how she felt about viewing a film after reading the related book, she stated, "I enjoyed the movie, but I was disappointed that some bits that were quite important that weren't put into it, so there's only a couple of bits in it."

Dash was genuinely angered by the manner in which the film version of one of his favorite books took liberties with the plot:

> One movie I don't like is *Eragon*, how they've changed a lot of the things that happened in it, in the movie, that they couldn't even make a sequel, in the same to the book, by killing off the Razac, which, yeah, and all sorts of ah, people that don't die. And they killed them off, and then at the end, they don't even do the fight scene right, where, one of the things when it happens, and, they don't do that, and it ruins the book—the movie quite a bit, because they can't make the sequel, everything grows up too quick.

Like Dash, some students required a high degree of plot faithfulness, such as Ingrid, who stated that "sometimes the movie's exactly like the book, which is really good, other times it's nothing like the book, and [I] just don't like it then." She preferred to read the book before seeing the movie.

Literacy educators can attempt to exploit this level of passion about textual fidelity to engage students in intertextual analysis. This can be more complicated than simple plot difference, as Jetnikoff (2005) explains:

> Rather than bemoan the differences, or notions of "fidelity to the original text" we could ask, "how close do film adaptations have to be?" To examine textual discourses, it can be pointed out that film adaptations are often changed or renegotiated according to cultural and historical contexts and audience pretexts. (p. 89)

Students' subjective opinions can be respected and encouraged, but the challenge for students is to articulate and argue the validity of their position and to understand the factors that may have contributed to the adaptation taking the form that it does.

Other students were more accepting of significant plot diversions. Layla described how the changes between the book and the film took her by surprise, explaining that "it's not what I expected. It's a good movie, but the characters, you know, like the characters are well done, but the actual story, the plot, the story ended where the book didn't end." She used this example to highlight her position on the order of reading and viewing that she felt most conducive to enjoyment, namely, "[R]ead the book, then watch a movie."

Pleasure

While a book and a film may tell the same or a similar story, the different modes will influence the reader/viewer differently. Some teen readers described there being far greater pleasure involved in the reading journey; for instance, Damien described books as offering a superior pleasure experience due to increased emotional engagement:

> I love reading books because it is an excellent hobby and passion and some books are really great. The difference between reading a book and watching a movie is that when you're watching a movie, you see what's happening; however, when you read a book, you feel what's happening.

Penny similarly explained why she read so many books rather than watching movies:

> I think it's just a way of . . . it's like some people, I dunno, watch television, or watch movies, 'cause, they forget the reality, and they start just—for me, it's just I escape in another world, and I don't have to worry about my problems, and I just—it's a feeling. So yeah, that's why I do it.

We cannot assume that all young people will necessarily find viewing more pleasurable than reading. It would seem that an assumption that all teens in the current generation will prefer movies to books, as movies are more modern, is currently not unequivocally supported.

Movies Are (Cognitively) Cheaper Than Books (and Shorter Too)

A ticket price to a movie can typically cost about the same amount of money as a book these days, so, unsurprisingly, financial cost was not raised as a preference for either mode. What was an issue, for some students, was cost in terms of the investment of time and effort. For some students, watching the movie was viewed as a better investment of their time, with one Year 10 student choosing to respond to his teacher's book recommendations by watching the related movies. This attitude was shared by a number of teenage interview participants, such as Gerome; when asked about how much book reading he did in his free time, he responded:

> **G:** I don't do it a lot, as much as other stuff, because . . . it takes more time than other stuff, like watching a movie only takes a short time, while reading a book it can take a longer time, much longer time, depending on the book, so I kind of feel against it, a bit.
>
> **I:** So, you'd prefer to do things that take shorter periods of time?
>
> **G:** Yes, and then I might lose concen—I might not concentrate, not on a book that's so long 'cause I might lose interest in it halfway so then I think, oh, if I find out it's a bad book halfway through it's been a lot of time wasted, whereas a movie, it would only be an hour wasted.
>
> **I:** What about *Hunger Games*? Have you read them?
>
> **G:** Ah, no. With—with those books, 'cause there's a movie, I'll find it easier, yeah, I'll just watch the movie and then I'll kind of know what the book's about, so, I don't— I'm just like, "It'll be shorter and I'll know the same stuff", so, no real point.

I then asked him if seeing a movie ever motivated him to read a book, and he explained his position:

> *Harry Potter* was like a massive thing, I read it and then, 'cause, when I was young, my parents said, "Oh, because you've read the other ones you're not allowed to watch the next one until you've read it," so, that kind of motivated me a bit. So, then I would see what the book was in comparison, but, now because school's got more homework and everything, it's more like, they will just be, wouldn't be wasted time, but it would be time that I could just use to watch the movie, and it would be over faster, so then, I get the kind of gist of it a bit faster than reading a book.

For Gerome, while time is a key factor, effort, in the form of required sustained concentration, is also outlined as an issue. A number of students identified concentration issues with their reading, which I explore in greater detail in Chapter 7, suggesting that this cost may be a significant inhibitor to reading. It is also interesting to view how, in Gerome's case, using the movie as a reward for reading has apparently not yielded a long-term interest in reading the book first. His concern about wasted time and effort and his eloquence when explaining his position suggest that the economic reasoning he applies to his time use cannot be underestimated as a disincentive to reading.

Just as most adults do not like to waste their time, neither do young people. Verdaasdonk (1991) provides an exposition of the economics of time and effort when adults are making entertainment choices, stating, "Consumers seem to be on a constant search for something new. On the other hand, consumers feel more and more pressure of professional and domestic obligations. Hence, they calculate which expenditures of leisure time should be made" (p. 408). The cost of reading in terms of time and effort has been used to support predictions of book reading as a "dying pastime" for decades (Changing Times, 1951, p. 42). The choice for the faster option may extend beyond simply weighing the benefit in terms of pleasure conferred or effort required. In addition to a number of recreational extracurricular activities, many of the students who participated in this study had heavy non-recreational burdens on their time, including homework, paid work, and sibling care, as I also explore in greater detail in Chapter 7. While movies can be cheaper than books in terms of time and effort, there is likely to be a cost of choosing the film over the book in terms of literacy benefit that has yet to be adequately quantified. The fact that students' themselves regard viewing as the path requiring the least cognitive effort and therefore, arguably, the least cognitive benefit suggests that further research is required, so that entertainment choices can be made in the light of full understanding of their consequences.

THE CHICKEN OR THE EGG?

So should young people read the book before the movie or after? As the interviews progressed, it became apparent that students who preferred to read the book before seeing the movie were more likely to be regular, keen readers, who valued the details that had to be omitted from the movie. For these students, a potentially enhanced emotional connection through heightened investment was also often apparent, as was enjoyment of textual juxtaposition as a shared social practice, as previously described by Zara.

Students who preferred seeing the movie first were a more diverse group, including keen, occasional, and reluctant readers. For some reluctant readers, seeing the movie was essential for subsequent reading; if they didn't see the movie, they would not consider reading the book. This would suggest that viewing a movie before reading a book could be a powerful motivator for reluctant readers.

Of course, pre-viewing may potentially lead to reading avoidance, and it therefore could subsequently impact negatively on literacy outcomes. Smith & Scuilli's

(2011) concerns that seeing the movie first would lead to many students avoiding reading the book were consistent with the attitudes of some of the students cited in this study, as they indicated that they used viewing the movie as a means to circumvent the necessity of reading, in order to access a story of interest to them without the effort. While this can be an advantage when attempting to teach higher-order ideas or concepts that might be otherwise inaccessible to some students, if viewing supplants reading, the impact of the comparatively reduced time and effort required may impact on literacy outcomes because, as described in Chapter 1, time spent reading is consistently positively related to performance on literacy indicators. On the other hand, reversing the accepted order by positioning the movie as a starting point could also potentially support reluctant readers to read more by using popular culture to engage their interest, providing a safe quality indicator, making classic texts more accessible, and providing a scaffold for imagining the characters that they will encounter in the book. While pre-viewing appears to offer much in way of both appeal and comprehension, until research explores the influence of pre-viewing on cognition, the impact of adopting this practice cannot be known. In the interim, I suggest that you will need to weigh these factors and do your own school-based experiments to figure out what works best for you, bearing in mind the complex interplay of factors that can influence students' experience.

4

Myths about Boys, and Why They Get Oxygen

The literacy performance gap between boys and girls has led to focused attention on how to improve the lot of boys. However, popular myths about boys and how to address this problem have the potential to further exacerbate this gap.

Boys can be readers. Indeed, if you have ever seen a boy devouring *Harry Potter*, *The Hunger Games*, or Andy Griffith's hilarious *Treehouse* books, the idea that boys might innately not be readers will also seem pretty strange to you. It is perfectly possible for boys to enjoy reading. For example, Scholes (2015) found that there is considerable variation in tween boys' attitudes toward reading, with many enjoying the practice.

But if boys reading less than girls is not just a natural thing, why do girls typically read more often than boys and show more positive attitudes toward reading in general? And I use the word "typically" freely here, as all of us who have worked with children know many girls who are reluctant readers, as well as boys who are avid readers. We need to understand the problem in order to meet the needs of boys, in order to be responsive to the gender gap in literacy performance and engagement that is pretty much consistent worldwide. As explored in previous chapters, not all young people can be characterized as keen book readers, and gender may influence this. Reflective of international research, boys may read less than girls and have a less positive attitude toward book reading (Merga, 2014c).

However, it should also be noted that for all the buzz around boys and books in the media, in the policy construction space and in educational research, the reality is that it is not the biggest gap of concern. The performance gap within genders, such as between high-achieving girls and low-achieving girls, is larger than the gap between genders (OECD, 2010), and race and SES-related gaps are also typically far more substantial (Martino & Rezai-Rashti, 2013). As such, the project should be to engage *all reluctant readers*, regardless of gender, so that disengaged girls are also supported. Due to the association between regular reading and literacy improvement (Neff, 2015), increasing engagement in reading (and particularly in fiction book reading as this is most strongly associated with benefit, as explored in Chapter 1), is desirable. The literacy gap is an issue that reading can help to close.

WHY THE GAP IN READING ENGAGEMENT?

If boys are not just naturally less likely to read because of their Y chromosome, we have to accept that culture and socialization play a part. Research suggests that the literacy gap between genders may relate more to sociocultural construction than to a biological basis. Reading may be culturally understood as a typically feminine practice (Martino, 2001; Morgan, Nutbrown, & Hannon, 2009; Nichols, 2002). Scholes (2015) contends that how tweens accept reading as part of their gendered identity is very much responsive to class issues as well. She found boys who quietly resisted the construction of reading as uncool for boys at lower-socioeconomic schools, terming these boys "Clandestine Readers," though she noted possible negative social outcomes for these boys, stating that "boys from The Clandestine Readers who positively positioned reading within their masculine identity, regardless of an unsupportive dominant peer group, may become further marginalized or conform to the policing of their popular peers" (p. 214). We need to raise the social status in our schools and homes to create school and home cultures that will encourage rather than stifle the reading engagement of boys, if we are to realistically support boys' achievement and engagement in reading.

In addition, the different socialization of boys and girls toward reading begins early. We do not treat little girls and little boys the same while they are young; parents are more likely to read with their daughters (Baker & Milligan, 2016), sending a strong and early message that books are for girls more than for boys, as well as equipping girls with a significant advantage in earlier development of literacy skills through earlier and more consistent exposure to reading experiences. The difference in the levels of encouragement seems to persist through lower school, as the WASCBR research with tweens found that even though boys read less frequently than girls, girls received more encouragement to read from their parents (Merga & Mat Roni, in press). If we invest more time and energy in fostering female readers than male readers, is it really very surprising that we observe a gender gap?

DO BOYS PREFER NONFICTION?

We may try to solve the problem using the same strategy that caused the problem in the first place—by pigeonholing boys as a homogeneous group. This has led to the popular myth that all boys prefer nonfiction and that nonfiction is the boys' genre. This has led to pink and blue stickers on books, pink and blue boxes of books, and the idea that boy-friendly literature is nonfiction. Again, those of us who know a boy who has been an avid reader of fiction (which is hopefully every reader of this book) may feel uneasy at this generalization. Literacy advocates who have a wealth of experience working with young people over a range of contexts tend to treat this myth with some degree of derision, having seen that many boys do enjoy fiction; however, others are still trying to be responsive to the pervasive myth around boys' preferences by coming up with pink and blue reading boxes as though book preferences are solely dictated by gender. This characterization, which exists ostensibly to help increase boys' reading and literacy scores, can potentially do the reverse.

When I read the literature on the gender gap, I was interested to discover that boys are strongly characterized as preferring nonfiction, based on a view of boys and girls that subscribes to a really outdated construction of biological determinism in which gender is conflated with sex. By "biological determinism," I mean that the problem tends to be treated as inherent, part of our innate and immutable nature as a product of our sex, and therefore something that we are powerless to change (Bastian & Haslam, 2006), ignoring the strong research-based evidence that places hegemonic masculinity at the root of most of the problems that boys experience in schools (Martino & Kehler, 2007). I do not think that we can overestimate how powerful and pervasive this myth is. Even the influential OECD refers readers to a Web site in one of their recent papers (OECD, 2015a), where boys are constructed as needing "boy-friendly non-fiction" (Scieszka, n.d.), despite the fact that the OECD's own research suggests that, when they have a choice, boys tend to choose to read fiction rather than nonfiction (Merga, 2017e; OECD, 2011d). That an organization as data driven as the OECD can ignore its own statistical evidence in favor of this myth illustrates how strong it is, also showing how strongly influenced educational research and data analysis are by popular fashions and ideas. Since conducting my own research in this area, further research evidence from the United States, suggesting that boys are not more motivated than girls to read nonfiction, has led researchers to conclude that "perhaps the traditional assumption that boys are more drawn to nonfiction than girls are is unfounded or is rooted in stereotypes rather than actuality" (Parsons et al., 2018).

While small, outdated qualitative samples may suggest that boys would rather read about trucks and cars than anything else, the characterization of boys preferring nonfiction is not based on strong empirical research. There is very little recent compelling evidence to suggest that boys do actually prefer nonfiction; however, the reverse has been consistently found (e.g., Coles & Hall, 2002; Harkrader & Moore, 1997; Manuel & Robinson, 2003; OECD, 2011d; Sims, 2012; Williams, 2008). Gender stereotypes about males' preference for nonfiction have also been soundly challenged by my recent research, reporting on my own research data (Table 4.1) (Merga, 2017e).

There is also a myth about boys' mode preferences, suggesting that boys typically prefer to read on screen. My most recent research challenges the notion that boys prefer to read on screens (see Chapter 6 for further details).

Table 4.1   Book Genre Preference of Male Identifying Respondents

Study	% Prefer Fiction	% Prefer Nonfiction	% Prefer Either
WASCBR	48	8.6	43.4
ISABR	49.4	17.2	33.3

I would strongly suggest that instead of telling boys and girls what they like, we need to ask young people about their preferences and accept that these will vary at an individual level, that they will also change over time, and that they will be responsive to cultural, social, and individual factors, as well as to a range of other influences such as resourcing and access factors that can constrain exposure and opportunity. When tween boys and girls are asked about their reading preferences, it becomes clear that they are not homogeneous groups. For example, Nathan explained that "I think that reading Tom Gates is fun, but not reading informational [sic], and I would rather play soccer," and Tania described how her attitudes toward reading are dependent "on what types of books you give me. I like reading books about adventure, mystery and nonfiction. Reading fairytales, I find, is quite boring to me." As some young people do prefer nonfiction, and reading across diverse genres can expose students to a range of text types and ideas, we need to make sure that young people have access to a range of interesting books that they self-select, with support if required. In the absence of supporting evidence, at this stage we really need to shelve this myth because, as I have explained, the perpetuation of such myths may contribute to male reading infrequency and social reinforcement of unhelpful stereotypes of masculinity.

ARE FEMALE EDUCATORS AND MOTHERS INEFFECTUAL WITH BOYS?

While I am sticking pins in gender myth balloons, I would like to challenge the belief that female educators and mothers cannot shape boys' attitudes toward reading. After a recent conference visit in Sydney, one of the teacher librarians, an enthusiastic and hardworking educator, somewhat nervously asked whether I felt that she had any hope of influencing the boys in her charge to read more, on account of the fact that she was a woman. This was not the first time I have been asked a similar question by a female educator; there is a pervasive idea that boys need men to influence them and that female educators are ineffectual. Tied into the discussion of boys and reading is the myth that boys need male teachers and that consequently the contributions of female educators, whether they be parents, teachers, or librarians, are relatively undervalued in the context of instructing boys.

At the International Literacy Association conference in 2017, I was again asked whether I felt that paternal support was essential to fostering boys' engagement in reading. I was careful to explain that while I felt that support, modeling, and encouragement from fathers and male teachers were highly valuable, that did not mean that male role models were essential for boys to become keen readers. Mothers can still make a difference, such as Shiva's mother, who raised a passionate reader through her powerful example.

> **I:** So . . . can you remember anyone influencing you when you were young and learning to read?
>
> **S:** Well my mum really likes reading, she reads a lot of books, and I think I just picked it up from her, really; watching her read, perhaps. Just before going to bed, she'd be just sitting there and I'd crawl up next to her and pick a book myself and start reading, yeah [laughs].

I: Lovely. And what about your father, does he enjoy reading?

S: I'm not too sure about that, yeah, we don't live together.

To be clear, while I understand and endorse raising awareness of the role that fathers can play in supporting the reading of their children of both genders, I do not believe that research suggesting boys need supportive fathers to become readers is robust. Plenty of boys become readers through support from their mothers, including my own sons (my husband is not an avid reader).

I am unhappy to note how this particular myth has led to female educators and mothers doubting themselves and their efficacy. Surely mothers have enough maternal guilt to contend with, without adding a myth such as this to the pile? My own research has tracked powerful reading apprenticeships between mothers and sons, as well as between fathers and daughters (Merga, 2014a). I have evidence that mothers can make a difference, and boys have described being positively influenced by female teachers as well as male teachers in my research, so I have limited patience with what seems to be yet another gender hang-up in the reading space. As previously explained, a wide range of potential social influences can have an impact on young people's attitudes toward reading for pleasure. While support from fathers is clearly beneficial, it is not essential to create a reader.

As with all of the myths I encounter in the reading research space, I always look for the initial basis of the myth so that I can figure out where it comes from and pull on that thread. In this case, a sustained argument has been established in the education research suggesting that boys are more engaged in literacy when taught by a male and that the paucity of male teachers, particularly in lower schools, disadvantages boys. Before we buy into this line of argument, we need to understand that "implicit in this argument is a condemnation of women teachers who are assumed to be unable to relate to boys, to inspire their interest, stimulate them to learn or manage their behavior effectively" (Skelton, 2012, p. 1). Beginning in the late 19th century, there have been calls to improve male participation in teaching, and "the main argument for doing so was the call for male role models, driven by an anxiety about the 'feminization of boys', who would be less able to develop their masculinity without appropriate role models" (Neugebauer, Helbig, & Landmann, 2011, p. 5). Once we understand where these ideas come from, it becomes easier to confidently resist them.

Do not despair over your ability to influence boys if you are a mother or a female educator! The substantiating research in support of the same-sex educator ideal is not strong. The research papers that support this myth often have very small quantitative samples and inconsistent results, and/or they are very outdated; for example, Shapiro (1980) analyzed a sample of just 141 students, finding that while boys had better attitudes toward reading in classes taught by male teachers, so did girls. In such a small sample, it would be reasonable to assume that individual teaching styles would play just as significant, if not more significant a role in determining student attitudes than the gender of the teacher. More recent findings challenge the idea that for boys, same-sex educators alone are influential. A study with a similarly sized sample found that, "[d]espite the call for more male teachers in the classroom and the proposed move to more 'boy-friendly' pedagogy as a means of tackling boys' reading underachievement, . . . neither male reading teachers nor computer-based reading had a significant effect on boys' reading performance when compared with the alternative" (Sokal & Katz, 2008, p. 88), and another similar analysis of a slightly larger sample found that boys responded better to female teachers (Sokal, Katz, Chaszewski, & Wojcik, 2007), completely subverting the myth. However, to really examine the veracity of this myth, we need to examine studies with very large samples to counter the effects of individual teaching styles.

The largest recent study I have found in this area draws on a robust sample of 5,858 German students from 166 schools, and this study strongly refutes the myth of same-sex teacher advantage (Neugebauer et al., 2011), finding that "both boys and girls who were taught by a male German teacher for 4 years (56 percent of the sample) had significantly less well developed reading skills than students who were taught by a female German teacher for four years" (p. 20). So again, the same-sex educator idea has not only been contested, it has potentially been subverted, though I am not interested in proving that women are somehow superior, as to be honest, I do not really see the point in the research question other than to debunk gender-based myths in this area. There are excellent male teachers and excellent female teachers, supportive mothers and supportive fathers. Rather than focusing on paren-tal or teacher gender, we should put our energies into being the best reading sup-ports that we can be. Surely in 2018, it is time to discard the idea that men learn best from men. Female educators, whether they be teachers or parents, can be powerful literacy advocates in the lives of young men. This is not to suggest that male teachers may not play a valuable role as models and advocates; rather, the assumption that they are *necessary* to boys' achievement in literacy has not been proven, and therefore female educators and parents should not underestimate the potential of their contribution.

5

Powerful Parents

Parents can be extremely valuable literacy supports, though they do not always understand the impor-
tance of their role or how they can be most effective.

Parents typically want the best for their children, and we tend to try to shape their
ideas and attitudes based on our own values. For example, the dad who wants his
daughter to be a future basketball star may spend hours training with her, taking
her to her games, and cheering enthusiastically from the sidelines. This shows her
what he values and what characteristics he seeks to foster in her.

As parents are usually relatively time-poor, we tend to invest our time with our
children quite strategically, so we tend not to expend time and encouragement on
things that we do not really believe are important for our children. Our children
are able to gauge what is important to us by the choices we make in our own lives,
as well as the encouragement and support we give them to pursue different activities in their daily lives.

As our children get older and move into the tween and teen years, we may wonder about our ability to influence their behavior. Just how far beyond our influence
will our children travel? First, we need to understand that it can be contended that
adolescence is socially and culturally constructed (Brown, Larson, & Saraswathi,
2002), so the widespread generalizations that we make about tweens and teens as
mulish, intractable, and autonomous youths should be questioned. There is considerable variation in how different children negotiate the adolescent years, even
within the same gender.

As such, I do not think that we should take the popular generalization that teens
do not read as an immutable given; even though teens do generally read comparatively infrequently, this does not mean that there is nothing we can do about it. We
also need to know that the idea that a breakdown in parent–child relationships in
adolescence is the norm is actually an outdated throwback to positions in 1950s and
1960s psychology, leading Steinberg (2001) to conclude that "while storm and stress
may be the norm in families of teenagers with depression or conduct disorder, conflict is not normative in average families" (p. 4). We still have the capacity to influence and socially support our children into their adulthood, and we both *can* and

should be a significant influence on their reading engagement beyond the early years. Klauda's (2009) review of the role of parents in teen reading motivation and engagement found that:

> parent support may be an important factor in helping address current, widely held concerns about adolescent reading engagement and achievement. That is, many studies reviewed here indicate that parents' support for their children's reading continues to relate positively to children's motivation to read in adolescence, despite the common view that parents play a less important role in their children's lives in many ways during this developmental period. (p. 358)

As such, at the outset it is important that we make parents aware of the important roles that they can play as their children grow older, preventing expired expectations, as previously discussed.

My research into parents' roles in supporting their children to read beyond the early years aims at keeping reading as a priority and part of the ongoing parental support activities and strategies. However, research suggests that parental engagement in fostering reading may decline at a very young age, with family engagement in shared reading and home activities decreasing in early childhood from 2 to 6 years of age (Hayes, 2015), suggesting that withdrawal of encouragement is not just associated with the later years of lower schooling. We were surprised to find that nearly a third of the tween respondents in the WASCBR were not perceiving any encouragement to read (Merga & Mat Roni, in press). Where children were receiving encouragement, mothers (91 percent) were the most common source, followed by teachers (66 percent) and fathers (62 percent). Our findings suggest that, while infrequent readers tend to receive more encouragement from their parents than frequent readers and therefore encouragement is typically focused on the children who need it, a puzzling gender disparity exists. As previously mentioned, we found greater parental encouragement for girls, despite the research suggesting that they read more frequently in general (Merga & Mat Roni, in press). The lack of encouragement for boys and gender-based limitations on encouragement are both concerning.

Parents can make a real difference to the reading engagement of their children, regardless of age and gender. Parents' attitudes toward reading are closely related to their children's attitudes and reading behaviors (Petscher, 2010), and adolescents whose parents were encouraging and showed confidence in their child's reading are far more likely to have children who identified as readers (Clark, Osbourne, & Akerman, 2008). Tweens also value the support they receive from their parents at home and recognize their disadvantage when they do not receive this support. For example, Jody explained that "when I was 7, my dad or mum didn't teach me how to read, so it was harder when I got in Year 3." Jody compared herself unfavorably with peers who had the advantage of support for learning to read at home. As I have previously mentioned, Year 3 is currently the first year of high-stakes reading testing, which is probably why Jody felt her relative disadvantage in Year 3, even though this interview was taking place in the following year. Scrutiny on her reading performance was elevated as she was suddenly required to be measured against her peers on a national level.

I suspect that one of the reasons that parents withdraw encouragement toward tweens relates to the fact that parents' role beyond the early years may typically be poorly defined. Nieuwenhuizen (2001) explained that the transition to high school can lead to a notable change in parental involvement, as "very few parents continue to read to them, and many no longer actively encourage reading because they feel that the skill is acquired, and they can see the child reading school texts, which is considered to be sufficient" (p. 6). As previously explained, this is an instance of expired expectations. Research suggests that parents are far more likely to read with primary-aged children than those in high school, and they are also more likely to encourage them to read and to talk about reading with these younger children (Clark & Foster, 2005). As a result, it is important that we make parents aware of the importance of continued engagement and that we outline how this can be most effectively achieved.

So what do parents who successfully support their children's reading into the teenage years do so effectively? My research has found that parents who continued to support their children's recreational book reading into adolescence were encouraging and responsive to their children's individual taste and preferences, which can support the provision of informed recommendations, and were active in modeling keen reading, providing for their children, and facilitating access to books (Merga, 2014a). Reading aloud beyond the early years has also been deemed a highly supportive practice (Merga, 2017f). If we want parents to prioritize these literacy-promoting practices in their busy lives, we need to recruit them early as allies and continue to provide them with ongoing advice and support. We cannot just assume that even highly educated parents understand the ongoing importance of reading. Also, ideally all family members in a parental role, whether they be partners, guardians, or wives and husbands, should try to be consistent in their encouragement and support of reading.

On a related note, they should also be united in their positioning of the importance of reading among other recreational pursuits, with online media ideally limited to make some time for reading. Recent U.S. research (Mares, Stephanson, Martins, & Nathanson, 2018) found that where parental disparity over media rules existed, outcomes for children were less than ideal. While these researchers were focused on limiting screen-based media use rather than on encouraging book reading, it is useful to note that "one parent's media rules interacted with the other parent's rules" and children were particularly responsive to this united front (p. 184). So where parents, partners, and guardians can be united in their support of reading, this could exert a beneficial influence and encourage children to value and make time for reading in their daily lives.

PROVIDING ENCOURAGEMENT THROUGH SHARED SOCIAL PRACTICE

Reading should ideally be something that is enjoyed as a family and something that we share together. Books should inform our social exchanges, and, where finances, access, and time permit, books should have a strong physical presence in our home on our shelves, whether we purchase them or borrow them from the library. We should be talking about them, not just to the children. When parents discuss books in the context of pleasure in front of their children, it can have a lasting effect, as described by a German ISABR respondent who reflected on the earlier social influences that shaped a positive attitude toward reading in adulthood:

> My parents read a lot and talked enthusiastically about the books they were reading. When I was very young and wanted to know what they were talking about, they used the oldest trick ever and told me I was too young to understand. I guess that was how I got curious and wanted to read myself as soon as possible. (Merga, 2017f, p. 10)

In this case, it was actually exclusion from discussion that motivated reading engagement, within the context of reading being explicitly valued by influential family members. We also know that where parents were able to engage their children in discussion about particular books that dealt with shared interests and were able to recommend books to their children, a strong shared social context for reading was often developed (Merga, 2014a).

For example, Dash highlighted his strong supportive home context as motivating him to embrace reading at an age when many others would typically be disengaging from the practice. He described comparative disinterest in reading for recreation in the earlier years of schooling. Once he moved into the tween years and he was deemed old enough to read young adult and adult books, his father introduced him to his collection of fantasy books. What was really interesting about Dash was how motivated he was to read by his social supports as a teen, despite the high degree of difficulty he encountered attempting to read books that were beyond his skill level:

> Around Year Five I started reading a lot of Dad's books, because all of his are teenage to adult fiction, so, yeah, he didn't really give me the *Dragonlance* until about Year Seven, 'cause *Dragonlance* uses a lot of complex words and . . . I would have to read a chapter, and then I would go back and read the chapter again, because I didn't understand what happened in it. So, it's . . . most of the books he has have really adult words and stuff like that, complex.

Dash was motivated to persist in this extremely challenging reading of complex and lengthy texts (the first book in the *Dragonlance* series is 448 pages long, a significant commitment for a young person who was still establishing his reading skills). He used persistent rereading practices to strengthen his reading comprehension skills because reading was important to him. The strong supportive encouragement he received from his father was enough to support the development of an ongoing love of reading. While his friends were not generally readers, he was a passionate reader who shared the experience with his father, explaining that "once we're reading a book or that, and once we've both finished it, we like talking about what happened it [laughs] and, yeah, if he's read it before me and I get up to a certain part, I'll say something and he'll laugh at that" (Merga, 2014a, p. 158). While his mother was disinterested, his aunt also shared in these interests and discussions:

> [M]y dad reads a lot as well. He likes the same books as me, and so does my aunty, so . . . she normally gets the books from me or my dad, but my dad always puts me

onto a good series that he reads. Like, there's one I've still gotta read about an assassin or something like that, from Brent Weeks, the first one he wrote, so. Yeah, my dad wants me to read that eventually [laughs].

I particularly like using Dash as an example because he was also a highly motivated and successful athlete, and thus he could not be readily characterized as an introverted book reader. He was outgoing and so enthusiastic about books and reading, he gave me a list of additional books to read at the end of the interview. He introduced me to the *Spook's Apprentice* and *Ranger's Apprentice* book series, and so while he was an interview subject, he also ultimately influenced my own reading. Subsequently he also influenced the reading of my sons, both of whom have now read all of the books in the *Ranger's Apprentice* series, and my eldest also really enjoyed *Spook's Apprentice*. I was never able to follow up with him and tell him this, as he was an anonymous participant in the research, but I hope that someday he will come across this paragraph so that he knows that I did pursue the books the suggested!

While we know that parental encouragement of reading can have a positive influence, as parents we should be aware that not all of the behaviors that we may deem encouraging are necessarily equally well received by young people (Love & Hamston, 2003). For example, nagging children to read in order to improve their testing grades is unlikely to work; as previously explored in Chapter 2, expectations or demandingness needs to be coupled with responsiveness. A focus on reading purely to improve academic outcomes tended to be poorly received by teens. When parents just reminded their children to read, without positive encouragement, this often did little to foster motivation for reading. For example, tween student Tyson's parents provided encouragement "by saying 'just read' a couple of times a day" (Merga & Mat Roni, in press); however, this only occasionally influenced his reading behavior. There were probably many reasons for this, the most obvious being that this demandingness was not accompanied by any more responsive encouragement. In addition, Tyson noted that his parents were not really avid readers; children were often acutely attuned to parental hypocrisy in this regard. Therefore, while expectations can be valuable, expectations in isolation may be insufficient to foster a love of reading.

Sometimes parents selected reading materials for their children without considering their children's reading preferences. For example, as previously mentioned, teen Gerome described being expected to read nonfiction at home with his parents, whereas he greatly preferred reading fantasy fiction, and this had a detrimental impact on his enjoyment and frequency of engagement (Merga, 2014a). Where possible, tweens and teens should be encouraged to self-select reading material, but where parent choice is necessary or requested, every effort should be made to match the reading material with the young person's interests rather than exclusively providing materials that parents prefer or deem most educational.

MODELING

Whether they choose to or not, the reality is that parents have some influence over their children's reading outcomes simply through their own reading-related knowledge and practices, with research with younger children finding "a significant and sustained relationship between parents' reading-related knowledge and their children's reading outcomes" (Segal & Martin-Chang, 2018, p. 14). While there is less research looking at how parent's knowledge influences the reading outcomes of tweens, we do know that the practices that parents model and value in their own lives are noted by their children. As such, not all encouragement is explicit, interactive, or put into words; simply modeling is an important practice. Where children see their parents reading for pleasure on their own, they are transmitting the valuing of the practice.

Unfortunately, the reverse is also true, and young people can be somewhat startlingly perceptive. In the 2016 WASCBR, I was surprised by the number of tweens who smirked in the interviews when I asked them about their parents' reading habits. By the end of the data collection, I was just about able to identify what I coined the hypocrisy detection face; tweens were happy to critically expose their parents' double standards when it came to reading, even though I did not explicitly ask them about double standards as such. It made me aware of how we are always teaching our children through our behaviors, even if we do not want to be. If parents wish to influence their children to be avid readers, ideally they need to be readers themselves. As a parent and an educator, I am aware that a lot of our reading may occur during the very limited "me" time we have during the day, which unfortunately often coincides with children's sleep periods. If we are not seen to be readers, young people cannot be influenced by our modeling behaviors. In addition, mothers are far more likely to model positive attitudes than fathers (Merga & Mat Roni, 2018b), suggesting that fathers could and should do more to act as effective models.

So we are not just trying to encourage young people to read; we are trying to encourage their parents to read too, where possible. This modeling is felt to potentially affect the way we engage with our children in several ways, and it can also influence our willingness to engage with our children around books. Firstly, we are more likely to talk to our children about books if we feel that reading serves important personal needs of our own (Bus, Leseman, & Keultjes, 2000). Our own knowledge of books, particularly fiction books, may account for a noteworthy percentage of children's basic reading skills and oral language, supporting intergenerational literacy transmission (Mol & Bus, 2011). We also know that young people are more likely to be readers if they have parents who clearly and explicitly prioritize reading as a recreational pursuit (Strommen & Mates, 2004). So rather than reaching for the remote or our phones on the weekend when we have a moment between the seemingly endless household and work tasks, if we choose to pick up a book instead, we are potentially helping to support our children's literacy without saying a word. Some schools have developed creative ways to help to engage their parents in reading. For example, one school that I recently visited encourages and allows staff, parents, and students to borrow books from their libraries. This may be well beyond the realistic resourcing scope for many schools, but it is certainly a worthwhile goal to strive for: school libraries that serve the broader school community.

We also know that modeling is influential from the comments made by adult readers who reflected on the social influences that shaped their attitudes toward reading. It was very interesting to hear older avid readers account for the role that modeling had on influencing them to become a keen reader. In the ISABR, adults who loved reading reported indirect avid reader influence, such as modeling, as being a key shaping factor fostering their avid reading motivation. Indirect socialization, such as having parents who model reading, was felt to exert a positive effect that was sometimes crucial to adopting a lifelong reader identity (Merga, 2017f), as also found by others (Mancini & Pasqua, 2011; Mullan, 2010; Wollscheid, 2013). One of the most fascinating examples of parental modelling emerged from the ISABR data, where an avid reader described the influence that her father's passionate love of books had on her in her childhood:

> He would be always ready to suggest a book to read, to discuss books or simply dismiss a book as "hairdresser literature", but he never pushed books onto his children. Books were just there, part of our life and draining on our budget. I recall him coming from the bookshop with a box full of books, at times, and my mother (who never had time to read, in spite of being a book lover herself) pulling her hair over the budget. We were under the communist regime, where everything was scarce, but, whilst many people befriended food shop assistants, my father was befriending the bookshop ladies. (Merga, 2017f)

This choice, despite the political challenges and shortage of resources, to privilege books above even food, had a powerful effect on this reader. However, I am not suggesting that you emulate the father in this wry recollection and spend all of your food budget on books (however tempting they may be) just to set a good example for your children. What the example clearly illustrates is that modeling not only shows young people how to be a reader—what reading looks like and the time and level of concentration involved. It also communicates a strong valuing of the practice, as parents, who are often seen as perpetually busy and often battling with limited resources, are choosing to invest valuable and limited time and money in the activity, and therefore it must be important and interesting. This is why some of my research respondents reported being powerfully influenced by models who may not have ever given explicit verbal or material encouragement; the indirect encouragement conferred through exposure to an influential model, can, in some cases, independently shape a lifelong reader.

Tweens and teens also reported this powerful socialization effect. For example, teen student Sara explained, "I've always had family members, like my grandmother's always been, she's very into reading books, so I guess I've always had grandparents, parents, they've always read, and I guess I've just picked that up" (Merga, 2014a, p. 155). An adult respondent in the ISABR described the power of paternal influence through modeling, explaining that "my father led by example—he constantly had a book in his hand." As such, modeling is an essential component in any parent's strategy to improve a child's reading engagement.

However, we also have some insight into why modeling can be such a challenge for parents, even when they have a genuine interest in reading, the literacy levels required to read fluently, and the resources to continue to access books. Time was recently cited as the most significant barrier for modern parents seeking time to read for pleasure, with the time and energy commitments of parenting often creating a barrier where there had been no previous significant impediment. For example, this parent struggled with reading comprehension due to fatigue and time constraints:

> My partner and I both have studied literature at tertiary level. We love to read. Before having children, we both had more than a couple of books on the go at a time. We would spend a lot of our quality time together discussing books and other material (short stories, poetry, non-fiction etc.) that we had read. Since our kid was born, I [mum] have GREAT difficulty reading. I read a paragraph and have to go back and re-read it because it didn't sink in! I read and produce a lot of written material for work but am usually too tired to read for pleasure. My partner still reads but less than before and I would say in shorter pieces (criticism and journals, magazines etc.) or longer works—but that takes a lot loooooonger to finish. (Merga & Ledger, in press)

As such, even avid readers may lose their habit due to the pressures of modern parenting. This response reflected comments or views of avid adult readers in the ISABR, when asked about the most substantial barrier to their reading. For instance, this Australian mother described her children as being her most significant reading impediment:

> My kids. They're little, they need attention; I have very little free time. I used to read on average a book every two or three nights, often one a night. Nowadays I get patches when I can read and I might get through three books in a week, but then not get to read any more books for another four or six weeks. Books of my own, that is. I read the kids' books to them for a typical amount of half an hour a day [in] general plus twenty-ish minutes at bedtime. If I start reading a book of my own, they jump on me, climb on me and bring me their books. The oldest is just starting to read books . . . without my participation and it's amazing (and relieving!) to see. There may be light at the end of the tunnel! (Merga, 2017d, p. 14)

While the mother's frustration here is apparent, it is very interesting to note that when she attempts to read independently, it motivates her children to instigate a reading experience of their own volition, providing an excellent example of the efficacy of modeling.

Reminding parents that it is important to make time to read for themselves where possible and stressing the benefits of modeling can help to keep reading a priority for parents, but we do need to acknowledge the significant constraints that parents are often laboring under and ensure that tweens and teens have exposure to positive reading models in the other areas of their lives, such as schools and libraries.

PROVIDING ACCESS

If you do not have a book, you cannot read a book, but access does more than just provide the means to read. Like modeling, it also indicates strong valuing of the practice, as the financial and/or time resources dedicated to sourcing books are being allocated to making reading happen. Parents who supported their tween's access to books in the WASCBR were seen as encouraging, whether the books are part of the parents' collections, given as gifts, or sourced with parents from the library.

Sometimes, a pile of new books, coupled with parental encouragement, could awaken a love of reading. For example, Zac explained that a substantial gift of books was a turning point in his attitudes toward reading, as "I remember after I was about four, they bought me a lot of books . . . and then I started off with those. And then I really liked them, and then my mum used to read them to me, and then I tried to read them myself again to myself without telling my mum" (Merga & Mat Roni, in press). Similarly, a respondent from the United States described how her mother and grandmother had been significant influences on her positive attitude toward reading into adulthood through their provision of books from the library and as gifts:

> My mom has had the biggest influence on my reading since she taught me to read and encouraged me to read for enjoyment from a young age. When I was growing up, we often went to the library together to pick out books, especially in the summer when I was out of school. My paternal grandmother also had an influence because she often gave me books as gifts.

Partin and Gillespie (2002) also found that giving books as gifts and having home libraries both fostered a positive attitude toward reading, whereas subscriptions to newspapers and magazines did not have the same positive effect. This might be something that schools and libraries can remind parents of before or during different cultural gift giving seasons.

Just having the books sitting on the shelves can make a difference. An Icelandic respondent in the ISABR described how having books in her home as a child shaped her attitudes toward reading, explaining that "growing up we had a room full of books that made me feel they were important right from the start. I have very fond memories of picking books with my parents." When parents provide access to books in the home, their children display a greater motivation to read (Aðalsteinsdóttir, 2011; Gambrell, 1996), and increasing access to reading materials such as books can have an independent, causal effect on students' motivation to engage in reading (McQuillan & Au, 2001). My research with teens supports previous international research linking books in the home to improved attitudes toward reading and frequency of engagement in reading for recreation (Merga, 2015a). In addition, access to books at home can offer literacy benefits, as a book-rich home environment is associated with a range of skills: "vocabulary, information, comprehension skills, imagination, broad horizons of history and geography, familiarity with good writing, understanding of the importance of evidence in argument, and many others" (Evans, Kelley, Sikora, & Treiman, 2010, p. 19). The benefits for literacy skills and attitudes have been found to remain consistent even when controlling for socioeconomic factors (Chiu & McBride-Chang, 2006; Clark & Poulton, 2011; Evans et al., 2010). Young people who maintain a love of reading into adolescence typically have books in their houses. However, while access is essential to enable reading to occur and also communicates valuing in the home, it is also important for parents to use more active strategies, such as reading aloud or talking about books, so that the books are not just taken for granted or just part of the furniture.

I discuss reading aloud in greater detail in the next section; however, access to books plays a vital role in enabling this to happen in homes, and we cannot ignore the impact of SES on potential access to books. Recent U.S. research explored the impact of poverty on the availability of books for young people, finding "disparities in access to print for children living in high-poverty neighborhoods compared with those who live in borderline communities" (Neuman & Moland, 2016). While children in high-poverty areas were notably worse off, the authors note that:

> none of these communities, whether borderline or high poverty, were actually well-equipped to support children's early literacy skills and interests in learning to read. None appeared to have an abundance of reading resources or adequate choice of book titles for children. (p. 16)

While this research focuses on outcomes for younger children than I focus on in this book, it is likely to hold relevance for older children, and it highlights that access issues do not only affect those living in the lowest-SES contexts in our communities. Neuman then went on to perform an intervention in which books were introduced into low-SES communities in book vending machines, in order to experiment with ways in which to address this access issue. The research suggested that:

> children's books were accessed and valued in these communities. Evidence for this claim was demonstrated throughout this study in several highly visible ways: by the sheer volume of use with more than 64,000 books selected from machines over an 8-week period, and by the number of books selected for children at all age ranges, from birth through the teenage years. Furthermore, we found no indications of "intervention fatigue"; to the contrary, evidence from the machine counts showed sustained interest in accessing books throughout the summer. These results help to disrupt the deficit perspective, the view that low-income parents care less about their children's education. (Neuman & Knapczyk, 2018, p. 22)

Making books available in local contexts was important, as "the close proximity of books to where people were likely to traffic clearly had its benefits to many in these communities," and "many regarded these resources as a welcome contribution to the local neighborhood, and a necessary support to help spark their children's interest and skill in reading" (Neuman & Knapczyk, 2018, p. 22). Thus, access to books for all is clearly a foundation factor without which a range of the other suggestions mentioned in this book cannot be realized. It should be one of the first considerations of any literacy educator or advocate.

READING ALOUD

There is something about listening to a well-read book that can have a transformative effect and transport the listener into a different world. When I reflect on the time I have spent reading with my sons over the years, I remember the love and the shared enjoyment. We would emerge from the reading experience together, having traversed through a world under London, or having battled a Rakshasa army, or having ridden on the back of a whale. I know that these are memories that I will treasure as long I have them.

In addition to often affording a great degree of pleasure, the act of listening to language offers great benefits for enabling young people to develop an array of literacy skills. It is important that we understand and acknowledge these benefits, because, if we want parents to read to their children more often and for longer, we need to be able to communicate the benefits of this approach. A recent meta-analysis of 19 interventions involving 3,264 families concluded that parent–child book reading is significantly beneficial for the psychosocial functioning of both children and their parents (Xie, Chan, Ji, & Chan, 2018), and while the literacy benefits of reading aloud with children are noteworthy, these psychosocial benefits should not be understated. Reading aloud builds reading skills and acts as a bridge to higher-level reading. We know that when parents and teachers read aloud to their children, in addition to sharing a pleasurable social interaction, they are supporting the development of vital foundational literacy skills (Duursma, Augustyn, & Zuckerman, 2008; Swanson et al., 2012). While reading aloud has been consistently associated with vocabulary development, recent research suggests that it may also support grapheme awareness in young children (Wesseling, Christmann, & Lachmann, 2017). This advantage can be measured; children who are regularly read to have been found to achieve higher than average results on standardized tests in both literacy and numeracy (Kalb & Van Ours, 2014). Hutton and colleagues (2017) argue that reading aloud in childhood "is considered among the best means to provide constructive cognitive stimulation promoting healthy brain development" (p. 8).

Literacy ability builds confidence, which is motivational in itself. For instance, a U.S. ISABR respondent explained that her mother "started reading to me at a very young age. When I was three she started teaching me. When I reached kindergarten, I was reading on a second grade level. I've had a love of books since then." Recent research finds a relationship between engagement in the reading aloud experience and literacy benefits, suggesting that there may be "a neurobiological mechanism by which greater child engagement during shared reading may directly influence or 'turbocharge' the development of foundational emergent literacy skills, particularly comprehension" (Hutton et al., 2017, p. 9). While the sample studied were preschool aged, these findings suggest that further research with older children could be beneficial for increasing our understanding of how the quality of the reading aloud experience influences the benefits for young people.

Sharing reading aloud influences young people's attitudes toward reading. We know that parents who read aloud to their children are supporting a lifelong reader identity development; children who experience enjoyable reading opportunities at home are more likely to read both in childhood and beyond (Baker, Scher, & Mackler, 1997), with parental involvement in reading aloud leading to greater reading engagement in children (Loera, Rueda, & Nakamoto, 2011). We also know that the previous findings from the ISABR suggest that reading aloud was felt to play a key role in fostering lasting positive attitudes toward book reading that extended into adulthood; for example, one adult U.S. respondent who identified as an avid reader explained that "my mother always read to me before I went to bed as a child. As I learned to read myself, I adopted this ritual as my own. Books and stories have since retained their comforting and constant presence in my life" (Merga, 2017f, p. 12). Similarly, a young adult from New Zealand described the influence of her father, who "would always read to me before bed from the age of probably zero until I was a teenager, and this was invaluable to me." An investigation into reading aloud in the WASCBR found that interactive reading experiences are complex and diverse social and educational events, with opportunities for shared reading experience related to growth in skill and confidence, and early cessation at home and at school is described as compounding anxiety toward reading aloud, as well as constituting lost opportunities for shared enjoyment (Merga, 2017a).

When you read aloud with your children at home, you are giving them a valuable opportunity to improve their reading skills, and when you allow them to read aloud to you and you listen supportively, you enable them to develop both confidence and reading skills. When children's only reading aloud opportunities occur at school, they can fall behind their peers both in confidence and proficiency. Opportunities for reading aloud at home also prepared students to read aloud to others at school, potentially alleviating anxiety by building both confidence and skill in performance of the practice (Merga, 2017a). Tween respondents in the WASCBR related reading aloud opportunities to educative benefit, such as Sarah. Sarah used self-initiated reading aloud opportunities to develop her reading comprehension, relying on her mother's support. If Sarah read a book:

> not [of] my age group, and like, I can read every word, she can help me like understand, like what I'm saying, and she can help me think of what I'm reading and stuff in my head, instead of having to stop and think and think and think about what I'm reading. (p. 10)

The opportunity to seek clarity around meaning, when required, was an invaluable advantage, and Sarah was able to develop both fluency and comprehension skills.

Theo also enjoyed reading aloud, as it gave him the opportunity to strengthen his oral fluency and pronunciation. He explained that he would "sound out" difficult words with his mother, who provided strong support, as "if it's right, she says 'Good boy', or she says the word, or otherwise she says 'Good try'" (Merga, 2017a, p. 10). In contrast, students without this opportunity to build their reading skills in relation to oral fluency were at a distinct disadvantage in relation to their peers. For example, Hayden felt a sense of deep anxiety about reading aloud. Hayden's anxiety around reading aloud at school related to his lack of confidence and to his propensity for comparing his skill level with that of his peers "because I'm always standing up there shivering, my hands are shivering, I just don't want to read, so I just start reading. And I sound pretty weird" (Merga, 2017a, p. 11).

Hayden didn't look at his issues with oral reading fluency and attribute them to the comparative lack of opportunity he experienced. Rather, he saw them as his own failings. This is why, where possible, parents need to provide opportunities for young people to continue to develop their oral fluency beyond the early years. Not all parents are able to do this, so other literacy advocates, such as teachers and librarians, also need to shoulder this responsibility so that students such as Hayden do not conflate their lack of opportunity with intellectual failing.

The benefits of sharing reading experiences with young people may not only be for them. While there is somewhat limited research investigating reading aloud with children beyond the very early years of schooling, research suggests that shared reading experiences between parents and children can have a positive influence on parental stress (Karrass, VanDeventer, & Braungart-Rieker, 2003), so the benefits of the practice are not necessarily confined to the child. In the WARAS, which I conducted with my colleague Dr. Susan Ledger, we explored the perspectives of parents, as well as those of teachers and children. We found that most parents enjoyed reading aloud to their child (96.7 percent) and that this enjoyment tended to relate to the possibility for a shared learning opportunity, for pleasure, and/or for interpersonal connection. For instance, one parent explained that "it's our quiet time before going to sleep, so we get all snuggled up, talk about the day we've had and what's happening tomorrow, then read some books. It's a wonderful way to wind down and bond, and help my son feel calm and relaxed" (Merga & Ledger, in press). Unfortunately, we found that while most parents reported reading to their children at home at least sometimes (90.8 percent), less than half of parents claimed to be doing this on a daily basis (43 percent) (Merga & Ledger, in press), suggesting that children are missing out on this experience.

As literacy advocates, we are aware that all parents may not have been read to as children and that, where this is the case, we cannot assume that parents will be comfortable reading aloud. Parents who have not been read to may not know what this looks and feels like, and they may not necessarily have competence attempting to share reading with their children, who are often at varying ages. One of the most interesting findings of the WARAS was that while nine out of 10 parents who agreed to take part in that study read to their child at least sometimes, a quarter of parents had not been read to by their parents. This meant that it had not been modeled for them. This was also somewhat exciting, as it was apparent that a number of parents who had not been read to were nonetheless reading to their own children, suggesting that intergenerational transmission of home literacy practices can be positively mediated by other factors. Just because some parents were not read to by their parents, this did not necessarily cause them to in turn not read with their own children. In the absence of an extensive, cross-generational longitudinal study that tracks reading at home practices over decades, these retrospective research findings should provide a valuable starting point for further deeper inquiry into this area, as we need to know *why* parents who were not read to decide to read to their own children.

Low literacy and lack of the experience of being read to are not the only impediments to shared reading. When we seek to increase parents' engagement in reading with their children, we need to understand the time and lifestyle pressures that many parents face, some of which may be insurmountable as they relate to things like caring for sick children in the hospital or working multiple jobs to ensure the family survives.

However, other barriers may be easier to mitigate. While WARAS research suggests that limited time was by far the biggest barrier parents perceived to their reading aloud frequency, misunderstanding the reasons for reading aloud and how literacy develops along a continuum was also a key reason for ending the shared reading experience. The WARAS found that more than a fifth of parents of children and tweens felt that reading aloud was not really necessary after children had learned to read by themselves.

This finding supported earlier suspicions that, despite the continuing value of reading aloud, its value beyond the point of independent reading skill acquisition is not necessarily well understood. This has also been found in other recent research; while children continue to enjoy being read to well beyond the early years, parents may cease to read aloud at home when children are still enjoying the practice (Scholastic, 2015; Scholastic, 2016a; Scholastic, 2016b). Recent research suggests that over a third of children aged 6–11 whose parents had stopped reading to them wished it would continue (Scholastic, 2016a, p. 30). It is important that parents understand the value of continuing to read to their children for as long as possible. Heavy curricular demands may limit children's experiences of being read to at school (Sanacore, 1992; Wasiuta, 2011); indeed, recent findings from the WARAS suggest that only 2.4 percent of the respondents in the tween years were being read to every day at school, which is a very small figure indeed (Ledger & Merga, 2018). Therefore, it cannot be taken for granted that children are experiencing regular reading aloud through others. Where possible, we need to share this responsibility; it should not be orphaned.

Shared reading is not just about reading skills; it is about sharing an experience of closeness and togetherness. While some children do not mind it when reading aloud ceases, usually because they are regular, rapid readers who feel that being read to slows them down, many more readers, some of whom are also very highly skilled tweens, are upset when their parents stop reading to them. For example, when asked about his parents reading to him, Jason explained, "they kind of stopped when I knew how to read. I knew how to read, but I just still liked my mum reading it to me [sic]" (Merga, 2017a). The WASCBR research found that tweens continued to enjoy the social element of being read to beyond the early years, though some also linked the practice with benefits for their literacy performance; tweens felt they learned a lot both from listening to reading aloud and from reading aloud themselves. While the academic benefits of exposure to reading aloud are increasingly apparent, the social and emotional benefits can also be significant. We need to have a broader understanding of the significance of the practice and the importance of its continuance.

While it might be tempting to have siblings read to each other to make the most of time and resourcing, this strategy should be approached with caution, as the WASCBR research found that it sometimes backfired somewhat badly, leading to a negative reading experience for both children. While time-poor parents may be tempted to outsource the reading aloud to their younger children's older siblings, this may not be the best idea, particularly if the children do not have a consistently harmonious relationship and/or if adult supervision is not possible. While some of the WASCBR tweens really enjoyed reading with or to their siblings and found it to be a mutually beneficial experience, others had negative experiences, trying to engage tired and angry siblings with little or no help from their parents. This did little to reinforce a positive attitude toward reading and, in some cases, unfortunately contributed to quite a few bruises, with showdowns between siblings:

> [N]ot all interactive reading experiences with siblings could be characterized as educative or enjoyable. Diana's sister's behavioral issues were challenging. Diana explained that when tired, her sister "gets a bit angry, so she can't sit and she won't

read". When this happens, Diana was left to autonomously mediate the situation, with limited parental support. Rough play or even violence marred the interactive reading experience in some instances; Jason also described reading aloud to his brother as challenging, as "sometimes he's being annoying, rolling all over me when I have to lay in bed with him, to read it to him", and Bruce's brother frequently kicked him. Karen felt that her unpleasant experience reading to her little brother was probably due to her being viewed as an unacceptable replacement for her mother. (Merga, 2017a, p. 8)

It is easy to imagine how quickly things can deteriorate between two tired children, often reading together at the end of a long school day. Parents should retain responsibility for facilitating shared reading experiences or at least stay vigilant over them where possible. That said, some tweens did enjoy the opportunity to share reading with their siblings, with some looking forward to it at the end of the day, such as Jaye, who said, "I like to read to my two little sisters before we go to bed!" While this can be an enjoyable and rewarding experience, it may not be appropriate for all times and for all children. Some degree of parental monitoring should be retained, so that we know that the children are enjoying reading together, not just punching each other under the bed covers.

FIVE TIPS TO HELP PARENTS MAKE THE MOST OF READING ALOUD TO THEIR CHILDREN

I am often asked how parents can most successfully implement reading aloud in the home. Parents want practical suggestions, not just research. I was asked to write the following piece for *The Conversation*, and, with my colleagues Paul Gardner, Saiyidi Mat Roni, and Susan Ledger, we crafted the following recommendations for parents. Feel free to share this advice with your parent allies:

1. **Give it all your attention:** For many people, the best time to read with their children is at night, once the children are in bed. But if you find your children too cranky and disengaged at this time (or if you are feeling tired yourself), you might want to try reading to them earlier in the day.

    Whatever the time, it is important to give the book and your children all of your attention. Phones and other devices with enabled notifications should be switched off. Everyone should be comfortable, and the children should associate time spent being read to with enjoyment.

    Where possible, we strongly suggest making reading to your child part of the daily routine. The more often children are read to, the more substantial the benefits are (e.g., Penno, Wilkinson, & Moore, 2002). Reading to children is both an opportunity to model how the written word sounds and a chance for family bonding.

2. **Engage with the story:** Children do not typically enjoy having the story stopped every few seconds for comprehension checking, so we suggest you keep interruptions to a minimum.

    Recapping is useful when picking up a book again after a break. If parents let their children provide this recap ("So, where are we up to?"), this also enables informal comprehension checking. Opportunities for prediction are also beneficial ("Wow . . . what do you think might happen next?").

Sharing your response to a book and encouraging children's responses can stimulate critical thinking. These techniques and others can enhance learning and comprehension, but they should not upset the fluidity of the reading experience or turn it into a test.

You can share the task of the reading itself with your children if they want to. This is beneficial for a range of reading skills (e.g., Nation & Snowling, 2004), such as reading comprehension, word recognition and vocabulary building.

3. **There is no age limit:** You can start reading to your child from early infancy to support their developing language abilities (Karrass & Braungart-Rieker, 2005), so it is never too early to start. The skills infants and young children develop through shared reading experiences can set them up for literacy achievement in their subsequent schooling years (Duursma, Augustyn, & Zuckerman, 2008).

Reading to your children remains important beyond the early years, too, with continuing benefits for literacy development (Fox, 2013) and cognitive skills (Kalb & Van Ours, 2014).

We should read to young people for as long as possible (Merga, 2017a). There is no age where the benefits of being read to completely expire.

Very recent research in the UK found struggling adolescent readers can make remarkable gains on their reading comprehension when books are read to them at school (Westbrook, Sutherland, Oakhill, & Sullivan, 2018). This is perhaps due to the opportunity for students to enjoy books that are too hard for them to read themselves.

4. **Pick a book you both enjoy:** We suggest you select a book that interests both you and your child. Reading together is a great opportunity to share your passions while broadening your children's horizons through making diverse book choices.

Do not be afraid to start reading books with chapters to your children while they are still very young. The age to begin this will vary depending on your child's attention span, but it is often possible to begin this with preschoolers.

As long as the story is not too complex, children love to be taken on an enjoyable journey into books that are too hard for them to read independently. This can also help to extend children's vocabulary, among other benefits.

It is a good idea to take your children to the library and model how you choose interesting books for shared reading. Research shows many tweens (Merga, 2017c) and teens (Merga, 2016a) are easily overwhelmed by choice when they attempt to pick what books to read independently, so helping them enables them to gain a valuable skill.

5. **Do not worry about your style:** Not all of us are destined to be award-winning voice actors, and that is okay. It is great to use expression and adopt different voices for the characters in a book, but not everyone will feel able to do this.

At multiple points in our research, we have come across people who have praised the reading efforts of parents who were not confident readers but who prevailed nonetheless. For example, in our recent paper, a respondent described being read to by her mother who struggled with dyslexia (Merga, 2017f). This mother and many other parents have inspired a love of reading in their children through their persistence.

Being taken into the virtual reality of story is a memorable, pleasurable experience that stays with us forever. Reading aloud provides parents with a valuable opportunity to slow down, relax, and share the wonderful world of books with their children.

(Adapted from Merga, Gardner, Mat Roni, & Ledger, 2018; reproduced under Creative Commons license)

6

The Myth of the e-Book-Loving Digital Natives

The popular branding of all young people as a homogeneous group of digital natives is increasingly contested in recent times. Encouraging children to read books on screens may seem intuitively appealing, but the issue is more complex than it may seem.

Teachers, parents, and librarians are encouraged to keep up with the latest trends in educational technology. The rhetoric around this sometimes suggests that adults are a bunch of out-of-touch dinosaurs who need to keep up with the times in order to meet the needs of young people. This positioning may encourage indiscriminate choices, and it ignores the reality that it is virtually impossible to keep abreast of every technological advance and that many adults these days are also relatively young people who grew up with the Internet in their homes. Age may not be as significant a factor as we think, as digital proficiency is not necessarily related to age; older people sometimes have to show younger people how to use the technology. For example, I recently encountered a tween who had outstanding skills on PlayStation and Xbox, though he struggled to perform simple tasks in Microsoft Word. Both young people and adults can be typically patchy in their digital literacy, understandably stronger in the areas with which they have the most experience and where they perceive the most value.

As I have mentioned previously, the celebration of screen-based technology as uniformly superior has led in the recent past to paper books being often positioned as antiquated or even dead (Price, 2012). It seems that e-books were supposed to modernize books, to make them more appealing for generations who have grown up with technology, but sometimes the urgency with which technology is promoted is reminiscent of the latest diet fads: They both try to make the audience feel guilty for being deficient in some measure. The anxiety to remain abreast of current trends can be exploited by commercial entities to sell new educational products that may not yet be robustly associated with benefit, such as apps that claim to teach your child to read without any adult intervention needed. As technology tends to advance faster than research, we chase the benefits of new technologies before we can assess their advantages and risks. As research typically trails behind innovation in this area, we are often left making resourcing decisions based on intuition, optimism, or the loudest or most sensational views of others.

There is also a tendency to buy into the conceptualization of the current generation of young people, who are viewed as Digital Natives. While this construction tends to present young people as a group of individuals with uniformly high interest in and ability in engaging in technology, research suggests that, in reality, young people are a far more diverse group, with different digital literacy skills and interests (Leonard, Mokwele, Siebrits, & Stoltenkamp, 2016) and that they may make use of a relatively limited scope of digital technologies (Thompson, 2012).

We are also increasingly aware that they do not always make good use of technologies; this is often discussed in the media, such as in a recent article explaining how "public school students were handed more than 2000 suspensions last year for offences such as cyber bullying, using mobile phones to film fights or sharing hateful or inappropriate material online" (Hiatt, 2017). Cyber bullying, which includes "sending offensive or threatening messages, spreading rumors, displaying personal information or images, or excluding an individual," is a serious and pervasive issue (Lee, Hong, Resko, & Tripodi, 2018, pp. 12–13).

One of the biggest risks for educators appears to be the potential to go off task during learning time, which has been a risk in moving to higher levels of device use in learning contexts, with the multitasking capacity of laptops offering high potential distraction (Fried, 2008; Sana, Weston, & Capeda, 2013).

We also need to consider the potential consequences of encouraging young people to move from an off-screen book reading mode to an on-screen mode, letting our common sense have as much leash as our enthusiasm for new technology. The amount of time young people spend on devices is increasing both at home and at school (Merga & Williams, 2016). It is not just parents and homes that are lax in setting screen time limits: very few (18 percent) of Australian schools place limits on the amount of time young people can spend in front of a computer, which is very low when compared with other nations (Fraillon et al., 2014). Along with computer vision syndrome, other risks can be created or exacerbated by increased screen time: cardiometabolic syndrome, obesity, spinal and postural issues, sleep disorders, and Internet addiction (Merga, 2015b; Merga & Williams, 2016), and while my previous research with young people did not focus on this area, anecdotal discussion of eye strain in particular was mentioned in relation to paper book and e-book mode preferences, with screen-based reading found to cause discomfort for some (Merga, 2014d).

This is not to say that all students who move from paper to screen-based reading will suddenly become ill—some of the risk factors, such as sedentary behavior, could foreseeably be comparable. However, whenever we adopt an exciting new technology, it is important to consider both the benefits and risks. Young people are already exceeding the screen time guidelines; only a third of young Australians were meeting this guideline in 2007 (Commonwealth Scientific and Industrial Research Organisation, 2008). More recent findings suggest that three-quarters of upper school students exceed the two-hour recommended limit (Hardy, 2011), and "regardless of socio-economic status, students in Australia spend about 2 hours and 30 minutes on line every weekend day, on average—more than the OECD average" (OECD, 2015b, p. 1). Recent U.S. research suggests that "adolescents who spent more time on electronic communication and screens (e.g., social media, texting, electronic games, Internet) were less happy, less satisfied with their lives, and had lower self-esteem, especially among 8th and 10th graders" (Twenge, Martin, & Campbell, 2018, p. 8). These U.S. researchers also found that:

> adolescents' psychological well-being suddenly decreased after 2012, possibly due to their spending more time on electronic communication and less time on non-screen activities such as in-person social interaction. The rapid adoption of smartphone technology in the early 2010s may have had a marked negative impact on adolescents' psychological well-being. (Twenge et al., 2018, p. 12)

While more research needs to be done to investigate the causes of the decrease in teen well-being, this research may lead us to question the logic of the bookless library, which forces young people into increased screen time without offering a paper option. A number of the young people I collected data from self-identified as highly distractible by social media, such as the teenager who explained that "I really do enjoy reading. However, because of social networking sites I get distracted, I think that's for most teenagers [sic]." I feel it is likely that the students with these attention issues are most likely to be disadvantaged if we offer them books only on devices that allow for multiple off-task affordances.

International research suggests that extensive screen time can negatively influence students' sense of well-being and educational engagement. A recent OECD report suggests that "in most participating countries, extreme internet use—more than 6 hours per day—has a negative relationship with students' life satisfaction and engagement with school" (OECD, 2017). OECD analyst Alfonzo Echazzara further explores the findings:

> In every school system, students who reported using the Internet more frequently, particularly on school days, scored lower in science than students who reported using the Internet less frequently. These results are not necessarily a call for digital abstinence, but rather a call for moderation, as students who reported using the Internet moderately—up to 30 minutes on a typical weekday at school, between 1 and 4 hours on a typical weekday outside of school or between 2 and 4 hours on a typical weekend day—scored above students who never used the Internet or used it more intensively. Using the Internet intensively is also associated with less satisfaction with life, arriving late for school and lower education expectations. (Echazarra, 2018)

As such, rather than looking for ways to increase our students' online time by encouraging them to move from paper books to e-books, a more measured approach that recognizes the value of moderation can be beneficial.

However, some school and public libraries in the United States and Australia have already gone to extremes, removing all access to paper books and replacing the collection with e-books only (Merga, 2014d). Even putting aside the importance of moderation, this seems also to have the potential to exert an adverse influence on student literacy. Simply, while it is not yet proven that all young people prefer to read on screens, such an extreme action as removing every paper book runs the risk of limiting young people's access to a potential preferred mode. This could, in turn, influence reading frequency.

In addition to there being a somewhat limited amount of data that gives insight into children's use of traditional and new book modes, some of the research collecting attitudinal data around young people's book use is inextricably complicated by funder conflict of interest or by teacher advocacy, which can lead to young people satisficing to deliver what they think the researcher wants them to say (Merga, 2015e). If we prime our research respondents to love or hate a certain book mode by telling them what they should think before we collect data from them, the data is useless. When we present e-books as an exciting new development rather than simply as another reading possibility in a study funded by e-book providers or device manufacturers, again, we cannot really use this data. Researchers in this space need to be employing a design that allows and encourages findings that confound their expectations.

While sharing research that challenges the primacy of the e-book has led to me occasionally being labeled a technophobe, this is not true. Personally, while I typically read paper books more frequently than e-books, and I do personally prefer to read paper books, I do regularly read on my e-reader, and I also occasionally read on one of the multiple e-reading apps I have added on my tablet. The benefits of the different modes lend themselves to different scenarios in my case; if I need a book instantly or if I am travelling for work, I will tend to read on a device; I love that I can bring an entire library with me on a work trip because it saves me having to choose, and because I am a fast reader, I need a couple of books to get through a long-haul flight. If I am reading for pleasure at home, I will tend to read paper books that I buy or borrow from the library.

I have reviewed the benefits as well as the potential limitations afforded by e-book modes and recognize that, in addition to portability, e-books can make book formats more accessible for students with vision impairment or some learning disabilities (Camardese, Peled, Kirkpatrick, & Teacher, 2012). They offer an intriguing resourcing possibility whereby children can potentially bring a great volume of books on one device into an otherwise bookless home (Mackey & Shane, 2013), which is important, as the WASABR found that around a third of teens had fewer than 50 books in their home (Merga, 2015a).

I have an open mind toward book mode preferences, and I have a strong appreciation for the unique affordances that e-books can offer, as well as an optimistic disposition toward what they may offer in the future. However, noting the trend toward the bookless library, it is important to gauge whether or not young people really prefer to read books on devices, particularly in light of the strong pressures that schools, libraries, and parents may face to adopt e-books (Merga & Mat Roni, 2017a). We need to know more. Increasing our resourcing of e-books and concurrently limiting or removing our resourcing of paper books for young people is a good idea only if:

- The young people in question prefer to read on these modes, and
- The devices support equal or increased reading frequency, and
- The devices do not facilitate off-task behavior, and
- The screen-based reading can be deemed equal in benefit to paper-based reading, which is still not known (Giedd, 2012; Liu, 2005). (Paper-based reading

may be more strongly associated with reading comprehension [e.g., Mangen, Walgermo, & Bronnick, 2013].)

It is particularly important to emphasize this last point. In Raynaudo and Peralta's (2018) recent small study comparing learning on e-books and paper books, they found:

> Without denying the importance of technology in the XXI century, in this study, we found that using a book can lead to similar results, or maybe even better, than those reached with an electronic book. We conclude that electronic enhancements are not necessarily per se improvements over previous methods. From our perspective, the debate is not only about using or not new technologies in educational environments but about how to use them to offer meaningful and different learning experiences compared with the ones traditional media already provides. (pp. 10–11)

There are three things of interest in this paper. First, the findings; second, the valuable literature review suggesting that e-books do not necessarily provide a superior educational experience; and third, as can be seen in the preceding quote, the almost apologetic tone that the researchers adopt when concluding that paper books may still provide the most powerful learning experience. Like me, they need to apologize for findings that challenge the myth of screen superiority. My own research primarily focuses on reading mode preferences, access, and reading engagement, as I outline next.

ARE THEY READING ON SCREENS?

To date, research generally suggests that where tweens and teens have access to e-books, they still typically choose to read on paper books. While digital reading technologies may be intuitively appealing, teens do not necessarily find e-book reading more appealing than reading paper books. In general, where teens read books frequently and had access to devices, they did not make frequent use of them, suggesting that having high device access does not mean that reading books on devices is a favored pastime (Merga, 2014d), a finding that was further confirmed in our subsequent research (Rutherford, Singleton, Derr, & Merga, 2018).

However, we need to look more closely at the data to make sense of it. While teens tended to underutilize e-book readers, tablets, mobile phones, and computers as book reading devices even when they had access to them, this finding could be the result of teens just not choosing to read books with frequency. As such, when analyzing the WASABR data, I also looked specifically at the device use of teen readers who reported reading books at least twice a week. Again, where they had access to these devices, they were not often using them to read books:

> While avid readers predictably had higher rates of device usage for book reading, only 59% of these students had access to an eReader device, and only 24% of these students frequently read books using the device. While 98% of avid readers had access to a computer, only 12% of avid readers frequently read books on it, and while 88% of avid readers had access to a mobile phone, only 7% used it frequently for reading books. It can thus be assumed that these frequent book readers exhibit a continued marked preference for traditional book reading practices. (Merga, 2014d, p. 32)

While access was high and these teens were regular book readers, most were not reading on their devices very often, with some notable exceptions.

I wondered if these findings would differ for tweens, who would theoretically have been exposed to a broader range of technologies from young age. However, when analyzing the WASCBR data with my colleague, Dr. Saiyidi Mat Roni, we found that, again, they also generally fit the profile of the infrequent user, even when they were daily book readers (Merga & Mat Roni, 2017a).

We also wanted to find out whether access to devices had any impact on how often young people would typically read books. We conducted additional analysis to determine the effect of device ownership on reading frequency. Arguably the most important finding in our study was that reading frequency was less when children had access to a greater range of these devices, with mobile phone owner-ship particularly associated with reading infrequency (Merga & Mat Roni, 2017a). This meant that the more devices young persons had access to, the less likely they were to read books, suggesting that buying your child a device in order to increase their reading frequency is likely to have the opposite effect.

We decided that these findings were too important to just share in the form of an academic journal article, so my colleague Dr. Saiyidi Mat Roni and I also released a piece in *The Conversation*, which explained the significance of our findings for the general public and finished with some tips to encourage reading engagement (Mat Roni & Merga, 2017).

To our amazement, this has reached many more readers than we ever anticipated, and the article also appeared across a range of other newspaper articles and radio interviews. We used these media opportunities to argue against the assumption that all young people prefer to read on screens and to suggest that, while a general pref-erence for reading paper books seems to prevail, at least some paper books remain available to young people. It was really exciting to see our research challenging the myths and misconceptions that can flourish in this space and to give literacy advocates who were skeptical of the generalizations made an opportunity to draw upon recent data to resist unnecessary changes.

More research needs to be done into why e-books have not surpassed paper books in popularity at this stage despite their numerous advantages. Most of the research in this area has been done with adults and young adults (Johnson & Buck, 2014), and it has also predominantly found a continuing preference for paper books (Tor-res, Johnson, & Imhonde, 2014). This preference for paper books may typically relate to the following factors:

- Greater perceived comfort in paper mode reading (Evans, 2017; Fortunati & Vincent, 2014)
- Improved comprehension (Jeong, 2012) and retention of what has been read in paper mode (Baron, 2013)
- Less immersive involvement in the e-book reading experience (Wagner, Ben-lian, & Hess, 2012)
- Reliance on electricity and Internet access to use an e-reading device (Taipale, 2014)

- Ease of annotation in paper books (Fortunati & Vincent, 2014)
- Other issues, such as eye strain in screen-based reading (Jeong, 2012)

It is realistic to anticipate that some of these issues (such as eye strain) may be mitigated as the technology continues to improve; indeed, we have already experienced significant advances in this area with the development of e-ink (Benedetto et al., 2013). However, it is not known whether we will ever achieve parity in terms of satisfaction. In addition, some of these research samples were quite small; now that we have a broader understanding of the possible range of issues, a greater body of quantitative research in this area would be beneficial. However, further qualitative research is also indicated, as we cannot assume that the issues faced by older people are the same as those experienced by tweens and teens. We need a great deal of further research with robust sample sizes to ensure that the findings hold currency, relevance, and generalizability moving forward.

When we try to understand the continuing use of paper books in the context of increasingly high availability of e-books, we need to speak directly with young people in order to learn about their preferences. The WASABR research collected some relevant insights from teens about their e-book usage in the interviews, with issues such as struggles with the technology emerging. For example, Layla talked about how the books available online for free download are typically older, and she found negotiating the unfamiliar technology quite discouraging, as after downloading an app to her iPod, she had difficulty using it to read a book. She explained that this was "really confusing because I thought you could read books on the app, but . . . I opened the app and it was like . . . download the book. so, I was like, 'okay, we'll see about that'" (Merga, 2014d, p. 34). Issues with gauging the thickness of books and access were also raised, though the desire for an actual physical book remained for its permanence, as described by the next teenager:

> I also read a lot of books online, but it's not as good as having an actual book to hold and mark your page. It's also great having it to keep, not like an online book forum where they could get lost if something was to happen to the website. (Merga, 2014d, p. 34)

Walter found issues with tracking his progress and maintaining his place in the book, explaining, "I prefer reading in books than my iPad 'cause it's easier to know where I'm up to, 'cause, when, on the iPad you can put a bookmark on it, but it doesn't always stay there. It's annoying, so that's why I'd rather read books." As such, just because technological affordances may try to mimic what is on offer in the physical form, such as the possibility of bookmarking, this does not mean that young people will deem these features equally useful.

DOES GENDER MAKE A DIFFERENCE?

Boys are characterized as being "into" their technological toys, and some have hoped to harness this enthusiasm and direct it toward reading. For instance,

Table 6.1   Percentage Daily Reader Device Use by
Gender Where Access Is Available

	iPad/Kindle	Computer	Mobile Phone
Girls	8.5	5.3	10.9
Boys	6.4	2.1	4.1

Source: Adapted from Mat Roni & Merga, 2017.

Harrison (2016) speculates that "it is certainly the case that there are gamelike features in using a laptop, a tablet, or a phone, and these may enhance boys' motivation" (p. 222). As previously discussed, there are a number of popular myths about boys and reading, spurred by the performance gap between the male and female genders. When analyzing the data, we collected from tweens in the WASCBR, we decided to split the data for gender in order to determine whether speculation that boys would prefer to read books on screens could be proved in our data.

We wanted to start with an overall picture of what boys may prefer. Before the analysis, we tried to source research data looking at boys' reading mode preferences, but again, what is available is quite heavily weighted toward research where children were possibly primed to deliver a favorable response toward e-readers through an e-reader company funding of the project and other mitigating factors such as teacher advocacy around e-reading before and during the project; for further detail about these issues with the literature, refer to the paper (Mat Roni & Merga, 2017). Once this data was discounted, there was not much literature left to review, though we did find some possible trends. When data were found that were not specific to intervention contexts, boys may not read e-books more frequently than girls, with previous UK research suggesting that 8 percent of girls read e-books compared with 7.7 percent of boys (Clark, 2012).

Our research found that when boys and girls identified as daily readers and when they had access to devices, boys were less likely to use their devices for reading than girls. As such, rather than e-books being more appealing to boys than girls, we actually found the reverse (Table 6.1).

IS IT TIME TO EMBRACE THE BOOKLESS LIBRARY?

These findings have implications for parents, librarians, and educators wishing to match resourcing with student reading preferences, and they are particularly pertinent in the context of the movement toward so-called bookless libraries (Merga, 2014d; Merga, 2015b). At this stage, the suggestion that all young people, boys in particular, will prefer to read books on screens is not supported. If this myth persists and if many young people continue to retain a preference for paper book reading, this could potentially lead to negative consequences:

• First, the trend toward the "bookless" library may be further advanced, potentially limiting young people's access to a preferred reading mode (Merga, 2014d; Merga, 2015b). An imagined progressive privileging of e-books over paper books has already led to money being cut from paper book resourcing in school and public libraries, as mentioned earlier.

- Second, while questions exist about the comparability of the book reading experience on paper and on screens with regard to attention and concentration, as well as the body of research exploring negative associations between sustained screen time and health, social and educational outcomes, encouraging young people to embrace the on-screen mode remains questionable.

- Finally, the generalization feeds into a homogeneous construction of young people and gender stereotypes that, at this stage, is not an accurate representation of reality, and it also potentially reinforces these stereotypes. Indeed, the myth of children preferring to read books on screens will become a self-fulfilling prophecy by default if young people simply can't access paper books at their "bookless" library.

In the e-book/paper book discussion, we may also wonder about the comparative research around using these forms for reading aloud. Early research suggests that in the case of reading aloud, book mode may make a difference. Reading aloud from e-books is not necessarily a comparable experience to reading aloud with paper books. Research suggests that there is less beneficial parent–child discussion about the book during reading when an e-book is used. While this was initially linked to the affordances of interactive features that could distract from the story, recent research in this area suggests that, even when these features are strictly limited and like-for-like texts are compared, less discussion was still occurring (Revelle & Bowman, 2017). More research needs to be done in this area, comparing use of the same text in different modes.

It is also important to mention that some tweens and teens *are* very keen e-book readers. For example, teen student Hattie read books on her iPad to meet her voracious demand, storing about a hundred books on her tablet, which she shared with her mother. Also, reading on her tablet enabled instant access to a new book, preventing a gap between reading experiences, as "when I finish the one I'm on, which I've only got a few pages left, I'll get a new one soon," often with no real gap (Merga, 2014d, p. 33). So, for Hattie, e-books were important for supporting her reading volume and frequency. While most young people prefer paper books, e-books should also be available where possible to support the reading engagement of young people who prefer to read e-books.

ARE THEY TALKING ABOUT BOOKS ONLINE?

When I need a new book, I often jump onto Goodreads.com and click on my recommendations, or I read the reviews of my Goodreads friends. This enables me to hit the bookshops or the library armed with a list of must-reads, and if it is a real book reading emergency (I must read this book within the next 24 hours, or I will die of curiosity), I will go to the online store and get it on my e-reader or tablet app. I really value the role that online Web sites and social networking sites play in lining up my next book so that there are no gaps in my reading because, like many people, I like to have a book in progress at all times.

Young people are typically characterized as technologically savvy and heavily involved in social networking online, so I wondered whether young avid readers would make the most of the opportunities to talk about books online. However, the WASABR research found that teens who read a lot have a lower frequency of engagement in social networking than infrequent readers, with some students resistant to social networking in general (Merga, 2015c). Some students had no idea where to go online to find out about books, with one teenager commenting, "I wish there was a site where you could find books, and do a quiz to find a perfect book for you," which I found surprising, as quite a lot of information is available online, though perhaps not in the preferred form.

While some of the teens who took part in the WASABR described a similar attitude to mine, where social networking was primarily used to source new books to read, others were even more avid in their social networking engagement (for instance, one young teen described a great love of Quotev, which she used to read and to generate fan fiction). That said, overall, social networking opportunities were felt to be underutilized in my study, though this usage data was collected through qualitative interviews and therefore is not definitive or widely generalizable. For some teens, this was due to a tendency to "prefer to maintain book reading as a solitary pastime, or they prefer to engage in social networking around books offline" (Merga, 2015c, p. 12).

While I am wary of encouraging readers to spend more time online and aware of how easy it is to get distracted in this space, as I have highlighted elsewhere in this book, many young people really struggle with choosing books, and social networking about books can provide an excellent support in this area. I feel that this is an area that will probably be subject to change over time, as young people become increasingly aware of the possibilities online, and I look forward to tracking the developing research in this field.

A FINAL COMMENT

I am not for a moment suggesting that e-books do not have a place in contemporary libraries and in young people's hands. I also know that my research is the last thing people wish to see when they have just spent thousands on e-readers for their students, consigning the paper books to the recycling bin. However, as contended elsewhere, it is important that we determine our students' preferences and aim to meet these, while at the same time ensuring that devices are being used for the intended purpose, and that we are not forcing young people into increasing their screen time, particularly if it will send them off task or pose risks to their well-being. For example, if silent reading of self-selected books happens on tablets instead of paper books, vigilance needs to be in place to ensure that book reading is occurring. Otherwise, instead of silent reading, students are doing silent browsing or even silent gaming, both arguably less beneficial for student literacy. In addition, if, as research suggests, the mere presence of a smartphone on our person detrimentally impacts our available cognitive capacity, even when switched off (Ward, Duke, Gneezy, & Bos, 2017), I feel that we should first ascertain that young people will not experience the same effect if they migrate their reading from paper books to reading on devices.

7

What Would Make Young People Read More Books?

Tweens and teens had no difficulty describing exactly what they felt would make them read more.

When I was still in high school, I began my first teaching job, tutoring the sister of a friend in English. I was very pleased about this turn of events, as my pink- and purple-colored hair and other notable eccentricities in my appearance were not really socially acceptable at that time, so it would have been hard for me to obtain and retain a regular casual job involving interaction with other people. I quickly picked up additional students, and before I knew it, I found myself a teacher, pretty much by accident.

I did not ever treat my students like empty vessels, to be filled by my knowledge, as my students were only a few years younger than I was. I had no choice but to accidentally adopt best practice, working with these young people, as it was obvious that relationship building and listening to my students were essential for me to be able to keep convincingly impersonating a teacher and somehow grow into the role before parents noticed that I was an imposter and stopped paying me money.

Luckily, I pulled it off. As part of my strategy, while I worked closely with my students to improve their structural and grammatical skills using targeted instruction tailored to meet their individual needs (see, now I know some of the buzzwords for what seemed intuitive at the time), I quickly found that the most rapid and consistent improvement could be achieved when I managed to get my clients hooked on reading. It seemed to me that getting them to read had an almost magical impact on their literacy abilities, and the entertaining discussions we had about books helped to deepen their reading of the text, fostering critical understandings that they may not have previously considered. Most importantly for my 17-year-old self, it was also fun, and therefore I was getting paid to have fun. I recommended books, we talked about books in the context of excitement, we argued about the appeal of different characters, and we agreed to disagree. Through these enjoyable exchanges, critical inquiry and literary analysis skills were fostered, and, amazingly, all of these early students made significant gains in their grades.

Many years later, after years of tutoring and classroom teaching of English as an Additional Dialect and English (Language Arts), when I decided to undertake a PhD, I found myself returning to that same exciting realization, the knowledge that if we can simply encourage our students to read more, a resultant transformative impact on literacy skills can typically be achieved. I read the research that supported the magic that I observed; many people had reached the same conclusions that I had using a range of research methods and informing theoretical frameworks, and the groundwork had been done for me with regard to establishing benefit. So what did I have to offer as a researcher? What more did we need to know?

I thought about the multiple facets involved in "getting them reading." It seemed to me that this was a somewhat complex endeavor, though intuitive to a lifelong reader like me, and I was particularly concerned about our sense of efficacy in our role as literacy advocates. Among the myths and the pessimistic contentions that it is not worth the effort because the book is dead, how can we know that we can make a difference, and how do we know the best areas in which to exercise our efforts? This is why I decided to focus on *who* could make a difference and *how* in order to inform future interventions in this area and to build the sense of efficacy in teachers, parents, and other literacy advocates such as librarians. I also explored the changing environmental and resourcing factors that influence reading engagement. I did not want to constrain myself to a purely qualitative or quantitative approach, seeing the value in using different approaches for different questions. Indeed, some of the quantitative research that I read seemed to be asking the wrong questions and would have benefited from current qualitative research to reexplore the field, and some of the qualitative research was in need of follow-up quantitative exploration to allow for generalizability.

When focusing on the who and the how of reading influence, one of the ways I investigated the how, in both the WASCBR and the WASABR, was by simply asking tweens and teens, "What would make you read more?" in the context of book reading. I liked this idea as it enabled young people to tell me what they really thought rather than limiting their responses to the range of things I thought would influence their reading, based on the previous research in this area. While a few students needed to give this question a bit of thought before responding, all were able to articulate at least one notable barrier or enabler that they identified in their own lives, while I was careful to avoid prompting them or guiding them in any specific direction.

Responses for tweens and teens were quite similar. Teens claimed that they would read more books if they had better strategies for choice, access to attractive and diverse books, time availability, time allocation, concentration, and encouragement (Merga, 2016a). The subsequent investigation into what would make tweens read more found five recurring themes: finding engaging books, series adherence, challenge seeking, skill deficit, and time availability (Merga, 2017c). These findings indicate optimal avenues for future research and educational intervention to foster increased engagement in reading, as well as providing a basis for further quantitative research in this area to find out how widely generalizable these ideas were. What I found most interesting, as I analyzed the data, is the fact that I could clearly see a capacity for social influences to mitigate the barriers and support the enablers that were raised. This is one of the numerous reasons that I can clearly state that social influences like you can make an important difference in this area, once we understand exactly what they felt would make them read more. As you read through the subsequent section, you'll probably find that you are already addressing many of these points in creative ways.

STRATEGIES FOR CHOICE

How good are you at choosing a good book? What knowledge, skills, and interests do you draw on when making this decision? We probably do not often think about how we go about this process. I am not going to pretend for an instant that all books are entertaining and that all books can appeal to all people. Being stuck reading a bad book can be like being forced into a long-winded conversation with someone who drones on in a monotone about something very boring. Most of us would look for a way to escape such social horrors, which is why I do not force myself to read a book if it does not work for me past a certain point, and I do not expect my students or children to persist past a reasonable point either. Because of my experience, I am able to avoid these bad matches for the most part, and I have relatively sound strategies for choosing, as I do not want to waste my time on something that I will find deeply annoying.

Young people do not necessarily have very good strategies at their disposal when choosing books. The reality is that many *adults* find it difficult to choose when overwhelmed by a large and diverse quantity of books, so we probably should not be surprised that many young people have poor, limited, or a deficit of strategy for choosing books to read, particularly when they are fortunate enough to be faced with the expansive possibilities of a well resourced library. While we know that it is important that young people choose the books that they read for pleasure rather than having the decision imposed upon them (Edmunds & Bauserman, 2006; Krashen, 2004), not much research has really looked closely at how young people go about selecting books, though the fact that this skill is not always effectively taught in schools has been noted (Mackey, 2014).

The lack of strategy for choice was a barrier when some teens sought a book to read for pleasure. I found that many respondents had poor or ineffectual strategies for choosing books, and many of them did not know about existing Web sites and tools that could support their search, such as Goodreads. Difficulty finding an engaging book was identified as a barrier to reading more, highlighting the importance that this skill be explicitly taught either at home, in the classroom, or ideally in the library. Where young people are not highly motivated to read, helping them to find a book that meets their interests is very important, as they will not necessarily persist if not immediately engaged, as explained by this teenager:

> I often don't read because I'm not interested in any of the books in my house. When we go on holiday or camping I usually buy a book to read beforehand, but don't return to it after the holiday. There have been some books/series that I've been into in the

past, like *White Fang* and the *Alex Rider* series, but I find it hard to find a good book, let alone get into it before I lose interest.

For this student, access to interesting books in the house was clearly also part of the issue, but this quote also highlights the window of opportunity that a book has to engage young people before they disengage. As I have illustrated previously, I think that this is reasonable; however, it also highlights the importance of helping students get "into" books that suit them.

As might be expected, the tweens interviewed for the WASCBR study also tended to have limited choosing skills, and they also did not describe making much use of available supports in this area, such as library catalogues. When Saiyidi and I analyzed the data around how these students chose books, we found the following recurring trends, which we present here with an example:

- **Random/no strategy:** "I just pick a book, any book, and then walk off, and then read it, and if not, it's not good, I'd get up again and read it, and if not it's not good, I'll get up again, and get my own another book, and yeah, until I get a good book" (Gary).
- **Color:** "I look at mainly the chapter books, and if I see something like a black or cool color, kind of thing, that I like, then I look at it" (Jason).
- **Back cover text:** "There's something on the back, and that normally tells you about the book, and sometimes in bookshops they get so interesting that I start crying over which one I should choose, 'cause I love books so much. That happened to me in a [name of bookshop] before" (Sarah).
- **Title:** "If it was the school library, I would normally get a browser, and like I'd just look through, and if there's something interesting, like if I find an interesting title that makes me want to read it, I'd take it out, and I'd put the bookmark in, and I'd go sit down and start reading, and if it's an interesting book, sometimes I'll . . . rent it or something" (Kara).
- **Genre:** "I used to go [to] the dinosaurs and look at them. And then I went to the space which are over there, then I would go into the natural disasters which are there" (Lucian).
- **Points:** "So on AR quizzes we get points and so far, I'm the highest out of the class. So, I like to get big books that give me good points because you can get books but they give you zero points" (Karen).
- **Size:** "I usually start with the fiction ones, and I just look for a really thick one, 'cause I read really fast, so my teacher told me to look for a really thick one, and eventually I'll find a few really thick ones, and I'm like, 'Okay, I'd like this one.' And I'll try and read it. And that's how I got into the David Clement-Davies series" (Matt).
- **Page sampling:** "Usually I would read the first to second page of the book and just read it and see if it makes sense, if it's an interesting book and never judge a book by its cover" (Tyrone).
- **Author familiarity:** "I choose them by the authors I know because I like those specific authors, like Roald Dahl and Paul Jennings and things like that. I'm

into those sorts of books so I know Roald Dahl. And then my friends introduced more books to me so I get a wider variety" (Rose).

- **Repeat reading:** "I normally choose one I haven't read in quite a while. Because sometimes—I've read most of my books, most of the books I like—but then I go and read other ones I haven't read in a while and then I come back to other ones like, I go in a circle" (Neil).

- **Series reading:** "Because with the *Dork Diaries* there's lots of a different series and there's always new series coming out with all of the series books and I find it really interesting to read each one of them and see what's next in the series" (Samara).

- **Supported choice:** "My dad knows where all like the mystery sort of books are. And I like books without pictures, just big chapter books, I like reading those, and my dad always goes there, so he just knows, and then I go and choose the right one" (Clare). (Merga & Mat Roni, 2017b)

Some of the strategies listed here that tweens were using, such as choosing a book based on its color, were likely to be pretty ineffectual, both in the short and long term. You will have also noticed that many of the tweens had just one strategy; when you think about yourself as a reader, and how you choose books, there is probably more than one strategy that you employ.

Overall, when looking at the range of strategies that young people used, we found that familiarity, complexity, and interest tended to guide choice when a formal or informal strategy was used (Merga & Mat Roni, 2017b), though the focus was often on just one of these elements. As such, we have to teach children how to choose and to use multiple strategies to find books that are both interesting and realistically readable.

Take the point of complexity. As I describe later on, challenge is really important to some children, whereas others may be quick to capitulate should they encounter difficulty, so what constitutes readability will be very much dependent on individual students' skill levels, attitudes, *and* sense of self-efficacy in reading. There is no blanket approach. We need to show them how a reader chooses: We need to scaffold choosing skills, and we also need to make young people aware of the existing, free, and often readily accessible supports available to them. When even avid readers are underutilizing social networks to support choice (Merga, 2015c), clearly greater awareness of these tools is necessary if we want students to use them.

Familiarity could be both a blessing and a curse as a guide. Risk-averse children were particularly reluctant to read outside their often limited scope of experience, leading to some tweens and teens confining themselves to series selections and familiar authors, and in the case of repeat reading, reading the same books over and over. We will need to be particularly careful to pay close attention to individual preferences when coaxing risk-averse repeat readers out of their comfort books into broader reading. For these students, opportunities to expose them to potentially appealing books beyond the scope of the familiar, through opportunities such as book discussions and recommendations, can be important to keep young people reading once the familiar has been exhausted.

Tweens also often had quite specific requirements in a book, just as many adults do. For example, Naomi felt that "sometimes when books are too long and don't have any pictures to entertain you, kids might find it a bit boring and might not read the book, even if it's a good book." Naomi's instincts would appear to be sound; three-fifths of the tweens in the WASCBR said that they would prefer a book with some pictures, with around half this percentage wanting a book with no pictures, and nearly 10 percent wanting a book with lots of pictures. The extent to which tweens are still reliant on images to support their reading comprehension may be poorly understood.

Tweens also often had clear preferences for plot, author, and genre. For instance, Samson explained, "I like the idea of a cliffhanger. When you never know what is going to happen and there are so many ways the story can go." While some children were somewhat inflexible about their genre choices, others, such as Julian, were more amenable to being coaxed into other choices:

> I would like to say that I love books such as James Bond, Lee Child and *Skullduggery Pleasant*; they are very entertaining, because I enjoy movies like *Olympus has Fallen*, but I want to read it. I pretty much like staying to my genre, but I don't mind getting out of it because I guess I just love reading.

Similarly, a teen respondent in the WASABR had a clear idea of the books that they preferred, sharing this anonymous insight in the open field of the survey:

> I love reading books all the time, I'm just a slow reader. I enjoy going to the library, but most the books I read are old ones my mum read when she was my age. I like to read horror books and ones where bad things happen to good people, and ones that are sad. I love reading.

If we listen closely, we can help to guide their choices, while also equipping them with strategies for choice so that they can self-source books. As per above, it is clear that many young people are clearly able to articulate what they are looking for in a book, even if they cannot always easily find a book that suits them, though luckily the student who enjoys books where "bad things happen to good people" will never run out of reading options!

ACCESS TO BOOKS

Children need opportunities to access books in order to support their reading, which I know is kind of obvious, really, but worth saying anyway, as it is a continual reminder as to why it is so important to keep both school and public libraries open and available in our communities. Researchers have measured the degree of advantage conferred through access to books. For example, difference in levels of access to books is felt to be the key reason for summer reading loss, with Allington and McGill Franzen's (2017) analysis of the body of research in this area leading them to conclude that the comparatively restricted access to books and other reading material experienced by children from low-income families is at the root of the problem; this limited access is unsurprisingly associated with reading infrequency. Neuman and Knapczyk (2018) are critical of the assumption that all young people have equal access to a range of age-appropriate, high-quality literature.

Providing access to books is an important equity consideration that has a measured and cumulative influence on young people's literacy levels. As U.S. research has found, while we know that greater access to books results in more reading, students do not have the same level of access to books in their homes, and they also do not have equal access to well resourced libraries (Shin & Krashen, 2008):

> Teens raised access to attractive, relevant and diverse books as a limiting factor on their reading. Relevant, relatable characters were sought; one student felt he would read more if he could find more books about "stuff what—that's happening, like with boys my age, and stuff—something that", and another student commented that "I like reading books a lot but there needs to be more books, teenage books, because I'm running out of books to read very quickly". (Merga, 2016a, pp. 415–416)

Similarly, some tweens in the WASCBR found that access to books limited their reading volume and frequency:

> For Max, access was the key issue. Max felt that he would read more "if I had the book I wanted to get", though he found it hard to obtain access to his preferred reading materials. When asked why, he explained that "I can't really find them in the school library or other libraries", and that appealing to his mother had also been unsuccessful, as "I have told my mum that I want to get it, but she won't let me buy it". Max knew what he wanted to read; he simply could not gain access to these books. (Merga, 2017c, p. 214)

While many of the children in my research seemed to be able to access books, economic resourcing was identified as an issue by some students, such as this respondent:

> I know this is a very hard thing to do and it probably can't happen, but I believe if books were cheaper more parents wouldn't mind buying books at a cheaper cost. That way more kids get to enjoy reading.

While parents should take some responsibility for this where resourcing permits, this is not always possible, so schools, led by both teachers and librarians, should continue to take responsibility in this area by sending books home, as I explore later on in this book. As this is an area where a number of key social influences can take the lead, it also runs the risk of being an area of orphaned responsibility, so it is important that if your children or students cannot have regular (and by that, I mean daily) access to books in their homes, we need to ensure that someone else in their lives is doing this, and not just hope or assume that they are. Library visitation access is also relevant to this discussion, so I encourage you not to skip Chapter 9.

TIME AVAILABILITY

Young people are busy, and in addition to the recreational pursuits that they engage in, many of them have pressing and genuine demands on their time that they have limited power over. I have previously explored time availability as a barrier to reading, and it was raised when young people were asked what would make them read more. Time availability differs from time allocation, as time allocation is due to *choice*, whereas time availability relates to required activities (such as sibling care, homework, and employment) that act as barriers to spending time on a

Table 7.1   Teenager's Self-Reported
Free Time on a Weekday

Answer	%
None	1%
0–1 hour	6%
1–2 hours	15%
2–3 hours	17%
3–4 hours	19%
4–5 hours	17%
5–6 hours	12%
6–7 hours	6%
More than 7 hours	8%

recreational pursuit such as book reading. Distinguishing the two is necessary, even though, where students experienced a time barrier, it often incorporated both.

I asked the teens in the WASABR to let me know how much free time they typically had on a normal weekday to try to gauge the time availability of this group, and the results in Table 7.1 show that there was quite a bit of variance, with 21 percent reporting less than two hours of free time in a day, while 26 percent had more than five hours. The reading expectations that we could realistically have of these groups would be equal, but their capacity to fulfil these expectations is very different.

Limitations on the time availability of teens were varied. For example, Tranh had to babysit his brother while his mother worked, and his father was away from home, working at the mines, and Dash sometimes felt overwhelmed by homework and sporting commitments, even though he enjoyed reading when he had the chance. He spent four to five days a week training in his preferred sport, and while this might have been a choice, it also may have been related to parental expectations and vocational goals, so the difference between time availability and time allocation was not always clear-cut and could not necessarily be sufficiently investigated in one interview. When I asked Dash if he read more now or in lower school, he explained how the greater homework load in upper school influenced his time to read:

> I'd have to say less now, because with homework and assignments, I do a lot of them, and I get a lot of them going at once. Like, last week I had a science assignment, an English essay, a maths assignment and an S&E assignment. Maths and S&E [were] due on Tuesday, the science due on Wednesday, and the essay for English due on Monday, so [laughs] I was pretty hectic right then. And playing in a competition in [country location] for tennis, and . . . I got home and I hadn't finished [laughs] writing the essay for English on Sunday, so . . . yeah.

The demands of paid employment were also sometimes significant. I experienced a memorable interview with Zara, a teen who was juggling three casual jobs. She worked every day of the week apart from Monday while attending school full-time. It sounded as though she was working harder than I was, and at that time I was doing my PhD while also working part-time and raising two young children. If we just looked at Zara's reading frequency and made a judgment about her reading attitude based on that, we would come up with the wrong conclusion. Despite experiencing difficulty concentrating, she quite enjoyed reading, and she kept purchasing books that she simply did not have time to read. She explained, "I'm either working, or I've got school, or school homework or exams or something like that. There's always something, so I hardly ever have time" to read books.

Tweens such as Neil were also experiencing an issue with time availability:

> Well, if I had more free time because sometimes I do have homework, sometimes I have to go in Mathletics and do that sort of stuff, and other times I have to unpack my bag, do things like that. And just help my sister because she just hurt her leg recently, and so if I had more time then I would read more. (Merga, 2017c, p. 217)

Like the previously cited teen respondent (Zara), Neil also enjoyed reading; he just experienced time constraints that limited his opportunity. While sibling care and homework were again barriers, I was interested to discover employment was also an issue for some tweens, though it may have been unpaid. For instance, "Maria's daily assistance at her mother's shop was her most significant barrier, involving sweeping, cleaning the floor, polishing surfaces, and moving furniture as required" (Merga, 2017c, p. 217). Others also described the difficulty finding opportunities to read.

Just as if we want children to read for recreation, they need access to books, we also need to ensure that they have opportunity for recreational time for reading. Many young people indicated that they would consider using a greater amount of free time to read: 48 percent of teens in the WASABR agreed that they would read more books if they had more time, and 77 percent of WASCBR tweens selected "yes" when asked if they would read more books if they had more free time. The paucity of time that some of these children could call their own also has implications for the importance of providing school-based opportunities for recreational reading, an idea that I will return to later in the book.

TIME ALLOCATION

When you decide what you will do with your free time, what factors come into play? If it was as simple as preference, many of us would be lying on an island beach somewhere, reading a book and relaxing; however, sadly, preference alone will not get us there. As I have mentioned previously, choice is rarely as simple as preference alone; a number of factors influence time allocation. For example, tween Quentin explained, "I love reading books, but sometimes it is hard for me when video games are distracting me." Time allocation is also influenced by the relative easiness of competing tasks, as well as the rewards for participation and a range of other factors such as access and resourcing.

As I explored in Chapter 2, preference or time allocation remains a key reason for reading infrequency, so we need to understand why young people choose to exclusively invest their time in other recreational pursuits when reading books is an option for them. When we do not anticipate enjoyment from an activity, we are less likely to engage in it, such as the teenager who made the following comment in the open field of the survey, which I have presented verbatim with errors intact: "reding books is really boring. i would prefer to do other things with my time :P."

Time allocation was an issue for both tweens and teens. While the WASABR and WASCBR were not designed to pursue students' nonreading recreational pursuits in detail, the study nonetheless yielded insights into these habits. Many young people described preferences primarily for spending recreational time engaging in a variety of leisure activities on devices, whether they be mobile phones, computers, tablets, or gaming consoles, though some were also involved in organized sports and other non-screen based pursuits such as surfing or dance. For some, reading was something that was done only when the preferred recreational pastime could not be accessed. For example, when I asked tween Tyler how often he read, he explained, "[N]ot too often, but when I can't do something on the computer, then I'll go into my room and read a book." On the computer, he would enjoy first-person shooter gaming and viewing videos. Anna's response to the same question was very similar, stating, "Well . . . I like reading . . . [S]ometimes I get a little bored when I'm reading . . . but to be honest I prefer playing on my iPad."

For some respondents, not only did they not allocate time for reading, their allocation of time for recreational pursuits such as texting on mobile devices could be considered excessive. For instance, teen student Walter described engaging in social networking for three to four hours per night, sleeping with the phone "permanently on in the background" (Merga, 2016a, p. 418) and sleeping with it next to the bed. He would occasionally receive and respond to a late-night text message or phone calls that disturbed his sleep. Walter would be considered increasingly typical in the context of research suggesting that "mobile telephones may be having a major impact on the quality of sleep of a growing number of adolescents" (Van den Bulck, 2003, p. 263), and an association between use of electronic media at night, particularly use of phones, suggests that this electronic media use is related to sleep disturbance, and, in turn, it potentially can perpetuate depressive symptoms (Lemola et al., 2015). With screen-based recreation presenting as a strong mitigating factor to young people's engagement in reading, children need to be encouraged to make balanced choices, addressing the potential effects of extended screen time (as previously explored) and increasing exposure to literacy benefit. It is also worth critically considering the influence that the creation of movies based on books can have on students' engagement with the source books before exposing your children or students to film adaptations prior to reading the source novels. For some students, this can be really motivating; for other young people, the availability of a movie or television show that covers the content of a book means that there is no longer a need to read the book, making reading seem pointless.

Why do *you* like reading? Also, if you prefer to read a book rather than see a movie, why is this? While there are a great many reasons for adult reading motivation, the opportunity for escape is a strong motivating factor for many readers (Merga, 2017b), but are all young people cognitively equipped to enter so deeply into a book that they can escape in it? Do they all have access to environments where such escape is supported by quiet and comfortable surroundings? If we want young people to enjoy reading, they might need some extra help in accessing and/ or building the internal and external factors that support the activity, factors that we typically take for granted until we are trying to read a book on a train with a person sitting next to us, loudly discussing their infected toenails or complicated love lives. So, while finding books that are really interesting to young people is essential, we need to be careful not to take other factors for granted when we are looking to foster increased motivation to read. In the next section, I will talk more about the demands of concentration, which are closely linked to time allocation.

CONCENTRATION AND MULTITASKING

It is hard to read if you cannot concentrate, as reading is not an activity that allows shallow focus on the task at hand; I personally know this because I have tried reading while cooking and reading while on the treadmill, and I have failed badly at both activities, as you might imagine. If you try to read while doing other things, you are likely to have to read the same page over and over again until you apply the required amount of concentration that reading demands. Over two-fifths of adult avid readers who responded in the ISABR had experienced difficulty concentrating while reading. These respondents were asked to indicate the reasons why, allowing for multiple selections. While tiredness and a noisy environment were the most common causes for difficulty in concentration, around two-fifths of these respondents who had experienced difficulty concentrating while reading indicated that it was because they were attempting to do other things at the same time.

Concentration is an issue for many young people, not only because poor concentration inhibits reading but also, as I have mentioned, because it makes reading hard work, it can lead to young people choosing to pursue easier activities in their recreation time. For example, one teen who participated in the WASABR explained that book reading constituted a comparatively high cognitive investment, which was not worthwhile in his view:

> But then like, sometimes reading is an effort because you've still got to use your brain, but if you sat down and watched TV, you can like, you don't really have to concentrate, but you can't sit down and read a book and not concentrate, because then you get halfway through the book and you're like, 'What's going on?' (Merga, 2016a, p. 419)

While we might not start out with the concentration levels required to read a complex book, luckily there is something we can do about this. The idea that we need to build reading stamina in order to read effectively is not new, with researchers such as McCracken (1971) contending that opportunities for sustained silent reading were important in order to foster students' ability to read for a sustained period. We know that in addition to needing to be able to read fluently and deeply in order to optimize academic performance in schools, many jobs will require these abilities, so fostering reading stamina and concentration can do more than potentially increase reading engagement—it can also help us to achieve better outcomes in our everyday lives.

The world in which we currently live is not necessarily geared toward helping us in this regard; just look at the number of people "face-planting" in the general public as they attempt to send text messages while walking up the stairs. The current environment in which we live is unlikely to be conducive to building sustained capacity for attention, and if classroom-assigned books are the only sustained text we read, in a textual diet otherwise dominated by short-text forms such as text messages, online news articles, and social networking posts, we are not likely to be building and sustaining reading stamina. We actually tend to gear our lives toward practices that may worsen rather than strengthen our attentional capacities; for example, current home and school contexts often require multitasking activities. However, we know that across a broad range of possible tasks and with few exceptions, our performance when we multitask is less efficient than when we are just performing one task, and we also know that multitasking is even harder for young people due to their immature cognitive processes and attention (Courage et al., 2015).

My research suggests that concentration is not an issue that can be confined to struggling or even young readers. Issues with concentration when trying to read have also been reported in the predominantly adult sample who took part in the ISABR, suggesting that adults who love reading books may struggle with this issue (Merga, 2017d). This is not just an issue for nonreaders; environmental factors such as background noise can play a part. Media multitasking, where individuals attempt to undertake a variety of screen-based pursuits simultaneously, for example, texting friends on a phone while watching television or actively contributing on social networking while streaming music videos, is both popular and contentious.

These activities actually tend to make young people's concentration worse over time, and young people who claim to media multitask frequently may have difficulty distinguishing between relevant and irrelevant environmental stimuli (Ophir, Nass, & Wagner, 2009), and they may experience issues with concentration and sustained attention (Cain & Mitroff, 2011; Ralph, Thomson, Cheyne, & Smilek, 2014), With U.S. research finding that over half of teens engage in media multitasking while reading (National Endowment for the Arts, 2007) and that the extent of media multitasking is increasing (Rideout, Foehr, & Roberts, 2010), this can have a detrimental effect on their overall ability to focus for the required length and depth to really engage with a book, though we do not know enough about the long-term impacts of such multitasking on young people's developing attention and learning systems, as research in this area is still insufficient and often contradictory. We also need to learn more about causation: does media multitasking cause neural and behavioral differences, or are these differences preexisting and leading young people to attempt media multitasking more often (Uncapher et al., 2017)? More needs to be known in this area, and until this research has been undertaken, limiting the amount of time young people spend in media multitasking is a good idea.

We need to be aware and to make our young people aware of the potential trade-offs at play; where and how we invest our attention can shape what we can subsequently use it for, as explored by Doidge (2010) in his interesting book on neuroplasticity. As such, the themes of time allocation and concentration are closely related and need to be considered together, and reading stamina and concentration may be issues for most of us to contend with as some point in our lives if we want to both sustain and build optimal attentional capacities. Though as previously described, book reading can support cognitive stamina into old age, the possibilities of book reading to mitigate the effects of the shallow attentional lifestyle that many of us lead is not yet fully explored.

My research recorded some interesting reflections in this area. For teen Ciara, book reading was one of her only opportunities to apply sustained attention to one task, due to the lure of media multitasking:

> I cannot sit and watch—I can't even sit and watch TV without doing something else. I have to either be there on my phone, or else I will get bored watching TV. It could be the funniest thing on Earth, and I would actually get bored. So, it's really hard to do. So even when I'm reading a book, I kind of have to listen to music, but, then it makes me think, I could be reading, but concentrating to the music, so I'm trying not to listen to music. So, I think books are one of the only things that will make me do only one thing at a time.

In addition to literacy benefits, reading may offer attentional benefits that can help us to meet the emerging challenges facing young people today. More research needs to be done to explore this possibility.

ENCOURAGEMENT

This section on encouragement is a little lean as it has been a recurring theme throughout the book so far, and I do not want to bore you with repetition. So what I present here is a further development on what has been explored previously, in relation to the data provided by tweens and teens when they were specifically asked what would make them read more. As previously discussed, expired expectations, where children no longer receive encouragement and reminders of the importance of reading, can lead to children viewing the practice as no longer important for them. Some teens also indicated that they would also like to receive this encouragement and support from their peers, explaining that this would inspire them to read more. For example, a student explained that:

> maybe if we could discuss books in class, maybe if . . . yeah, if, for even five minutes of the lesson, our teacher could be like, "Who's got an interesting book that they've read recently?" And someone could bring it up, and obviously, we'd all be like interested, if they described it well, we'd obviously go have a look at it, so yeah, even like five minutes of someone saying, "Oh, I read this book on the weekend", or "I saw that book", or "I find this interesting, I saw it was in the newspaper, I saw it was online", I think that'd be really helpful. (Merga, 2013, p. 240)

As such, encouragement was related to expired expectations, but it was also related to positioning the book as an item worthy of discussion and social exchange. When I looked more closely at who was providing encouragement across the teenage samples, there were some interesting implications. Only 48 percent of high school English teachers were felt to provide encouragement, though they were second only to mothers (49 percent), and nearly a third of teens felt that no one encouraged them. While in some cases, this could be because they were already perceived to be readers, these low levels of encouragement are worth noting.

SKILL DEFICIT AND CHALLENGE

One of the challenges for literacy educators seeking to meet individual needs is the diversity that we face, not just in terms of interests but also in relation to young people's skill and motivational issues. As I have discussed previously, these are often but not always related. We may have a child whose reading skill level is two grades below average sitting next to a student who is two grades above average. When these children peer surreptitiously over each other's shoulders to gauge where they are in relation to their peers, one of them may be very discouraged. It was not surprising that the children who took part in the WASCBR identified skill extension or challenge, as well as skill deficit, as factors that motivated or constrained their reading.

Students with skill deficit understandably saw their struggles in reading as a real barrier to reading more, and it is hard for these children to retain motivation, particularly as they tended to compare themselves to others who were achieving at a higher level. For children who struggled with reading comprehension and fluency, awareness of their issues, particularly when in comparison with peers or siblings, was demotivating. Both teens and tweens did this. For instance, tween Josh explained, "I don't really read very fast, I like to check myself a little bit, so I know what I'm reading. 'cause like my sister finishes a book in like five minutes . . . really fast." Teenager Nigel also described comparing himself to others:

> I'm not very fluent reader, either, and I'm quite slow reader. Like when we . . .'cause every Tuesday we go to the library, and read a book, and it takes me . . . when people have read 60 pages, I'm still on my 30th or whatever, and they're just . . . a bit faster than me. When I read out loud to the class I'm not as fluent, either.

It was interesting to note that there was also some awareness that the best way to improve was through increased regularity of engagement in reading, and the advantages of early literacy exposure were also recognized. For example, Anna would read more "if I was faster at reading, and I know my mum always says if you read more, then you're faster, so . . . but I'd like to read if I was faster" (Merga, 2017c, p. 216), and Dana explained that "reading books is not that fun if you don't know how to read books and spell when you are young." Skill deficit could also prevent students from reading the genres that they preferred; for example, a tween in the open field of the WASCBR wished that we could "make more adventure books easier," with others disappointed that even thin books can be hard to read. With these students, we might be very cautious not to extend them too far, as we want them to develop confidence in their reading and not have their sense of inefficacy further compounded through inability to read a text.

Conversely, we have other students who actually *want* to be given books that may initially seem too hard for them. Some tweens felt they would read more if they were supported to find and engage with more challenging books, seeking books that are "longer," "big," and "a challenge" (Merga, 2017c, p. 216). Sigrid explained, "I would read more books if they were harder. I love reading James Bond books. I would read all the books in the world if I had the time to read all of them." Catering to these students involves a different approach, and it further highlights the importance that we, as literacy supports, be wide readers. Sometimes this challenge seeking was linked to a desire for further skill development; for example, Vera stated, "I believe that reading improves your vocabulary, therefore you should read as often as you can."

While I think that sometimes this challenge-seeking behavior may be partly driven by a desire for praise, motivation research suggests that the motivation can tend to be more intrinsic in nature, with some children strongly motivated by opportunities to challenge themselves through their reading and by achieving satisfaction through learning complex ideas (Wigfield & Guthrie, 1997). These children may need further support to choose more complex texts in their preferred areas of interest. An issue arose when children sought appropriately demanding books that were at the same time deemed thematically inappropriate. For example, Sarah was an avid reader who experienced issues when trying to read her mother's books:

> I'm always trying to sneak into Mum's room and try and get her book, 'cause I've read most of my books, so I'm trying to sneak into her room and get all her books, not reading mine over and over again, 'cause I like reading new books and seeing what happens instead of knowing what happens again . . . I can read them, just a few of the words I have trouble with, but then sometimes when they're about romance I put them down because that's just gross and . . . I don't like that.

As Sarah was only 9 years old, it is unsurprising that she disliked reading content with explicit adult scenes. As such, when we are transitioning children into more challenging materials, we need to take their thematic preferences and maturity into account. With contemporary adult material in many cases quite reliant on the shock value afforded by graphic rape, incest, and torture scenes, literacy advocates will need to find and maintain a body of complex and interesting texts that do not feature these plot twists for tweens and early teens to enjoy when they are advanced readers.

I wrote about skill deficit being a barrier for teens also in the context of infrequent readers in Chapter 2, explaining that 13 percent of adolescent respondents agreed with the statement, "I am not good at reading." It is also worth noting that later on in the survey, I asked *all* of the students to indicate their level of agreement with the statement, "I would read more books if reading was easier." It was interesting to note that 13 percent of the whole group agreed with this statement, suggesting that it is not just infrequent readers who are aware that skill issues are acting as a barrier to their reading.

BROADENING THE READING OF SERIES ADHERENTS

I am not a big fan of plane travel, though my job occasionally requires it so that I can share my research findings and collaborate with other researchers. So to make the time go faster, I usually load a whole book series onto my e-reader and plough through it. Strangely, it is usually a series that I have already read because I will not risk being stuck with bad books at 35,000 feet above the Earth's surface. This approach makes long-haul travel go quickly and easily because, while my body is being carted around the world, my brain is flying on dragons and learning to use my newfound magic powers and rescuing a loved one from a fate worse than death (naturally depending on the series). I choose to read a series rather than a stand-alone in this context because I find travelling a bit challenging for my concentration, so I need to go deeply in my book and to be able to build on the prior knowledge of characters that I develop as I move through the series journey.

Getting young people hooked on a series seems like a great entry point to reading. A number of children and teens described series as lighting an ongoing passion for reading, such as Layla:

> I never used to like reading before, but since Year Seven, last year, we started reading *Tomorrow When the War Began*, John Marsden, the first book, and since then I've kind of been really enjoying reading. I finished the series, and, reading different books.

Students said how much they enjoyed connecting meaningfully with characters, but series completion was also seen as an achievement. I noticed that younger students often seemed very pleased with their accomplishment when they read an entire series, such as Timo, a tween who proudly explained, "I just read a whole series of *Big Nate* the other day, and *Diary of a Wimpy Kid* twice."

Both boys and girls enjoyed series in my studies and those of others (Hopper 2005; Maynard, Mackay, & Smyth, 2008; Worthy, Moorman, & Turner 1999). In the WASABR, many teens described preferring the security of adhering to a series, as this reduces the potential risks of choosing a book that was not enjoyable. For example, a teen explained that he preferred to read from a series "because then you kind of know the books—you're gonna like the next books, so you can just go straight into them" (Merga, 2016a, p. 414). Tweens in the WASCBR described this in similar terms, such as Matt, who explained, "[I]f you're reading one series and it ends, you kind of want more books in that series, so you want them to go back to that series and write more about it" (Merga, 2017c, p. 215). The reading of a series was described in terms applicable to an ongoing friendship, bringing to mind the motivations of some adult avid readers who tend to describe books, authors, and/or key characters as actual friends in their lives, such as the respondent who reads "because I feel that the characters are good friends of mine that I need to catch up with" (Merga, 2017b, p. 152).

We need to consider, however, one significant snag involved in hooking young people onto a series. One of the key barriers that emerged to wider reading was the somewhat self-imposed limitation experienced by children who were *exclusive* series adherents. These students were not really interested in reading stand-alone stories. This was also the case for some of the teenage respondents. For instance, Gerome explained, "I'm a very picky reader and I don't normally find many good books that I like, but if I found like a long series that I like, then I'd probably read more," Hattie described the link between series reading and social possibilities, where she was motivated by the reading of peers, as "like a short series, if there's one book and some people have already started reading the next one, and I want to get with that, then I probably will."

Despite the powerful role that series reading can play in fostering reading motivation, exclusive dependence on series reading can potentially lead to reduced reading frequency if alternative books and series are not sought or provided once the series is exhausted. In some instances, rather than trying to establish a new relationship with key characters and plot in a different series, students would sometimes choose instead to simply discontinue their reading. While further research is needed in this area, it is possible that series readers may struggle to transfer their interest to nonseries books, as "the close relationship that some children develop with key characters over a series may not be hastily replicated in stand-alone encounters" (Merga, 2017c, p. 215); it is sometimes described as an issue of fidelity to these characters and fear of risk in encountering new material that may not be enjoyable. So, while I think that we should keep using series as an excellent entry point, we also need to promote stand-alone books and to do what we can to make them appealing to series readers, which may involve making explicit bridges of commonality with previous works that we know that they have enjoyed.

We also need to know where to direct a young person who likes a certain kind of series onto a similar series; for example, I recently suggested that a young fan of Patricia Briggs *Mercy Thompson* series move onto the *Vampire Academy* series, which they then followed up with the *Bloodlines* series, both by Richelle Mead. While they deal with similar themes, they have strong female characters and a powerful emphasis on friendship, not just romance. The recommendations worked in this instance. I also recently suggested that a boy who had enjoyed *The Girl with All the Gifts* and *The Boy on the Bridge* by M. C. Carey move onto the *Blood Red Road* series by Moira Young, after I discovered that what he liked best was not necessarily the zombie element but the survival element; this child had also enjoyed reading *Hatchet* by Gary Paulsen. Broadening the reading of series adherents really does feel like matchmaking, though we are unlikely to see a reality television series based on it in the near future.

8

Reading Is for Pleasure, Not Just Testing

School librarians work closely with teachers to support student literacy; however, while teachers tend to focus on supporting skill development in their students in order to meet curricular demands, supporting the development of the will to read is important to ensure its continuance beyond the early years. In schools with a strong testing orientation, school librarians may play a valuable role in reminding students that reading is about pleasure too.

I really shrink at the idea of adding anything additional to the typical workload of educators. As a former classroom teacher, I know that the demands placed on contemporary teachers are overwhelming and is one of the main reasons that so many people do not remain in the profession, with workload a commonly cited cause of attrition from teaching (Buchanan et al., 2013). However, I really believe that the suggestions outlined herein will not only enhance young people's literacy learning but can also make teaching a more pleasurable experience through encouraging an environment where enjoyment and sharing ideas become central rather than peripheral to the learning experience.

As I have mentioned, supporting reading *will* is not really positioned as a curricular priority, particularly beyond the early years. Indeed, literacy development is more commonly associated with lower school teaching than with upper school teaching, despite the fact that it occurs across the schooling continuum and curriculum (Kell, 2009). When we measure the success of teachers as literacy educators, we may tend to review the results of their students on high-stakes literacy tests, and their students' attainment of the specified literacy skills as mandated in the curriculum. We rarely consider the impact that teachers have on their children's attitudes toward engagement in reading, even though we know how closely this is related to reading motivation and, in turn, to literacy success. It has been argued that contemporary educational policies may "view and treat the teacher as little more than a dutiful delivery mechanism for so-called proven literacy education programs and methods" (Brooks, 2007, p. 177), and teachers may be more confident and capable focusing on reading skill rather than reading will (Camp, 2007). While reading will remains off the agenda, it is unlikely to receive adequate attention in the classroom.

I am trying to change teaching role perceptions in my current position as a senior lecturer in teacher education. In this role, I have the opportunity to influence my students to try to ensure that my graduates go forth into their teaching roles with a sound understanding of how to foster literacy skills in diverse students and contexts, as well as how to effectively encourage young people to embrace reading beyond the classroom. I know that there is a real possibility that, once my students leave me, they may be pressured in their new school climates to teach to the high-stakes tests without giving the time to foster reading motivation (Polesel, Dulfer, & Turnbull, 2012). I know that as early career teachers they will be time-poor, so any activities that are not mandated or explicitly and broadly linked to the curriculum will probably not receive priority. I try to counter these obstacles by positioning the fostering of reading will, as well as reading skill, beyond the early years as a key part of good teaching in the English learning area.

I also notice that each year, my group of future teachers is a group of people with very diverse interests, backgrounds, and values, and not all of them are regular readers when they enter my classroom. We tend to assume that all teachers and prospective teachers must be keen readers, but if we do not explore the veracity of the stereotype of teachers as keen readers, we run the risk of assuming that all teachers are equally equipped to be strong reading models. My research (Merga, 2015d) and the research of others (Applegate & Applegate, 2004) tends to challenge this homogeneous construction of teachers, as I will explore further in this chapter. Tweens and teens did not always have teachers that they felt were readers; however, when asked, tweens were almost uniformly able to articulate what a supportive and encouraging teacher looked like. They clearly described the characteristics they perceived that informed how they determined a reading model (Merga, 2016b), as I will outline later in this chapter.

These insights offer important implications for teacher educators and current teachers alike, as even teachers who move into their profession full of enthusiasm to foster a love of reading can find themselves unsupported, fatigued, and stymied in the current educational climate, with its constant curricular change and high-stakes testing. Therefore, first, teachers of reading need to be wide and regular readers; reading needs to be embedded in the job description. Second, teachers need to model their keen reading attitudes and approaches for their students; how this can be most effectively done is explored in the chapter.

It may also be incorrect to assume that teachers encourage young people to read. The young people who took part in my research often did not necessarily feel that their teachers provided encouragement. As I previously mentioned, only 48 percent of high school English teachers were perceived to provide encouragement, and 45.7 percent of the tweens in the WASCBR sample felt that their teachers encouraged them to read, which was 66.3 percent of the just over two-thirds of respondents who felt that someone they knew was providing encouragement to read. As such, we cannot take for granted that teachers at any schooling level are being perceived as a strong source of encouragement for young people, and we need to change this, first by accepting that the old stereotypes and expectations may no longer stand and second by endeavoring to improve our encouragement and modeling.

MODELING, READING ALOUD, AND EXCITEMENT ABOUT BOOKS AND READING

Modeling is not just for very tall people who do not eat much. As we understand the link between attitudes toward reading and engagement in reading, we want to be teachers who foster the will to read, in addition to developing reading skills for functional and testing purposes. Seeing us as models of reading can play a key role in influencing young people's attribution of the importance of the activity, with Guthrie and Davis (2003) contending that "if students are to believe that reading is a valuable activity and a useful competence, they need to perceive this belief in adults or significant others who they trust" (p. 69), such as teachers and parents. While the stereotype of teachers tends to reflect a bookish personality, research suggests assuming that those of us who are teachers must like reading is flawed, and this is an issue when examining teachers' capacity for reading modeling. As Martin (2003) suggests, "the best teachers of literature are those for whom reading is important in their own lives and who read more than the texts they teach." When teachers choose to be readers, this not only has implications for their ability to be strong reading models, it also exposes them to a greater body of books, which in turn can enable them to make links to this literature and to recommend more books to young people for leisure reading.

However, as previously explored, not all teachers are readers. Aliteracy has been found to be relatively high in preservice teachers (Vansteelandt, Mol, Caelen, Landuyt, & Mommaerts, 2017), and only 25 percent of elementary teachers in the United States were found to have "an unqualified enjoyment of reading" (Applegate & Applegate, 2004). As teachers who value reading are most likely to use the best literacy practices in the classroom (McKool & Gespass, 2009), the importance of teachers' reading relates to pedagogy as well as to optimal modeling for their students. However, few studies focus on teachers' modeling of reading in the classroom context, with the limited available research suggesting that while teachers may believe in the importance of the practice (Loh, 2009), few teachers are regular reading models (Morrow, 1982). We can speculate on why we do not necessarily practice what we ostensibly value, and I imagine that time would be one of the most significant mitigating factors. In addition to potentially overwhelming curricular demands, the marking load for English teachers is often much higher than that of their colleagues in other subject areas due to the sheer volume of submitted writing. Not all teachers would necessarily easily find time to read unless they recognize it as a priority.

Unfortunately, we also know that teacher education programs do not always successfully communicate that the fostering of reading engagement falls within the scope of teacher responsibilities. For example, a recent study of preservice teachers in Singapore found that most did not feel that motivating students to read was applicable to their role (Garces-Bascal et al., 2018). One of the most interesting things about this Singaporean finding is that it could be subject to change in light of the recent innovations that have seen Singapore provide "a systemic and societal response to our earlier question concerning whose job it is to build lifelong readers . . . by promoting lifelong reading habits on a macro (i.e. societal) level"

(p. 7). As I have previously argued, this issue is certainly not unique to Singapore; reading engagement needs to be more central to teachers' roles as required by curriculum and literacy policy in contemporary schools.

English teachers are not necessarily effective reading advocates. When I conducted the WASABR, it became apparent that, according to the respondents, best practice for teachers wishing to encourage their teenage students to read more for recreation includes exhibiting personal enjoyment of recreational book reading. However, not all children perceived their high school English teachers as encouraging, with Shiva explaining that:

> some of them have been encouraging, some of them have just quite a neutral perspective on it, yeah. They don't like not recommend to us, but they don't go out of their way to recommend any books to us, or anything like that. (Merga, 2015d, p. 40)

Similarly, not all high school English teachers were perceived to be readers. When asked about their English teachers' attitudes toward reading, some students could not confidently affirm that their teachers actually enjoyed reading books themselves. For example, Dash explained, "I'm not sure how he likes reading books, because I've never really heard him talk about reading books, other than the ones we read at school, so, I couldn't give you a true opinion on that" (Merga, 2015d, p. 42). Sharna felt that her English teacher was not a reader, as she mostly talked about playing computer games in her recreational time, though she had a different English teacher on Mondays, and he recommended books. It may not be reasonable to assume that all English teachers enjoy books and reading; students from a diverse range of backgrounds, such as media studies, often become English teachers (Mayher, 2012), and many contemporary English teachers are teaching outside their area and therefore may not technically be fully trained to teach English (Weldon, 2016). We can't assume that even English teachers like reading. While many teachers do love reading and act like passionate reading advocates, the assumption that students chose English as a subject area due to an affinity with books may no longer hold currency in many cases.

Is this just an issue with high school teachers? I was interested to see if tweens viewed their teachers as readers or if there was a similar potential degree of ambivalence. I imagined that maybe these teachers would be perceived as more encouraging than their high school counterparts. When speaking with tweens as part of the WASCBR study, their typical stereotype of teachers as innate readers initially got in the way of the inquiry. When I asked them if their teachers were readers, they would often say "yes" without considering the question. For example, Veronica responded, "Well, she should because she's a teacher and all that," but when asked *how* she knew this, she revised her response to "I don't know" (Merga 2016b, p. 262). Some similar responses were recorded when I previously asked high school students how their English teachers felt about reading books, with Krysta explaining "but they're English teachers. They *all* like reading—I guess that's how I see them. English teachers like reading." While Krysta was not sure whether her teacher liked reading, she thought it was possible due to her attitude toward silent reading, and the fact that she is a teacher. With children struggling to look beyond the stereotype, it was a good thing that the question was asked as an interview item rather than as a survey question, as students would typically not give the question much consideration, tending to fall back on the bookish teacher expectation and stereotype.

Once students accepted that I would need them to explain their position beyond a stereotype, we were able to proceed. Some of the students felt that their teachers were readers, and while a number of students did not perceive their teachers to be keen readers, they were almost invariably able to recall a past teacher who could be easily discerned as an excellent reading model. Their descriptions made it possible to discern what a reading model looked like to children beyond assumptions and stereotypes. When I asked the students how they deemed a teacher a reader or not, three recurring traits were mentioned. I have shared these characteristics with interested educators in Australia, the United States, and Finland, and my audiences have tended to agree that while these traits seem obvious at the outset, as we move deeper into them, they actually yield novel insights, as each part of the characteristic is noteworthy. I explore them further in Figure 8.1.

Teachers wishing to be excellent reading models and to encourage their students to read need to let their enjoyment and connection show. The teenage respondents in the WASABR identified teachers' excitement about books and reading as highly encouraging (Merga, 2015d), and the tweens subsequently studied in the WASCBR also sought emotional connection in their teachers' reading aloud to determine that the teacher did in fact like reading. These teachers often also demonstrated a willingness to instigate and support student-centered discussion on books. In the following list, I highlight the three key points as identified by tweens in Figure 8.1.

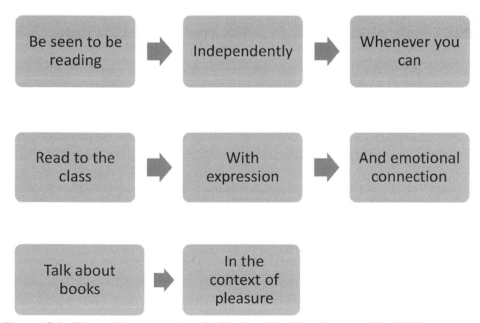

Figure 8.1 Three Characteristics of a Reading Model as Perceived by Children in Years 4 and 6

- **Be seen to be reading independently whenever you can:** Even if you are a keen reader who devours a novel every night after a long workday, if your children do not see you reading, you're not a reading model. According to the respondents, reading models read by themselves, not just to the class, and they also did so whenever the opportunity arose, not just during silent reading time.

- **Talk about books in the context of pleasure:** While you may talk about books every day, whether to point out nouns, or to highlight genre, or to consider audience response, all of the anatomical, measurable aspects of books need to sometimes be put aside to make space for discussion of reading for pleasure. I imagine that few students will look back on their schooling time and think fondly of the teacher who taught them about gerunds, whereas teachers who are passionate readers, who shared this passion with their students, and who encouraged their students to share their own book reading experiences are far more likely to be facilitating a transformative learning experience.

- **Read to the class with expression *and* emotional connection:** While some teachers read aloud and even read with remarkable expression, this was not enough to convince some children that the teacher really loved reading. For example, when Jason described his current teacher, he explained that "she does use expression and everything, and she is a good reader, but I just don't know if she likes reading books" (Merga, 2016b, p. 265). A previous teacher did all of that but also added something more, a genuine emotional connection to the book, which she used to more deeply engage her students. She was deemed to be a real reading model.

Reading aloud should not be curtailed in the early years, as reading aloud to tweens and adolescents is generally both beneficial and widely enjoyed (Krashen & McQuillan, 2007; Pitcher et al., 2007), with a U.S. study suggesting that it is the most enjoyed reading activity that adolescents experience (Varuzza, Sinatra, Eschenauer, & Blake, 2014). In addition, recent findings from the UK underscore the continued literacy benefits of reading aloud with tweens. In their study of the impact of reading books in the classroom at a brisk pace, Westbrook, Sutherland, Oakhill, & Sullivan (2018) found that the practice conferred remarkable reading comprehension improvement, with struggling readers showing progress of 16 months on standardized tests of reading comprehension after having two challenging novels read to them aloud over a 12-week period. Struggling readers are typically of the greatest concern to teachers, particularly due to the Matthew effect (Stanovich, 1986), where we see our stronger students improving at a far more rapid rate than our struggling students, so these findings are very promising indeed.

However, it is not always easy to implement pedagogical changes; if they privilege enjoyment, if they do not seem didactic and directly linked with testing, they may not *look* right to external observers. For instance, the participants in this recent UK study were somewhat nervous about participating in this practice, with reading aloud somewhat unconventional in high school. One respondent commented, "It's very tricky because if Ofsted [National Inspectorate of Schools] came in and saw us reading for forty minutes, what would they think of that lesson? But that's what [students] want to do" (Westbrook et al., 2018, p. 7). Reading aloud to children without constant 'educative' interruption does not look right, as books are more typically encountered "as fragments, a few pages read each lesson stretched over many weeks, the reading interrupted by oral and written literary analysis where teachers assume that students have comprehended what they read" (Westbrook et al., 2018, p. 1).

Reading aloud may also be less common then might be expected in the earlier years of schooling. In our recent study, Susan Ledger and I found that around a quarter of children felt that their teachers did not read to them often in schools, and our survey of teachers found that only a third of teachers used reading aloud as a daily classroom practice (Merga & Ledger, 2018). While this is probably reflective of the fact that reading aloud is not explicitly valued in our Australian curriculum, this needs to be addressed because, as previously explained, many children are not read to in the home. Both young and older children typically enjoy being read to (Albright & Ariail, 2005; Clark & Andreasen, 2014), and this is encouraging in light of the range of literacy benefits, including but not limited to vocabulary acquisition (Penno, Wilkinson, & Moore, 2002; Farrant & Zubrick, 2012), reading comprehension (Amer, 1997; Duursma, Augustyn, & Zuckerman, 2008), cognitive development (Mol & Bus, 2011), decoding skills (McCormick, 1977), and reading fluency (Chard, Vaughn, & Tyler, 2002).

The testing culture in our classrooms has had an interesting impact on young people's perception of their teachers as readers, which was all the more compelling because I did not mention testing to students as part of the interview schedule, so these were very much students' own ideas. One of the most notable barriers to the perception of teachers as reading models was the focus on reading for testing, which is why students often felt that their teachers believed that reading was *important* but not necessarily *enjoyable*. For instance, while Lucian did not know whether his teacher liked reading, he believed that his teacher viewed reading as important "because we're reading quite a lot this term and we've all had reading tests" (Merga, 2016a, p. 262). We do not yet have the balance we need between skill and will when supporting reading beyond the early years, and the growing emphasis on reading for testing can further challenge our ability to situate reading as a pleasurable pastime. We run the very real risk of children concluding that reading is an activity purely done for the purposes of assessment, and they are learning this from the powerful educational influences in their lives, their teachers.

WIDE READING, DISCUSSION, AND TEACHER RECOMMENDATIONS

In addition to modeling, reading aloud, and excitement about books and reading, to be able to engage students in books and reading, teachers need to be regular readers. They also need to know their students and be wide readers so that they connect young people with books relevant to their often diverse range of interests. Some teens had really diverse tastes, such as Hans:

> I've read quite a few different types of books. I've read *The Lord of the Rings* series and things like that; I've read a lot of fantasy. But I'm also a strange kid in the way that I've read all of the *Rich Dad, Poor Dad* series from Robert Kiyosaki.

Meeting the needs of students with eclectic or diverse tastes is one of the many challenges for all literacy advocates. There was also a number of tweens who described the importance of being quickly engaged by the books they selected. For example, Elly explained, "I like books that are interesting, but if they don't have sizzling starts then I don't like those books." As such, teachers need a wide repertoire of genres, pacing styles, points of view, and character types, as young people often have clear preferences in these areas.

There is something special about a teacher taking the time to get to know their students and to recommend a book to them that is broadly appreciated by young people. Teens were often willing to find and read the books their teachers recommended to them, particularly if they felt that this recommendation was responsive to a keen understanding of their interests and tastes (Merga, 2015d). Similarly, the tweens in the WASCBR were sometimes inspired to expand their scope of preferred genres in response to a particularly enthusiastic teacher. For example, Rachel found herself reading "war books" because she had a teacher who was effusive about the genre: "[I]f he likes a book, he would, you know, tell us about it, and say where he got it from" (Merga, 2016b, p. 263). Some teens in the WASABR study were similarly inspired by their teachers. Penny described the lengths her teacher went to provide her with appealing books in collaboration with the school librarian:

> When I went to the library, there was a whole table of separate books she told me to go look at, and that was in it. So obviously, I think she influenced that on me, helped me pick that, which is good. (Merga, 2015d, p. 43)

Book recommendations that meet the students' needs were generally well received, and where a librarian or educator was able to awaken an interest in a new reading area, this could also lead to young people expanding their scope of reading interest. To do this, teachers must possess broad knowledge of a range of texts, including but not limited to young adult texts, and keep abreast of new developments in youth popular culture. They also need to generate and facilitate student-centered discussion around book reading for pleasure. Typically, the school context promotes formal textual engagement and discussion, with personal interest and individual tastes not foregrounded (Guthrie & Davis, 2003). As I explained in Chapter 3, talking about books in the context of pleasure can increase students' level of exposure to potentially interesting and suitable titles (Gambrell, 1996), and it facilitates choice and reduces the risk of engaging with the unknown. However, not all teens have had this opportunity at school.

> [W]hen asked if they enjoy discussing books, Suresh stated that "I've never really talked about the books that I read", and Lachlan said that he was "not entirely sure since I've never really done that before". Simon kept an open mind despite his inexperience, explaining: "I have never actually done it, but I wouldn't mind it." In order to determine enjoyment of book discussion, students needed to have had an opportunity to engage in it. (Merga, McRae, & Rutherford, 2017, p. 11)

Similarly, recent research with tweens has found that book discussion is under-represented in the classroom.

> While some time seems to be often given to silent reading, book discussion of self-selected texts is neglected in the classroom, leaving only varied opportunities at

home and in the social space. Use of discussion about these texts in the classroom was so low, it brings into question how effectively the research in this area has been translated to the educator domain, beyond academia. (Merga, 2018)

As such, I suggest that we need to promote book discussion as a valuable pedagogical tool. Like reading aloud, it may be excluded as it may not fit the didactic mold, but these molds need to be challenged as we continue to expand and strengthen our understanding of what constitutes best practice.

Expectations and Rewards

I have previously touched on the importance of preventing expired expectations beyond the early years. I would also like to highlight the importance of effectively communicating expectations that students will read for pleasure both at school and at home, while at the same time reiterating that expectations need to be accompanied with both support and encouragement. We can require or suggest that our tweens and teens read, but if we do not facilitate access to books beyond the early years, this is unlikely to happen. If expectations become another scholarly, dry task to undertake as part of homework—devoid of expectations of pleasure, of the promotion of a positive social status of books, and of reading in the classroom—young people are unlikely to engage with much enthusiasm. Maintaining expectations that young people read is important. While intrinsic motivation is more strongly and typically associated with reading engagement than extrinsic motivation (Schiefele, Schaffner, Möller, & Wigfield, 2012), approval from key social influences has been found to be potentially motivating (Merga, 2017f).

However, while expectations are important, should we give rewards? We also need to give consideration to how we reinforce our expectations. Here, the debate around whether or not it is appropriate to give rewards for reading can be explored. Expectations may be related to extrinsic motivators in the form of prizes. Ryan and Deci (2017) explore how the influence of praise can be shaped by the type of praise given, with praise that is informational likely to foster intrinsic motivation, whereas praise that evaluates or controls is less likely to have a positive effect.

A distinction may need to be made between beneficial extrinsic motivation in the form of positive feedback and extrinsic motivation in the form of rewards, which are associated with a negative influence on young people's intrinsic motivation (Ryan and Deci, 2017). Like Ryan and Deci (2017), Krashen (2011) contends that "rewarding behavior that is intrinsically pleasant can extinguish the behavior because it sends the message that the activity is not pleasant and that people need to be bribed to do it" (p. 45). However, some research suggests that young people can value reading challenges and prizes (Merga, 2015d, p. 44) and find them motivating. For example, one student suggested that "maybe we could ask everyone to participate in a reading competition where you read for as long as you can without getting bored!" However, as my research is not longitudinal, it does not challenge the contention that extrinsic motivators in the form of prizes may not have long-term benefit. Many teachers and librarians have experienced success in engaging students to read through offering rewards, and until we have a considerable body of research that looks at the impact of such rewards on reading attitudes over time and with contemporary children I am cautious about suggesting that this practice has no merit.

A recent teacher librarian whom I spoke to as part of my current research project, Teacher Librarians as Literature and Literacy Advocates in Schools (TLLLAS), made a good point, explaining that she relies on prizes as she believes that the current generation of children may be particularly susceptible to receiving reward mechanisms, similar to how they receive constant rewards through online gaming experiences. This is certainly an area that I wish to investigate further with contemporary children.

I also wonder about the role that offering rewards can play in classrooms where reading books is not seen as being socially desirable. I wonder if the presence of rewards can have a protective effect for students who may wish to read but who do not want to be criticized by their friends; these students could gain some security by claiming to be reading just for the rewards. Therefore, at this stage, when people ask me what I think about offering rewards for reading, my responses tend to be ambivalent, as I think that rewards could serve multiple purposes. This is why I would like to do further research in this area before I get off the fence.

SILENT READING AND OPPORTUNITY

As a beginning teacher, I remember being nervous about introducing a regular sustained silent reading program in my classes, despite my strong conviction about its value. It felt like a risk. My school principal could walk past my classroom and see my students with their heads stuck in books rather than interacting in group work, or writing purposefully, or doing some other more active task to indicate that learning was occurring. Again, the question of employing practices that *look* enjoyable rather than didactic to the outside viewer came into play. While I had enough confidence in its importance to proceed regardless, I know that silent reading is a point of contention and even of conflict in some schools.

Research has found that use of silent reading as a classroom practice may be less common than we might expect, with less than half of teens experiencing regular silent reading. I also found that students in Year 10 were far less likely to have these opportunities that children in Year 8 (65 to 13 percent) (Merga, 2013). Similarly, recent research with tweens has found that silent reading was "popular but not always privileged in the classroom":

> [S]ilent reading was positioned as an optional extra in some contexts, which made it vulnerable to inconsistent delivery. Where silent reading was not privileged, and was readily replaced by other activities . . . this has implications beyond limiting students' opportunity to engage in the beneficial reading experience, which for some students was the only recreational reading they engaged in. Infrequent opportunity could also challenge students' abilities to remember and focus on the plots in the books they are reading, particularly if they are struggling readers and/or readers who are not willing or able to continue reading the books at home. (Merga, 2018).

Silent reading was certainly not off the agenda due to poor student enjoyment. Teens enjoyed silent reading for a number of reasons (Merga, 2013):

Better than working: Reading was not necessarily perceived as work. A student explained that "when you're reading a book, that you're enjoying it's not effort, 'cause you're enjoying it" (p. 235).

Relaxing: Reading was an opportunity for relaxation and "just chillin'" (p. 235).

Uninterrupted: Reading constitutes an opportunity for sustained immersion, particularly valuable for students with poor time availability, as "no one's gonna interrupt me and I can just read as much as I want" (p. 236).

Fun: Silent reading is an opportunity to enjoy reading; for some students, it was the only reading for pleasure that they did.

Since I began sharing my research with schools, I have become part of the support team for schools in some instances, where my papers have been requested so that they can be used to argue for the time and space for silent reading at school. This is an issue that never seems to receive universal support from school administrators. It is important that we continue to provide opportunities for reading for pleasure in school. While the validity of silent reading may occasionally be contentious (National Reading Panel, 2000), such challenges are often quickly and fulsomely dealt with (Garan & DeVoodg, 2008; Krashen, 2001). Most importantly, the benefits of reading frequency are well established (Clark and De Zoysa, 2011), and therefore providing opportunity for students to engage in greater reading frequency is likely to be beneficial, as it provides opportunity. Giving time to silent reading also communicates a valuing of the practice, as precious learning time is being given to an activity that is both educative and potentially enjoyable.

Teens recognized this attribution of value and described the opportunity to read at school as symptomatic of a valuing of regular reading. For example, Nigel felt that his teacher's decision to allocate valuable class time to silent reading in the library was indicative of his teacher's love of reading, explaining that "she loves reading. She's always going on about it. That's why we go to the library, I don't think any of the other classes do" (Merga, 2015d, p. 44). As long as an effective model of silent reading is employed, where students are reading and the enjoyment of reading is encouraged through the provision of an appropriate context and support, silent reading should be considered a valid component of learning at both the primary and the secondary levels (Merga, 2013).

When we implement silent reading, we want all of our students engaged in the experience, However, as any teacher knows, there are aspects of silent reading that some young people find challenging.

First, inasmuch as part of the purpose of silent reading is to support the development of the capacity for sustained, deep concentration, some students may struggle while building their concentration and reading stamina, with some students reporting a struggle to continue reading beyond their stamina threshold. The best way to address this issue is to actually read more often in order to increase reading stamina.

Additionally, while some teens reported that silent reading was occurring at school in an environment conducive to enjoyment and focus, environmental issues were raised by others who found the reading context unsuitable. Some students pointed out that they would prefer to read in the library, where book access was readily available and the atmosphere appropriate. In some schools where a whole-school approach to silent reading had been instituted, other subject area teachers were not facilitating access to reading material, and as a result, students reported that "'usually I've only got some Science books'" and "'cause we do it in SOSE (Society and Environment). So, we just have to, we get 15 minutes every Monday, to read, so we can't go and get a book to read" (p. 238). One of the concerns in introducing a whole-school approach, which has the potential to be highly beneficial and to situate reading as a school-wide priority, lies in ensuring that students have access to engaging books and ensuring that teachers in non-English areas understand best practice in supporting silent reading. Some schools were poorly resourced in general, with a student explaining that "they don't have any of the books I read in the school, so when Silent Reading came along, I just picked up a book that I didn't really like, and had to read it'" (p. 238). It is not always easy for young people to source their preferred reading materials in school.

Just as there is wide diversity in adult reading motivation (Merga, 2017b), young people read for different reasons and can have their reading fostered through varied approaches. Young readers are a relatively heterogeneous group; while some prefer to read in silence, without distraction, others like the opportunity to share exciting parts with a close neighbor. Howard (2009) created an interesting taxonomy of readers within a small research sample that highlights these differences. She developed the following categories of reader when exploring adolescents' willingness to share their reading experiences with peers: Avid Social, Avid Detached, Avid Solitary, Occasional Social, Occasional Solitary, Reluctant Social, Reluctant Detached, and Reluctant Solitary (p. 109). When considering how to create the best environment for silent reading that will lead to increased engagement in reading, it is useful to consider the needs of the Avid Social reader, for whom "reading exists in a "virtuous circle" in which friends encourage reading for pleasure and shared reading experiences solidify friendships" (p. 109), as potentially in opposition to those of the Avid Solitary reader in the Voluntary Solitary subcategory, those who "simply do not see any reason to share or discuss their reading with their peers" (p. 110), even though they may be receiving and appreciating a large degree of adult encouragement.

Within her sample, there were nearly as many Avid Solitary readers as Avid Social readers, suggesting that while social opportunities to discuss books during silent reading offer an exciting possibility to potentially further engage Avid Social readers, if this engagement were uniformly enforced, it could lead to the disengagement of Avid Voluntary Solitary readers, who would rather not be disturbed by others. Teachers should take these factors into account; the allowance of discussion before or after silent reading should support the needs of Avid Social readers, while not disturbing the reading experience of the Avid Voluntary Solitary reader and encouraging the social reader to read in a sustained manner. As I explain in my recent paper exploring tweens' attitudes, book discussion and silent reading should be mutually supportive strategies that are nonetheless best delivered separately:

> [F]indings would tend to suggest caution when considering blending silent reading with book discussion, with book discussion best situated before or after the silent reading experience, and minimized during. While some children enjoyed the opportunity for quiet discussion during silent reading, far more found this distracting. While this

research suggests that silent reading is favorably perceived, and that book discussion could be enjoyable for students, blending of the two is not advised. (Merga, 2018, p. 79)

I also think that it is likely that the categories presented by Howard (2009) can be subject to fluidity and can be environmentally responsive. For example, before I discovered Goodreads, I was far less influenced by my friends' reading; Goodreads supported my shift from a solitary to a more social reader, responsive to peer views and ideas.

I want to reiterate that, particularly as silent reading was, for some students, the *only* book reading they engaged in, when done well, this practice is highly valuable. However, it is important that this opportunity is offered regularly, ideally more than once a week, as students who are not reading the book outside this time may struggle to follow the plot of their book where significant gaps occur. For example, when discussing her issues with silent reading at high school, Ciara explained that "you get to that point, and then by the next week, when you go back, you forget where your book is, and you forget where you are, so, it just seems . . . like a lost cause."

A contemporary silent reading program has much to encompass and achieve. It is not simply a matter of putting aside time for students to read. Ideally, it should:

- Involve reading student-selected materials from a well-resourced library.
- Occur in an environment conducive to sustained attention.
- Involve some degree of teacher monitoring to ensure that reading is occurring and so that teacher encouragement and recommendations can be provided as required.
- Include the teacher modeling keen reading.
- Involve pre- or postdiscussion of books to build the social status of reading and to connect young people to books through recommendations.
- Occur consistently and for a sufficient period of time so that students can get "into" their books.
- Be part of a broader project to increase student engagement in reading, supported by other classroom practices, such as book clubs.

MORE ON READING FOR TESTING

Young people can be remarkably perceptive about the attitudes and values of key social influences in their lives, whether or not we want them to be. We know that the current high-stakes testing environment influences teachers' pedagogical approach (DeBenedictis, 2007) and that it has led to a focus on short-term, test-related gains (Polesel et al., 2012). It was interesting to note that, as touched on briefly earlier, students are fully aware of this pressure, to the extent that many of them conceptualize reading as a thing that is done to pass tests and meet academic requirements; this is the message they receive from their teachers, and this becomes what they individually internalize. While concerns were raised in the 1970s and 1980s about a prevailing view of reading as "merely an accumulation of skills"

(Raphael & McMahon, 1994, p. 102) that we measure, it would seem that little has changed as many students still view this as the sole purpose of reading.

When I asked both tweens and teens about how their teachers felt about reading books, reading was often seen as something done to facilitate testing. For example, teen student Craig explained that reading was part of "the grading thing," as "we have to do that, we get marked on that, so we have to read a few books, you know, if we want to get good marks for that." The pressure to meet testing requirements is related to high-stakes testing such as NAPLAN, but it is also related to gaining or maintaining a position in an academic extension program, with Craig describing a "threat" to perform to meet the grading requirements (Merga, 2015d, p. 45). Older teen Julio held a similar view, explaining that "in high school they expect you to just read mainly what you have to do for an assessment or something, but in lower school they'd always take us to the library, or get books out that *you* like," which is why he felt far more encouraged to read in lower school. However, as previously highlighted, many children in the tween years also felt that reading was very strongly associated with testing. Resisting this testing emphasis is about resisting powerful forces in the current educational environment, but it is necessary if we wish reading to be perceived as related to pleasure as well as to learning.

BEST PRACTICE

When we think about what kind of teacher we want to be, the idea of making a significant difference in young people's lives is often a driving force in bringing people into the profession. In 2015 (Merga, 2015d), I suggested that six qualities and practices typically characterize the *will*-supportive reading teacher beyond the early years. The subsequent research I have done in this field has led me to further expand, develop, and refine them. I have listed four examples to illustrate what this might look like in practice, but, of course, there are many more possibilities:

1. Personal enjoyment of reading is clearly apparent:
   - As a teacher, be seen to read independently where possible (e.g., during silent reading).
   - Show excitement and emotional connection to books when reading aloud or discussing books.
   - Do not discuss books only in the context of testing and explicit skill instruction.
   - Share recommendations that give insight into books that you have enjoyed.
2. Willingness to instigate and support student-centered discussion on books:
   - Create and facilitate student-led book clubs.
   - Encourage book discussions that are not confined to texts studied in class.
   - Model and allow differing views on books and characters.
   - Ensure that the discussion space is safe and lively.

3. Broad knowledge of both genres, young adult texts and youth popular culture:
   • As a teacher, read widely and share this wide reading approach with your students.
   • Keep abreast of the range of young adult texts, reading both literary and/ or popular texts in this genre (e.g., read the short list of the Children's Book Council of Australia).
   • Keep abreast of trends in youth popular culture through observation.
   • Read the books that your students recommend to you where possible.

4. Effectively communicate expectations that students will read at school and at home:
   • Remind young people that reading is important for social, vocational, and academic capital.
   • Expect that they fit it into their daily lives, with regular reminders of this expectation.
   • Communicate these benefits and expectations with parents, and ask them to reinforce them.
   • Ask students to regularly share book recommendations, which will require regular reading.

5. Knowledge of the interests and aspirations of the students:
   • Talk to students and listen to students' interests.
   • Tap into students' interests early and regularly, and use this data to inform text selection and recommendations.
   • Keep abreast of students' evolving interests.
   • Establish targeted recommendation systems on- or offline.

6. Provide regular interactive and silent reading opportunities:
   • Regularly read aloud to students with expression and emotional connection.
   • Provide self-selected silent reading opportunities as part of the class routine.
   • Encourage a whole-school approach to silent reading so that it is seen as a whole-school priority.
   • Build students' confidence in reading aloud by ensuring they have sufficient practice and encouragement before reading in front of peers, so that reading is not associated with fear.

7. Support access to books in the home:
   • Provide a regular time for students to visit and use a school or public library, for the selection of books to read for pleasure.
   • If possible, build a class library, ideally responsive to student suggestions and interests.
   • Ensure that students can bring their books home for a reasonable amount of time.
   • Do not limit students' access to libraries as they age.

8. Teach them how to choose:
   - Model your own choosing strategies.
   - Explicitly teach choosing strategies that balance interest and skill level considerations.
   - Model how long to persist with a book that is not immediately appealing.
   - Work with the school librarian (if possible) to support choice.

9. Build parent/guardian capacity:
   - Build parental efficacy, and let parents know what a supportive parent can do.
   - Encourage parents to continue to read with their tweens and even their teens, if possible, and to expect their children to keep reading.
   - Support parents to find work-arounds for low literacy, low time availability, and language issues (e.g., listening to audiobooks with children).
   - Offer training for parents who have not been read to in order to support them to meet challenges.

9

Libraries, Reading Spaces, and Choices

As libraries increasingly adopt a greater breadth of roles, are they still supportive places for readers? And what can librarians do to support young readers to increase their recreational reading engagement?

Both school and public library environments are constantly changing to meet societal and educational expectations, and school and public librarians are expected to do more with less. While libraries and their stewards can do much to promote reading engagement, they also face unique challenges that can both support and disable this capacity.

COMPETITION FOR SPACE FOR READING

The place of paper books in this contemporary context is not a given. To some extent, we are expecting our public libraries to be everything to everyone, and for a while it seemed that books might be pushed out to make space for all of these other services. The public library is supposed to act as a community center (e.g., Anderson, 1994), and, likewise, school libraries are expected to accommodate multiple scholastic purposes.

However, fortunately recent research suggests that a concerning movement away from book-related library space to privilege other roles may not be gaining traction. For example, while in 2015 nearly a third of American respondents agreed that "libraries should definitely move books out of public spaces in favor of using that space for other purposes," a year later that number dropped to 24 percent. Over the same two-year period, the percentage of people saying libraries should definitely not move books increased in 2016 to 31 percent, up from 25 percent in 2015 (Horrigan, 2016, p. 4). Clearly, it is not quite time to exhale yet, as that is still less than a third of the U.S. population surveyed who believe that books belong in the public spaces of libraries.

When I went to a conference in Vancouver in 2015, I learned about the libraries that had been responsive to the "modern" idea of the bookless or book-scarce library, with books removed or shunted into the backrooms. The constant reiteration that you have seen throughout this book on the importance of communicating our valuing of books and reading, when viewed against these trends, may be better understood. In our haste to remain current and meet the demands made of us, it is important that we not sacrifice essential services and materials that support reading engagement.

While there may be periods where the role of libraries as generous providers of books for pleasure reading may be unappreciated, it cannot be assumed that these trends, when observed, necessarily indicate a permanent or irrevocable frame of mind. I have suggested that while "libraries can actively support leisure reading," this role "is potentially under threat of being subsumed amongst the multiple roles and personalities a contemporary library is expected to accommodate and exhibit" (Merga, 2017c, p. 50). Readers' views should also be valued. Taking the opportunity to speak with readers, both young and adult, to ensure that libraries can continue to meet their needs is essential to moving forward. If the geography and features of the library are determined by people who do not use it to source reading materials and who may instead use it for services that could be replicated elsewhere, I am concerned that this could have a detrimental impact on retaining a space that can have such a potentially vital role for supporting community literacy.

LIBRARIES RESOURCING YOUNG PEOPLE'S READING

Our research supports the findings of others (e.g., Scholastic, 2015), suggesting that libraries continue to be an important source of books for young people. Some teens, such as Alisha, described their school libraries as havens of reading:

> I love coming into the library, especially since they've renovated it. It feels so homey, and I love just having your own book, that's probably my favorite cycle, 'cause you get to just sit there and read, and not having to do work or think. Feels so good.

However, we need to recognize that libraries are typically underutilized by young people, particularly as they age. Our research with tweens found that nearly 90 percent of students visited libraries at least sometimes to read books for enjoyment. However, most of the teens who responded to the WASABR study never visited a library in their free time to choose books (35 percent) or less than once a month (27 percent), with only 14 percent visiting a library at least once a week (Merga, 2016a, p. 416). While these two studies were not longitudinal, they raise questions about young people's library use as they move through the schooling years.

It is important that schools do not cut library hours as students move through the years of schooling; however many schools do this. Class time also needs to be allocated to visiting the library in high school so that teens maintain access to books. Our findings also indicate that schools with libraries are often seriously underusing them during class time, with nearly a third of these children not allowed class time to select books. What makes the availability of class time to select books all the more important is our finding that girls were more likely to visit a library in their free time than boys, so if we want boys to read with greater frequency, we should take that into account, giving young people time and opportunity to access books to read (Merga & Mat Roni, 2017b) and not curtailing this access as children move through the years of schooling. Findings from the 2016 WASCBR suggest that, as children grow older, they are less likely to visit libraries during their free time compared to during the school hours (Merga & Mat Roni, 2017b). This is a serious issue, as research suggests that young people who visit their library infrequently are over three times more likely to feel that that they cannot locate anything to read that is interesting to them (Clark & Hawkins, 2011); though this data was related to public library rather than school library use, it highlights the important role that library access in general affords young people. Not all families can afford to purchase books in the home, so, where possible, we need to promote awareness of public libraries where they are available.

THE QUALITY OF COLLECTIONS

While many schools are relatively well-resourced in terms of public library availability, unsurprisingly, where public libraries were felt to have poor collections and ineffective weeding, they were not positively viewed by young people. We know that strong resourcing of materials for young people is associated with young people's public library use (Joo & Cahill, 2017), so investment in quality resourcing for young people has been seen to be a worthy investment. A teenager described their local library on the open field of the survey:

> My closest library to my house is about 20 minutes away, and even then, the majority of the books are sub-par, 90's informational books that are not worth reading. I would read a lot more if I had access to a better library.

Other teens also had difficulty finding good books in their library, with another explaining that "libraries don't have interesting books. I would read more if the library had interesting and new books that we could borrow." Of course, we do not actually know whether these libraries were without potentially appealing books or these young people just had great difficulty locating them, returning to the importance of teaching young people how to choose books effectively. What we do know is that, in recent times, we understand the importance of young people's involvement in shaping our collections, as far as feasible. Aggleton (2018) positons this as imperative:

> [C]hildren should be consulted on collections that relate to children's culture. Collections of children's literature, whether in libraries or archives, can be seen as holding a dual cultural position, as both adults' and children's culture, provided children are interacting with the adult-produced texts. Therefore, if collections of children's literature are being used by children, these collections can be viewed as a site for the creation of children's culture, and children should be enabled to participate alongside adults in the development of these collections. (p. 15)

Where children are involved in the resourcing of their libraries, they can have a sense of ownership over and interest in those resources, as well as supporting the creation of their culture.

PEACE AND QUIET?

It is very much the fashion at present to mock the old-fashioned notion of librarian as a strict and sour old lady who lurks around the library, telling people to be quiet (see Black & Shaw, 2017, for recent media coverage) and to instead embrace the cool librarian who is totally fine with noise. Davis (2008) argues that librarians themselves are behind this effort at reinvention:

> Desperate to slough off the old limiting stereotypes of the stern bespectacled cardigan-clad shushing controller of books, librarians are clamoring to convince themselves, each other and the wider community that there is far more to the humble librarian than meets the casual eye. Numerous websites are devoted to extolling the glories and cementing the collective pride of the disaffected 'new' librarian of the 21st century—the "New Breed Librarian", "Anarchist Librarian", "'The Shifted Librarian", "Progressive Librarian", "Underground Librarian", "Street Librarian", "Belly Dancing Librarian", not to mention the "Naked Librarian" and the "Modified Librarian" boasting body piercings and tattoos. (pp. 57–58)

While this fashion is part of a paradigm shift inspired by a desire to maintain the relevance of the profession, we should avoid moving too far away from this idea of libraries being a space where silent and sustained reading can take place. We do not want to arrive at a point where it is no longer possible to read in a library because the environment is no longer conducive to the application of sustained attention. As such, we need to find out more about how both avid and reluctant readers navigate the evolving contemporary library; is the contemporary library reader-friendly?

Findings from the 2015 ISABR suggest that libraries should offer comfortable and quiet spaces that are conducive to reading for pleasure and that are responsive to the time and concentration barriers that avid readers face, and not assume that avid readers will easily adapt to multipurpose library environments with elevated noise levels (Merga, 2017d). Indeed, over two-fifths of self-reported avid readers sometimes struggled to concentrate while they read (Merga, 2017d, p. 57), though this issue was greater for avid nonfiction readers than for avid fiction readers (Merga & Mat Roni, 2018a). Tiredness and a noisy environment were the most frequently cited reasons for this difficulty in concentration (Merga, 2017d). Recent U.S. research with a group of 100 9th-graders supports the suggestion that environment may be important to facilitate reading, with Evans (2017) finding that "students who found quiet, comfortable spaces seemed to enjoy the printed text more" (p. 314). While we hurry to meet the needs of the imagined contemporary client, we need also to ensure that the more traditional possibilities of libraries do not in the process lose what they offer for readers.

One area in which both school and public libraries can apply immediate attention is to their advisory and choosing support services for young people. In relation to choice, as explored previously, not all young people have an effective strategy to select books (Merga, 2016a). Ultimately, children need to be explicitly taught how to choose books that meet their interests, skills, and security needs. As previously discussed, the motivations and strategies in choosing related to familiarity, complexity, and interest, but focus on just one of these dimensions can have potential influences on reading engagement; ideally students should consider all three in order to find a good match for them (Merga & Mat Roni, 2017b). We found that while some tweens "had no working strategy for selecting books, others used one or a range of strategies with varying success" (p. 18).

WHEN A LIBRARY IS A LEARNING HUB

I have also noticed a recent trend away from the school library and toward the learning hub or information center. For example, a respondent in the recent TLLLAS study described how the junior school library differed from her senior school library.

> **L:** [B]ecause it's such a big campus, that's way over the other side . . . but they call it a learning hub, and they don't have a qualified teacher librarian in there, and they're (a) brand new building this year so . . . a bit disappointing.
>
> **I:** So how did that come about?
>
> **L:** Because the person who had been in there for 27 years as a teacher librarian retired, and they wanted to do . . . a little shift in thinking.

A "shift in thinking" is typically inspired by a desire to be modern, where the popularity of STEM can be at the expense of the library as a place for reading. For example, in 2015 when two high schools decided to turn their libraries into "learning hubs," the following language was used to justify this decision:

> Both schools were keen to improve the education outcomes of the existing library/resource center. In their view, the education outcomes did not line up with the quantum of resources expended. Both schools were determined to create a new facility as the center for innovative pedagogy in the school. Both adopted the terminology of "learning hub" to emphasize the way influence from the center was to radiate out to the whole school. Both schools recognized the potential offered by new technology to re-design the existing library/resource center to meet their desired education outcomes. (Cashen, 2015, p. 1)

As there is no robust body of research at this stage proving that the learning hub offers superior "education outcomes" than the traditional library, it is clear to see that much of the energy behind the impetus for change may be rooted in the desire to be seen as progressive. I also wonder if when making decisions with significant financial implications about spaces that offer superior education outcomes, the benefits of libraries as spaces that foster literacy skills is taken into account, especially as I will contend that, at this stage, there is far more research supporting the benefits of the library (e.g., Lance & Kachel, 2018) than the learning hub. While I do not suggest for a moment that libraries should exist for the purpose of supporting reading only, this purpose should remain integral to any school library and that, before libraries undertake the significant transformative changes that we are often exhorted to make in the name of being progressive, we remain sensitive to the importance of making informed decisions based on research rather than trends.

THE NEED TO DELVE DEEPER INTO SCHOOL LIBRARY RESEARCH

In my research and research translation-related travels, I have met many teacher librarians, and it has really opened my eyes to the powerful role that these individuals can have, influencing both individual students' attitudes toward reading and the whole school culture. I have also heard tales of frustration around resource cutting and issues with poor teacher and librarian collaboration, as well as the impact of poor administrative and leadership support on librarians' roles and morale. These issues stimulate a great deal of discussion on networks such as the Future Ready Librarians Facebook page, where the daily challenges, inspirations, and aspirations of contemporary librarians in schools are shared in a supportive community.

We know that teacher librarians (TLs) and libraries can play an important role in supporting children's literacy. Lance and Kachel (2018) explain that "data from more than 34 state-wide studies suggest that students tend to earn better standardized test scores in schools that have strong library programs" (p. 15). We know that the presence of a certified TL is related to high graduation rates in the United States (Coker, 2015), and U.S. research has also found that reduction in the hours of school librarians typically exerted a negative influence on student achievement and learning (Dow & McMahon-Lakin, 2012). Librarians' level of skill and attainment does appear to be associated with students' outcomes, with U.S. research finding that "elementary students in schools with certified school librarians are more likely to have higher English and language arts (ELA) scores than those in schools with noncertified school librarians" (Small, Shanahan, & Stasak, 2010, p. 2). School libraries can play an important role in mitigating the impact of SES on student reading achievement, with libraries potentially playing a critical role in supporting children's literacy achievement. For example, a U.S. study found that elementary (primary) school students with certified librarians outperformed students in schools without a certified librarian on literacy scores, regardless of library resourcing (Small, Shanahan, & Stasak, 2010). Similarly, the most recent Australian research in this area found a positive relationship between library staffing numbers and results on high-stakes NAPLAN tests (Softlink, 2016b).

Educational benefits have also been specifically linked to literacy achievement. Previous research in the UK has found a very strong relationship between children's reading attainment and use of the school library (Clark, 2010), reflective of previous Australian research that found that "extensive use of the school library was associated with a difference of as many as 27 points to students' literacy achievements when compared with non-use of the library" (Masters & Forster, 1997, p. 207) and research reviewed by Chan (2008) that found that the majority of studies investigating the link between school libraries and students' academic achievement have found a strong positive association.

However, somehow this body of knowledge is not having the desired protective effect for the profession; TLs are still vulnerable to having their jobs diminished or cut entirely in schools. This may be due to a notable gap in the research that I am currently working to address: There is little information about the *specific role* that TLs can play in supporting literacy and literature skills and engagement in young school-based clients. It should also be noted that "in contrast to extensive research conducted in the US, Canada and Britain about school library impacts on student literacy and learning, only a handful of studies on this topic have been conducted in Australia" (Hughes, Bozorgian, & Allan, 2014, p. 34). In addition, the extensive research conducted elsewhere does not necessarily have much to offer in terms of highlighting exactly what TLs have to offer. This means that we can see that TLs offer real educative benefit; however, we do not necessarily understand what TLs do. While we know that TLs do much to manage libraries' resources, we do not fully understand the full scope of their daily activities. Unfortunately, if we do not know what TLs do, it is easy for administrators to erroneously imagine that their contribution is insignificant. The American Association of School Libraries (AASL) raises this issue in their recent advocacy document, noting that:

> The number of school librarians has declined nationally in recent years. When faced with difficult budget cuts, those making decisions often see the positon of the school librarian as an easier cut to make than other teaching or resource staff positions. (AASL, 2018, p. 2)

The three key reasons they suggest may underpin the lack of valuing of the school library all relate to those issues around understanding the role of the school library and librarian, arguing that the school community lacks awareness of what is offered in the school library program and that the roles and responsibilities of the school librarian are poorly understood and articulated by stakeholders, decision makers, and school administrators (AASL, 2018).

This has very real consequences for the profession. While we have failed to really adequately understand what TLs do to create this positive influence on young people, funding for TLs is increasingly diminished in Australia (Softlink, 2016a) and elsewhere (Kachel, 2015). School librarians have shown a tendency toward decreased funding, with over a fifth of Australian schools indicating a decrease in library staffing (Softlink, 2016a; Softlink, 2016c). They also experience time constraints, as TLs often enact multiple roles, and supporting literacy and literature skills is not their only educative role, as they are also concerned with the development of other skills, such as research and information technology (AITSL, 2014; Coker, 2015). The role of librarians in supporting literacy and literature needs to be fully understood so that the possible impact of this reduction of TL numbers on children's learning can likewise be understood. In this regard, the issue can be seen to incorporate a risk analysis component (Dickson, 1995), as it considers what can be lost in curtailing a role that is poorly understood and valued. As contended by Dow, McMahon-Lakin, and Court (2012), "While school librarians may be perceived by some as an expensive luxury, particularly when school budgets are cut, higher student proficiency rates at schools where school librarians are employed may be something schools cannot afford to do without" (p. 11). A 2011 Australian inquiry into school libraries and teacher librarians found that "it is indisputable that the value of teacher librarians' work has been eroded over the years and undervalued by many in the community, be it by colleagues, principals, parents or those in the wider school community" (House of Representatives [HOR], 2011, p. 117). Before we cut any further funds to TLs, we need research fulsomely exploring the value TLs provide for children's education.

We need to increase our knowledge of the literacy supportive role of TLs. It is this positioning of TLs as educators that is unusual, which is odd, as they are, after all, qualified educators. There have been recent attempts to bring this educative role to the fore and emphasize the importance of interprofessional collaboration between teachers and librarians (e.g., Pihl, Carlsten & Van Der Kooij, 2017). In the United States, TLs are increasingly recognized as playing an important educative role, with increased educational responsibilities and accountability and a growing requirement that they can demonstrate contribution to the continuous improvement of student learning (Scott & Plourde, 2007). U.S. research that looks at TLs' influence on student achievement tends to focus on information literacy and collaboration with teachers (as reviewed in Hughes et al., 2014), though, again, with little attention to their role in enhancing literacy and literature skills. In addition, as contended by Phillips and Paatsch (2011), "[F]ew literacy articles, policies or curricula in Australia mention school libraries. Teacher librarians have become virtually invisible in the literature and guidelines on literacy. Their work, absorbed into successful resource-based teaching and project-based learning, is invisible" (p. 31). While access to libraries is known to be beneficial for literacy outcomes, relatively little is known about the role that TLs may play as literacy and literature educators in contemporary schools.

U.S. researchers also recommend a stronger research focus on school library advocacy. It is argued that the body of empirical, peer-reviewed research is insufficient, with "evidence within the literature on the advocacy techniques that are most effective for positively influencing decision-makers . . . still relatively scarce" (Haycock & Stenstrom, 2016, p. 138). A meta-analysis of school library advocacy literature concluded that

> [O]f special consideration is the dearth of research literature about school library advocacy. Finding one research article published during the ten-year scope of the literature search suggests that the field must mature to include more research on the topic. (Ewbank & Kwon, 2015, p. 241)

Increasing the body of research in the field will not only increase the evidence that can be drawn upon when seeking to construct frames of best practice for TLs. It can also lead to greater valuing of the profession and further the construction of a professional identity that deserves to endure despite the crises of funding that barrage contemporary schools.

HOW DO TEACHER LIBRARIANS SUPPORT LITERACY AND LITERATURE SKILL DEVELOPMENT?

The role of librarians in supporting reading and reading engagement is positioned at the core of the profession in the United States and Australia. One of the common beliefs underpinning the U.S. *National School Library Standards* is that reading "is the core of personal and academic competency." This is described as follows:

> In the school library, learners engage with relevant information resources and digital learning opportunities in a culture of reading. School librarians initiate and elevate motivational reading initiatives by using story and personal narrative to engage learners. School librarians curate current digital and print materials and technology to provide access to high-quality reading materials that encourage learners, educators, and families to become lifelong learners and readers. (AASL, 2017)

The evidence standards for Australian TLs developed by the Australian School Library Association (ASLA) (2014) in collaboration with the Australian Institute for Teachers and School Leaders (AITSL) include reference to supporting this attainment of skills in literacy and literature under 2.5, "Literacy and Numeracy Strategies," in order to be deemed highly accomplished. TLs must have:

> a sound understanding of how children and young adults become independent readers and have a detailed knowledge of how to promote and foster reading. They have a comprehensive understanding of literacy and literature for children and young adults. They are active participants in the design, resourcing and implementation of literacy and numeracy programs within their schools. (ASLA, 2014, p. 8)

Similarly, the U.S. ALA/AASL Standards for Initial Preparation of School Librarians (2010) position literacy and reading under Standard 2:

> Candidates promote reading for learning, personal growth, and enjoyment. Candidates are aware of major trends in children's and young adult literature and select reading materials in multiple formats to support reading for information, reading for pleasure, and reading for lifelong learning. Candidates use a variety of strategies to reinforce classroom reading instruction to address the diverse needs and interests of all readers. (American Library Association & American Association of School Librarians, 2010, p. 6)

Clearly, supporting reading engagement is a requirement of the TL role. However, how this understanding manifests and is practically enacted across diverse school contexts in the daily teaching role of TLs is not defined. As such, relatively little is known about the typical scope of practice employed by TLs and their role in supporting implementation and exploration of the curriculum in relation to literacy and literature. The inquiry by the House of Representatives (2011) into TLs in Australia concluded that "it is not always clear exactly what role *they should and could* [my emphasis] play in schools to those outside, and even within, the profession" (p. 119). I think that we need to do a better job of making visible the work that TLs do in this space.

We need to define both the actual and aspirational roles of TLs as literacy and literature advocates, addressing this dual issue of "should and could" and placing the views of TLs as central to the research. For example, while we know that ideally TLs should read to students and facilitate opportunities to foster student discussion about books (Edmunds & Bauserman, 2006) and that librarians need to speak with young people to determine their interests, as well as supporting their access to these materials (Worthy, 1996; Worthy, Moorman, & Turner, 1999), we do not know much about how widespread their use of these practices is. In addition, the limited extant data in this area suggests that there could be a disconnect in role perception between teachers and TLs, with teachers and TLs having different ideas about their priorities (Small, Shanahan, & Stasak, 2010). Identifying both the actual and aspirational roles will also lead to the illumination of gaps and barriers, as subsequently explored.

EXPLORING THE TEACHER–TEACHER LIBRARIAN COLLABORATION

Of the potential shaping factors just mentioned, I am particularly interested in teacher–TL collaboration, including the role of the school in supporting this collaboration. While there is surprisingly limited peer-reviewed research exploring teacher–TL collaboration, research highlights "the need to examine the role of the librarian in the educational setting and to determine the most effective model of collaboration for librarians" (Montiel-Overall, 2005, p. 44). Subsequent research tentatively identified five key elements for successful collaboration: positive attributes of collaborators, school culture, management, communication, and motivation (Montiel-Overall, 2008). However, more needs to be known about the impact of collaborative practices on student achievement (Montiel-Overall, 2008).

My current project (TLLLAS) is exploring these collaborative relationships in more detail. While conducting research with tweens and teens from 2012 to 2016, I had many opportunities to converse with TLs, and I anecdotally noted great variation in the relationships that TLs had with other educators. While TLs may increasingly seek to optimize their educative contributions (Montiel-Overall & Hernandez, 2012), almost all of the research on teacher and TL collaboration is U.S.–based, and findings from studies generally "have not specifically focused on teacher and school librarian collaboration" (p. 2). Nevertheless, the extant research in this area suggests that levels of collaboration may be low (Mokhtar & Majid, 2006), with school librarians reporting that their teaching colleagues do not understand or support this collaboration (Moreillon, 2014). Models of successful collaboration, with attention to how this may be facilitated and what it may constitute, would significantly further knowledge in this area and provide valuable insights into improving collaboration. I am really looking forward to contributing to the research in this area through publication of the TLLLAS findings. In the interim, I strongly advocate for the strengthening of these collaborative relationships. Not only do they hold potential for improved student engagement and for the fostering of a school-wide supportive reading culture, but, as some TLs have already explained to me, the teachers with whom we collaborate can be invaluable supports, and in some instances, they are the only individuals within the school who have a realistic grasp for the full scope and potential of the TL role. As such, they can be supportive advocates when schools are conducting funding reviews, and they can help TLs hold onto their positions.

10

Final Thoughts

The research covered in this book is just a small part of the research concerns in this field. It does not cover everything. This chapter is here for the researchers who may have bristled their way through the book, annoyed with the paucity of direct quotes and footnotes, or for parents of illiterate tweens or teens, who will need to read beyond this book. This section can also help nonresearchers to be more discerning when determining the value of research they subsequently encounter in this field.

RESEARCH RIGOR

Like all research-based works, this book is not perfect or all-encompassing, just as, sadly, my brain is not perfect or all-encompassing. The book does not consider every piece of reading research in this area, and I employ a degree of selection of detail as I bring together the extant research to create a comprehensive but incomplete picture of what we know in this area. As I have already mentioned, I am constantly in the process of adding more to this body of knowledge, though I admit that it is a constant struggle to find funding for my research, perhaps as it does not fit neatly with the neoliberal agenda that still predominates in contemporary educational policy and pedagogy. If you are a researcher and your peer-reviewed research is missing, and it lends key insights into the areas I discuss, please feel free to send it to me for possible inclusion in future editions.

While I primarily make reference to peer-reviewed research, apart from key national and international research reports, the methods used by researchers are varied because they have to be. While we know that qualitative data (such as that obtained through interviews) is typically not as generalizable as quantitative data (such as that obtained through surveys), this does not mean that surveys are superior sources of research. If surveys measure students' responses to a question about their attitudes toward reading but the choices are not at all reflective of students' real range of attitudes, the survey data is not that helpful. For example, I ask you about your attitudes toward fruit, and I create a survey to measure your enjoyment of pears, oranges, and apples. If most of you select pears as your favorite fruit, this does not mean that I can then claim that all readers like pears more than any other fruit. I did not put every possible fruit choice on the survey; I am assuming, based on previous research, the theory I am testing or my intuitive feeling that your favorite fruit will be one of these three, so I do not ask you how you felt about mangos, plums, or a range of other fruits that you might like more. In this way, just as qualitative research has its limitations, quantitative research does too, and we need to take these limitations into account. We need studies using multiple methods to illuminate this area so that we have the breadth and depth needed and so that findings maintain their currency and are reflective of contemporary students' attitudes, values, and ideas in current and diverse contexts. As this is a book and not a research paper, I do not go into a great deal of methodological and theoretical detail and differentiation; however, I encourage those readers who are looking for greater detail to read my research papers, which I cite in the references list. I wanted this book to be accessible to a broad audience, so I hope that you have found it easy to dip into and out of and to use as a resource.

We also need to know that all research, whether it be qualitative or quantitative, is subject to noteworthy limitations, regardless of the sample size or demographic scope. I need to point this out as there are often vigorous debates in the field of reading and literacy around the validity of different methodological approaches, such as the contention around the value of sustained silent reading (as I explore in Merga, 2013) and the ongoing war between proponents of whole-word and phonetic approaches to learning reading (e.g., as explored in Watts & Gardner, 2013). Where these limitations are not mentioned, it does not mean that they do not exist. There is no such thing as a perfect research project or a perfect research communication. Even large-scale international research such as the OECD's PISA research, which is often the go-to research source due to the sheer size and geographic extent of the research (which enables generalizability), has limitations. For instance, a recent OECD paper drawing on Turkey as an example, found that existing OECD data has failed to accurately represent the 15–16-year-olds who take part in the study, as so many fall outside the PISA sampling requirements due to high levels of cessation of schooling or severe delay in schooling (see Spaull, 2017). Every research project ever undertaken has had its own set of limitations, including but not limited to methodological, resourcing, and theoretical limitations. There is no perfect research project that will be eternally generalizable. As such, while I have been discerning about the research inclusions here, I have no doubt that flaws can be found in the details; that is the imperfect nature of research. However, the main implication for you as a reader is to be as discerning as you can be when approached with the future body of research that emerges in this field, which brings me to my next point.

I have already discussed conflict of interest in relation to e-book research, and it is something that we need to consistently look at when consuming new research. Who funded the project? Does the method seem inclined to position young people to give a certain kind of response? By getting off the fence and writing this book, which undeniably adopts a position of advocacy, I am taking a risk. In order to continue as a researcher and to have integrity as a researcher, I need to be willing to completely debunk all of these findings. If I subsequently find that e-books have surpassed paper books as the preferred reading mode, I will report this as clearly as I have reported the reverse. I cannot be a researcher and wed myself to any position, and I need to continue to design and conduct research that allows for my current beliefs and ideas to be soundly challenged. At the extreme end, if in the unlikely event someday I find that reading is actually harmful for literacy, I need to be willing to share this finding with equal energy. Here lies the tension between the researcher identity and the advocate. I am an advocate because I do not see the point in research that meets no broader purpose, but I will continue to strive to adopt a position of critical consideration in my own work, taking as scientific an approach as is appropriate and possible within the constraints of my own cultural and social conditionings. I need to be a researcher first and foremost. In this vein, I acknowledge that conflict of interest can be an issue in some of the research included in this book. For example, when using data from the Scholastic reports, it's important for me to include an acknowledgment that they are a publishing entity and therefore may have vested interests in the influence the design of their data collection. As such, while data such as this is used because it is sometimes the *only* current and wide-scale data available in the area, it needs to be interpreted with this qualification acknowledged. I encourage you to use your own critical and discerning lens when reviewing my own work and the research included here.

SELF-REPORT AND SCHOOL-BASED RESEARCH

All of my research is constrained by the limitations related to self-report, and this can be a particular issue where asking respondents to recall earlier experiences in childhood (Merga & Moon, 2016). As contended by Polkinghorne (2005), "People do not have complete access to their experiences," and "[t]he capacity to be aware of or to recollect one's experiences is intrinsically limited" (p. 136). Not every respondent may have been able to accurately recall earlier and even present attitudes toward and engagement in reading. As I have stated elsewhere, I believe that longitudinal research that can track the changes in young people's attitudes over time would be highly beneficial, though it has rarely been attempted in this specific research area (Merga, 2015f).

All research conducted in schools is plagued by a trade-off that often excludes wider participation of the more vulnerable members of our community. This is due to the fact that, to meet the ethics requirements, written consent from both parents and children is almost always required for student participation in research. It has been acknowledged that "the added layer of human subjects protection associated with acquiring active parental consent for youths' participation, . . . can increase initial loss rates" (Esbensen, Melde, Taylor, & Peterson, 2008, p. 336). While this lowers overall participation rates, it can have a particularly deleterious effect on response rates from children whose parents have low literacy or poor English skills, both of which can be barriers to understanding the somewhat complex consent letters required. In Western Australia, health researchers have despaired over "the changing nature of school policy to mandate active consent procedures for all research activities" (Thomas, 2009, p. 73) and a decline in receptiveness to providing consent, which threaten research sample sizes and can also skew the samples so that they comprise of a greater portion of comparatively privileged children.

FOCUS ON WILL, NOT SKILL

This book does not focus solely on those who have not yet acquired foundational independent reading skills per se, and you will also have noticed that I have confined this book to principally focus on older children who have acquired independent reading skill acquisition, though this is not to suggest that they are all strong readers. There is a wealth of research focusing on specific issues that require teaching and learning adjustments, such as dyslexia, and this book does not focus on cognitive or physical disorders. Some children who experienced these disorders, however, could read independently and did take part in this study. While these children experience a raft of additional issues due to their circumstances, many of the ideas discussed herein will also be relevant to literacy advocates working with these young people. For further information about how to provide best practice support for students and children requiring teaching and learning adjustments due to diagnosed disorders, readers are strongly encouraged to engage with the literature in this area, so that they can tailor their support accordingly.

As you will have noticed by the time you have reached this point, the focus of this book is on children who can read but do not, for a range of reasons previously explored, rather than illiterate children. If your major concern is working with children who cannot read, you should read further in this area, and use the strategies in this book as supplementary support to more intensive interventions outlined in the literature around supporting fundamental reading skill acquisition beyond the early years, which is a challenging but essential task, one of the principal challenges being the low sense of self-efficacy commonly felt by children who have not achieved independent reading skill in the early years of schooling.

RECOMMENDATION FOR FURTHER READING: LOW-LITERACY AND DISADVANTAGED PARENTS

It is important for me to point out what literacy educators know: Children's home and social backgrounds tend to influence their literacy performance (Zhang et al., 2013). So, while my research does not focus on these factors and I have explored them in relation to reading for pleasure in Chapter 1, I encourage you to read even more broadly in this area to meet the needs of our diverse students. There is a growing body of research done in the literacy space that focuses specifically on parents and families in low-socioeconomic contexts; I have cited a very small sample in this work. While individuals from underprivileged backgrounds comprised part of the representative samples of my studies, they were not the primary focus, and I hope to further my investigation into this area in the future. The reasons for the comparative disadvantage are wide and varying, and parents from a low-SES background may also be more likely to have low literacy themselves, and this low literacy can influence parents' capacity to support their children in their literacy development. For example, we know that parents with low literacy are less likely to help their children develop their reading and writing at home (Bonci, 2008) and that they have less confidence supporting their children's literacy, and this in turn influences children's achievement.

As I mentioned in Chapter 1, despite this disadvantage, many of the issues that have been presented in the research were able to be mediated, at least to some extent, by intervention, suggesting that the effects of low socioeconomic status (SES) may be mitigated and perhaps in some instances entirely overcome. For example, parental responsiveness in discussions about books during shared reading with their children can limit the impact of SES on children's expressive and receptive vocabulary, suggesting that interventions that aim at equipping parents with skills and strategies to support literacy can be highly beneficial (Mol & Neuman, 2014). Though at this stage my research does not closely focus on this area, interesting implications emerged from the data that offer insights into ways we can mitigate disadvantage from parents with low literacy backgrounds. For instance, while it is unlikely that teachers who read aloud poorly would be very well received by their students, parents did not need to be highly proficient readers in order for their reading aloud to be highly appreciated by their children. When parents reflected on their experiences of being read to, what often stayed with them was the memory of the shared interaction with their parents. For example, one parent reflected:

> I loved it! Some of my fondest memories were of my dad reading to me. I loved that he used different voices for different characters. Mum was not so good at reading aloud. She stumbled and didn't have the right flow. But I enjoyed being close to her physically. It allowed me to cuddle, smell and get a close up look at her while she was reading. I got to know her while she was reading. (Merga & Ledger, in press)

This experience could be powerful enough to counter skill issues that parents with lower literacy skills might experience, as the possibility for warm and focused interpersonal interaction and the valuing the mother showed through her effort were both powerfully educative in their own right. I would like to do further research that examines the impact of increasing parental efficacy on their capacity and inclination to support their children at home, looking at parental SES and literacy both together and separately.

WHERE TO NEXT?

I have a lot of ideas for further research that I wish to undertake in this area, and I have mentioned some of them in the body of the book. If you feel that you have the time and energy to apply yourself to conduct research in one of the areas I have highlighted in the book or in another related area, I would love to hear about your findings. I look forward to presenting the findings of the study that I am currently undertaking into the role of teacher librarians in fostering literacy and literature knowledge and skills in young people, and I hope to continue to energetically apply myself to building research knowledge across the breadth of areas of inquiry that I have covered thus far. I also hope to branch out further and extend the scope of my inquiry, and I look forward to further opportunities to work with international collaborators. I recognize that the research presented in this book predominantly reflects experiences and contexts in the United States, Australia, and the UK, with other nations underrepresented.

I would like to finish the book with a number of questions we can ask ourselves as literacy advocates, whether we be teachers, librarians, parents, or other literacy support personnel:

1. Are we effectively communicating the value and the ongoing importance of reading books for pleasure?
2. Are we reading models? Do we read regularly, broadly, and deeply? Can we be seen by young people as readers?
3. Do we provide regular and effective encouragement to the young people in our lives?
4. Do we support young people's regular access to books?
5. Do we provide young people with opportunities to talk about books?
6. Do we know what the young people in our lives like to read?
7. Are we reading to our young people and providing safe opportunities for them to practice reading aloud?
8. Do we provide time and an environment conducive to reading?
9. Do we support young people's strategies for choosing books?
10. Do we take responsibility as a key reading support for our young people?

If we cannot answer honestly and unequivocally yes to all of these questions, all the time, we have a great starting point going forward. This gives us something positive to work toward in our professional and/or personal lives. I would also like you to think critically about the degree of influence that you can exert in your home, library, and/or school cultures. As explored in this book, so many factors and forces are eroding the recognition of the value of reading, despite its ongoing importance. I would love for you to get together with like-minded innovators educators and put together a battle plan to both preserve and extend the support for reading engagement fostered in the spaces over which you hold stewardship.

As explored in this book, there is so much you can do without needing extensive training, and you do not need to buy any programs or packages—just interesting and engaging books. What I am ultimately proposing is that we push for a cultural change. Many of us live in societies where literacy and literature are devalued, despite their ongoing importance, perhaps due to the fact that literacy is not sensational, new, or exciting. I am working hard to achieve this change, and I am sure that most of the readers of this book are working even harder. As I have explained at length in this book, the relationship between increasing reading volume and increasing reading engagement is both intuitive and supported by research, so this should be our first port of call moving forward. Now would be an excellent time for us to push for a greater focus on the educational approaches that *do* have sound research benefit supporting them, such as those outlined in this book.

I hope that you have found this book useful and that you use it as a springboard to influence those around you to move toward a greater understanding of the value of reading, and a greater level of engagement in the practice. If you have enjoyed this book and you wish to remain abreast of my research projects, I encourage you to follow me on Research Gate at https://www.researchgate.net/profile/Margaret _Merga.

Appendix: Research Projects

For further information about the theory and method underpinning the studies detailed herein, I strongly suggest reading the related research papers, which are listed on my Research Gate page. The following details are basic and intended only to give a brief outline of the projects that have been and currently are being undertaken.

2012 WESTERN AUSTRALIAN STUDY IN ADOLESCENT BOOK READING (WASABR)

Purpose of the Project

The WASABR aimed to discover current attitudes toward and levels of engagement in recreational book reading among Western Australian adolescents. It also examined the role of social agents in influencing the recreational book reading in this cohort, examining the influences of parents, English teachers, the peer group, and friends on adolescents' reading engagement in order to understand how adolescents' engagement is affected by social factors. These understandings were sought with a view to ultimately enhancing participation in regular recreational reading.

How It Was Conducted

The WASABR project ran from 2012 to 2014. A total of 520 adolescents in Years 8 and 10 at 20 Western Australian schools took part. The project was supported by an Australian Postgraduate Award. Schools were selected in order to achieve a sample representative of the diverse demographic profile of Western Australia, with one Year 8 class and one Year 10 class participating from each school where possible. There were more female (53 percent) than male survey participants (47 percent). Only 3 percent of participants were indigenous Australians; 14 percent of participants came from non-English-speaking backgrounds, and 21 percent of all respondents were born in a country other than Australia. There were more survey respondents from Year 8 (65 percent) than Year 10. Respondents were 13–16 years in age at the time of the study.

This mixed-methods project collected both survey data from all respondents and interview data from a smaller subset. The study was fully piloted in Term 3 of

2012, resulting in minor adjustments to the instruments. Data collection was fully undertaken in Term 4 of 2012. Surveys were primarily completed online in Qualtrics. Most of the 41 survey items collected qualitative data, though the survey also contained a qualitative field where students could contribute ideas that they wished to share, in addition to or beyond the scope of the survey.

After the surveys were completed, I randomly selected two participants from each school (where possible), controlling only for gender. These students then participated in a semistructured interview, which explored a range of issues concerning book reading practices in further depth. I performed all of the data collection, barring one instance where a participating school was beyond the distance of my travel capacity; in that case, I collected survey data only, with the survey being administered by the teacher. This doctoral project was supervised by Associate Professor Brian Moon, who was a coauthor on some of the publications.

2015 INTERNATIONAL STUDY OF AVID BOOK READERS (ISABR)

Purpose of the Project

This study sought to explore the characteristics of an under-researched group, avid book readers, with a particular interest in motivation, social influences, and preferences of avid book readers.

How It Was Conducted

The ISABR ran from 2015 to 2016, with data collection from September to November 2015. The project was funded by Murdoch University School of Education Strategic Funding. There was a total of $N = 1,136$ consenting respondents. Most (83.2 percent) were female, with 16 percent male, with fewer than 1 percent identifying as another gender orientation. Nearly two-fifths spoke English as an additional language. Respondents came from 89 countries, though Western countries were overrepresented. Dr. Saiyidi Mat Roni was a coauthor on some of the published works from this study and has played a key role in some of the data analysis.

The study was fully piloted with a small but diverse group of respondents before data collection. The project used a single-stage mixed methods survey tool hosted on Survey Monkey.

The international sample was recruited primarily through social networking and primarily through Facebook, though some participants were recruited through book-reading Web sites. Though a paid advertisement was placed on Goodreads .com, not many respondents clicked on this link (fewer than 170 of the total respondents).

2016 WESTERN AUSTRALIAN STUDY IN CHILDREN'S BOOK READING (WASCBR)

Purpose of the Project

The WASCBR sought to learn about children's reading and the social influences that encourage children to read for pleasure.

How It Was Conducted

This mixed-method project ran from 2015 to 2017, with data collection from March to June in 2016. Survey and interview data was collected at 24 public and private schools in Western Australia, with a total of 997 Western Australian children aged 8 to 12 surveyed, and 47 interviews took place. Where possible, two students were randomly selected at each school, controlling only for year group and gender.

All participants were in Years 4 and 6. The project was funded by the Ian Potter Foundation with a supplement from Murdoch University Research and Development. A diverse, representative sample of schools was recruited, and the total sample had an average Index of Community Socio-Educational Advantage (ICSEA) of 1040.9, slightly over the Australian average (1000).

The average respondent age was 9.8 years. There were a greater number of respondents from the younger year group (Year 4, 52.3 percent) than the older year group (Year 6, 47.7 percent), and more female (566) than male respondents.

2016 TEEN READING IN THE DIGITAL ERA

Purpose of the Project

To explore young people's reading engagement, frequency, and preferences across a range of contexts.

How It Was Conducted

This project was primarily run from 2015 to 2017 by Associate Professor Katya Johanson and Dr. Leonie Rutherford at Deakin University, and I was the primary investigative team member for the Western Australian component of the study. The project was funded by the Deakin University Central Research Grants Scheme and Copyright Agency Cultural Fund. A total of 13 secondary schools took part, with seven schools in Victoria and six in Western Australia. The ICSEA of these participating schools was just below average at 997.8. All participants were from lower secondary school (Years 7–10), with two classes typically participating per school, and most students aged 11–16. A total of 555 surveys were completed by students, with 37 interview respondents randomly selected, controlled only for year group and gender.

2016 WESTERN AUSTRALIAN STUDY IN
READING ALOUD (WASRA)

Purpose of the Project

The WASRA sought to gain insight into the following areas, as reported by teachers and parents:

- Frequency of teachers and parents reading to students across Years 1–6

- Duration of reading sessions when teachers and parents read to students across Years 1–6

- Barriers to frequency and duration of reading aloud.

How It Was Conducted

The WASRA ran from 2016 to 2017, funded by a Collier Charitable Foundation grant. Dr. Susan Ledger and I were co–chief investigators on the project. A total of 21 Western Australian public primary schools were involved in the final data set, with one additional school selected for piloting. Data was collected from June to December in 2016. Data was collected from two groups in order to reduce the burden of participation of schools. Mixed-methods survey tools were created and used, and schools were sampled to ensure representative diversity.

Group A: Seven schools were recruited for this group. A total of 91 surveys were completed in the early childhood group (Years 1–3), and 129 surveys in the middle childhood group (Years 4 and 6). Middle childhood students were able to fill out the surveys autonomously via a Survey Monkey online link. The younger children completed the survey face-to-face with a researcher.

Group B: Fourteen schools took part in this group, with 303 parent/guardian surveys and 101 teacher surveys being completed autonomously via a Survey Monkey online link circulated by the schools.

2018–2019 TEACHER LIBRARIANS AS LITERATURE AND
LITERACY ADVOCATES IN SCHOOLS (TLLLAS)

Purpose of the Project

The TLLLAS project is the project that I am currently working on (2018–2019). This project will determine how teacher librarians (TLs) in primary and secondary schools advocate for the reading of Australian literature (AL), as well as literacy and literature more generally. TLs' beliefs, practices, and experiences will be explored in in-depth interviews. The study aims to explore the scope of TLs' role in literacy and literature engagement and their perceived extent of influence and to investigate the degree of school culture and collaborative support for literacy and literature engagement. While this project is currently being conducted in Western Australia, I am hoping to conduct national and international follow-up studies on a larger scale.

How It Is Being Conducted

The TLLLAS project will run from 2018 to 2019, funded by the Copyright Cultural Fund. It involves in-depth interviews to illuminate beliefs, perceived barriers, resourcing capacity, teacher collaboration, and advocacy practices and experiences of TLs promoting literature and literacy engagement, including a subfocus on Australian literature. A total of 30 Western Australian TLs from across 30 primary and secondary school settings will take part, including staff of at least three rural schools. In addition to the interviews, which are conducted on-site, I make notes about observed situational and resourcing factors. At the time of submission of this manuscript, the project was well on its way toward completion.

References

Aðalsteinsdóttir, Kristin, Ed. (2011). *Learning and teaching children's literature in Europe: Final report.* European Union: European Commission Lifelong Learning Programme.

Aggleton, J. (2018). Where are the children in children's collections? An exploration of ethical principles and practical concerns surrounding children's participation in collection development. *New Review of Children's Literature and Librarianship, 24*(1), 1–17.

Aikens, N. L., & Barbarin, O. (2008). Socioeconomic differences in reading trajectories: The contribution of family, neighborhood, and school contexts. *Journal of Educational Psychology, 100*(2), 235–251.

Albright, L. K., & Ariail, M. (2005). Tapping the potential of teacher read-alouds in middle schools. *Journal of Adolescent & Adult Literacy, 48*(7), 582–591.

Alderson-Day, B., Bernini, M., & Fernyhough, C. (2017). Uncharted features and dynamics of reading: Voices, characters, and crossing of experiences. *Consciousness and Cognition, 49*, 98–109.

Allington, R. L. (2014). How reading volume affects both reading fluency and reading achievement. *International Electronic Journal of Elementary Education, 7*(1), 13–26.

Allington, R. L., & McGill-Franzen, A. (2017). Summer reading loss is the basis of almost all the rich/poor reading gap. In Rosalind Horowitz & S. Jay Samuels (Eds.), *The achievement gap in reading: Complex causes, persistent issues, possible solutions* (pp. 170–184). London: Taylor & Francis.

Allington, D., & Swann, J. (2009). Researching literary reading as a social practice. *Language and Literature, 18*(3), 219–230.

Alvermann, D. E. (2011). Popular culture and literacy practices. In M. L. Kamil, P. D. Pearson, E. B. Moje, & P. P. Afflerbach (Eds.), *Handbook of Reading Research: Volume IV* (pp. 541–560). New York: Routledge/Taylor & Francis Group.

Amer, A. A. (1997). The effect of the teacher's reading aloud on the reading comprehension of EFL students. *ElT Journal, 51*(1), 43–47.

American Association of School Librarians. (AASL). (2017). Common beliefs. Retrieved from http://standards.aasl.org/beliefs

American Association of School Librarians. (AASL). (2018). AASL advocacy toolkit. Retrieved from http://www.ala.org/aasl/sites/ala.org.aasl/files/content/aaslissues/toolkits/AASLAdvocacyToolkit_180209.pdf

American Library Association & American Association of School Librarians. (2010). ALA/AASL Standards for Initial Preparation of School Librarians. Retrieved from http://www.ala.org/aasl/sites/ala.org.aasl/files/content/aasleducation /schoollibrary/2010_standards_with_rubrics_and_statements_1-31-11.pdf

Anderson, B. L. (1994). The library as community center. *Library Trends, 42*(3), 395–403.

Anderson, P. (2016). Assessment and growth in reading comprehension. In H. Fehring (Ed.), *Assessment into practice* (pp. 108–114). Newtown, NSW: Primary English Teaching Association Australia.

Anderson, R., Wilson, P., & Fielding, L. (1988). Growth in reading and how children spend their time outside of school. *Reading Research Quarterly, 23*(3), 285–303.

Appel, M., & Mara, M. (2013). The persuasive influence of a fictional character's trustworthiness. *Journal of Communication, 63*(5), 912–932.

Applegate, A., & Applegate, M. (2004). The Peter effect: Reading habits and attitudes of preservice teachers. *The Reading Teacher, 57*, 554–563.

Australian Bureau of Statistics (ABS). (2013). *Programme for the international assessment of adult competencies, Australia, 2011–2012 (4228.0).* Canberra: Australian Bureau of Statistics.

Australian School Library Association. (2014). Evidence guide for teacher librarians in the highly accomplished career stage. Retrieved from http://www.asla .org.au/site/DefaultSite/filesystem/documents/evidence-guide_ha.pdf

Baer, J., Baldi, S., Ayotte, K., & Green, P. (2007). *The reading literacy of U.S. fourth-grade students in an international context: Results from the 2001 and 2006 Progress in International Reading Literacy Study (PIRLS).* Washington, DC: National Center for Education Statistics, Institute of Education Sciences, U.S. Department of Education.

Baker, L., Scher, D., & Mackler, K. (1997). Home and family influences on motivations for reading. *Educational Psychologist, 32*(2), 69–82.

Baker, M., & Milligan, K. (2016). Boy–girl differences in parental time investments: Evidence from three countries. *Journal of Human Capital, 10*(4), 399–441.

Baron, N. S. (2013). Redefining reading: The impact of digital communication media. *PMLA, 128*(1), 193–200.

Bastian, B., & Haslam, N. (2006). Psychological essentialism and stereotype endorsement. *Journal of Experimental Social Psychology, 42*(2), 228–235.

Batson, C. D., Early, S., & Salvarani, G. (1997). Perspective taking: Imagining how another feels versus imaging how you would feel. *Personality and Social Psychology Bulletin, 23*(7), 751–758.

Baumrind, D. (1971). Current patterns of parental authority. *Developmental Psychology Monograph, 4*, 1–103.

Baumrind, D. (1978). Parental disciplinary patterns and social competence in children. *Youth Society, 9*(3), 239–276.

Baumrind, D. (1991). The influence of parenting style on adolescent competence and substance use. *The Journal of Early Adolescence, 11*(1), 56–95.

Baumrind, D. (2005). Patterns of parental authority and adolescent autonomy. *New Directions for Child and Adolescent Development, 108*, 61–69.

Bavishi, A., Slade, M. D., & Levy, B. R. (2016). A chapter a day: Association of book reading with longevity. *Social Science & Medicine, 164*, 44–48.

Benedetto, S., Drai-Zerbib, V., Pedrotti, M., Tissier, G., & Baccino, T. (2013). E-readers and visual fatigue. *PloS one, 8*(12), e83676.

Berns, G. S., Blaine, K., Prietula, M. J., & Pye, B. E. (2013). Short- and long-term effects of a novel on connectivity in the brain. *Brain Connectivity, 3*(6), 590–600.

Bhattacharya, A. (2010). Children and adolescents from poverty and reading development: A research review. *Reading & Writing Quarterly, 26*(2), 115–139.

Bintz, W. (1993). Resistant readers in secondary education: Some insights and implications. *Journal of Adolescent & Adult Literacy, 36*(8), 604–615.

Black, M., & Shaw, S. (2017, May 24). 'The most loudest library ever': Booklover goes the way of shushing staff as community hubs take hold. *ABC News.* Retrieved from http://www.abc.net.au/news/2017-05-24/loud-libraries -signal-move-to-role-as-community-hub/8555112

Bonci, A. (2008). *A research review: The importance of families and the home environment.* London: National Literacy Trust.

Brooks, G. W. (2007). Teachers as readers and writers and as teachers of reading and writing. *The Journal of Educational Research, 100*(3), 177–191.

Brown, B., Larson, R., & Saraswati, T. S. (2002). *The world's youth: Adolescence in eight regions of the globe.* Cambridge: Cambridge University Press.

Brozo, W. G. (2005). Avoiding the "fourth-grade slump." *Thinking Classroom, 6*(4), 48–49.

Buchanan, J., Prescott, A., Schuck, S., Aubusson, P., Burke, P., & Louviere, J. (2013). Teacher retention and attrition: Views of early career teachers. *Australian Journal of Teacher Education, 38*(3), 8–25.

Bunbury, R. M. (Ed.). (1995). *Children's choice: Reading at home or at school.* Geelong, Australia: Deakin University Press.

Bursztyn, L., Egorov, G., & Jensen, R. (2016). *Cool to be smart or smart to be cool? Understanding peer pressure in education* (No. w23020). Cambridge, MA: National Bureau of Economic Research.

Bus, A. G., Leseman, P. P., & Keultjes, P. (2000). Joint book reading across cultures: A comparison of Surinamese–Dutch, Turkish–Dutch, and Dutch parent–child dyads. *Journal of Literacy Research, 32*(1), 53–76.

Cain, M. S., & Mitroff, S. R. (2011). Distractor filtering in media multitaskers. *Perception, 40*(10), 1183–1192.

Camardese, A., Peled, Y., Kirkpatrick, M., & Teacher, S. G. (2012). Using e-Readers to improve reading for students with mild disabilities. *Journal of the American Academy of Special Education Professionals*, Spring–Summer, 7–24.

Camp, D. (2007). Who's reading and why: Reading habits of 1st grade through graduate students. *Reading Horizons, 47*(3), 251.

Cashen, P. (2015). From library to learning hub. South Australian Secondary Principals' Association. Retrieved from http://www.saspa.com.au/2015/07/21 /draft-library-learning-hub/

Chan, C. (2008). The impact of school library services on student achievement and the implications for advocacy: A review of the literature. *Access*, *22*(4), 15–20.

Changing Times. (1951, December). Oddly enough, we still read books. *Kiplinger's Personal Finance*, 42–44.

Chard, D. J., Vaughn, S., & Tyler, B. J. (2002). A synthesis of research on effective interventions for building reading fluency with elementary students with learning disabilities. *Journal of Learning Disabilities*, *35*(5), 386–406.

Clark, C. (2010). *Linking school libraries and literacy*. London: National Literacy Trust.

Clark, C. (2012). *Boys' reading commission 2012: A review of existing research conducted to underpin the commission*. London: National Literacy Trust.

Clark, C., & De Zoysa, S. (2011). *Mapping the inter-relationships of reading enjoyment, attitudes, behavior and attainment: An exploratory investigation*. London: National Literacy Trust.

Clark, C., & Foster, A. (2005). *Children's and young people's reading habits and preferences: The who, what, why, where and when*. London: National Literacy Trust.

Clark, C., & Hawkins, L. (2011). *Public libraries and literacy: Young people's reading habits and attitudes to public libraries, and an exploration of the relationship between public library use and school attainment*. London: National Literacy Trust.

Clark, C., Osborne, S., & Akerman, R. (2008). *Young people's self-perceptions as readers: An investigation including family, peer and school influences*. London: National Literacy Trust.

Clark, C., & Poulton, L. (2011). *Book ownership and its relation to reading enjoyment, attitudes, behavior and attainment*. London: National Literacy Trust.

Clark, S. K., & Andreasen, L. (2014). Examining sixth grade students' reading attitudes and perceptions of teacher read aloud: Are all students on the same page? *Literacy Research and Instruction*, *53*(2), 162–182.

Cliff Hodges, G. (2010). Reasons for reading: Why literature matters. *Literacy*, *44*(2), 60–68.

Coker, E. (2015). *Certified teacher-librarians, library quality and student achievement in Washington State Public Schools*. Seattle: Washington Library Media Association.

Coles, M., & Hall, C. (2002). Gendered readings: Learning from children's reading choices. *Journal of Research in Reading*, *25*(1), 96–108.

Common Sense Media. (2014). Children, reading and teens. Retrieved from https://www.commonsensemedia.org/file/csm-childrenteensandreading-2014pdf/download

Commonwealth Scientific and Industrial Research Organisation (CISRO). (2008). *2007 Australian national children's nutrition and physical activity survey—Main findings*. Barton: Commonwealth of Australia.

Council of Chief State School Officers. (2010). Common Core state standards for English Language Arts & Literacy in History/Social Studies, Science, and

Technical Subjects. Washington, DC: National Governors Association Center for Best Practices, Council of Chief State School Officers.

Courage, M. L., Bakhtiar, A., Fitzpatrick, C., Kenny, S., & Brandeau, K. (2015). Growing up multitasking: The costs and benefits for cognitive development. *Developmental Review, 35*, 5–41.

Cunningham, A., & Stanovich, K. (1998). What reading does for the mind. *American Educator, 22*(1–2), 8–15.

Cunningham, P. M. (2006). Struggling readers: High-poverty schools that beat the odds. *The Reading Teacher, 60*(4), 382–385.

Cutchins, D. (2003). Adaptations in the classroom: Using film to "read" *The Great Gatsby. Literature/Film Quarterly, 31*(4), 295–303.

Daggett, W., & Hasselbring, T. (2007). *What we know about adolescent reading.* Nashville, TN: Vanderbilt University, International Centre for Leadership in Education.

Dai, Y. (1998). *Relationships among parenting styles, parental expectations and attitudes, and adolescents' school functioning: A cross-cultural study.* (Doctoral thesis). Retrieved from ProQuest Dissertations and Theses (UMI 9914478)

Darnton, R. (2011). 5 myths about the "Information Age." *The Chronicle of Higher Education.* Retrieved from http://www.chronicle.com/article/5-Myths-About-the-Information/127105/

Davis, C. (2008). Librarianship in the 21st century—Crisis or transformation? *Public Library Quarterly, 27*(1), 57–82.

DeBenedictis, D. (2007). Sustained silent reading: Making adaptations. *Voices from the Middle, 14*(3), 29–37.

De Naeghel, J., Valcke, M., De Meyer, I., Warlop, N., van Braak, J., & Van Keer, H. (2014). The role of teacher behavior in adolescents' intrinsic reading motivation. *Reading and Writing, 27*(9), 1547–1565.

Dickson, G. (1995). Principles of risk management. *Quality in Health Care, 4*(2), 75–79.

Doidge, N. (2010). *The brain that changes itself.* Carlton North, Australia: Scribe Publications.

Dole, J. A., Duffy, G. G., Roehler, L. R., & Pearson, P. D. (1991). Moving from the old to the new: Research on reading comprehension instruction. *Review of Educational Research, 61*(2), 239–264.

Dow, M. J., McMahon-Lakin, J., & Court, S. C. (2012). School librarian staffing levels and student achievement as represented in 2006–2009 Kansas annual yearly progress data. *School Library Research, 15*, 1–15.

Duursma, E. V., Augustyn, M., & Zuckerman, B. (2008). Reading aloud to children: The evidence. *Archives of Disease in Childhood, 93*(7), 554–557.

Echazzara, A. (2018). Taking a break from the Internet may be good for learning. *OECD Education and Skills Today.* Retrieved from http://oecdeducationtoday.blogspot.com/2018/04/internet-use-student-learning-school-pisa.html

Edmunds, K. M., & Bauserman, K. L. (2006). What teachers can learn about reading motivation through conversations with children. *The Reading Teacher, 59*(5), 414–424.

Esbensen, F., Melde, C., Taylor, T. J., & Peterson, D. (2008). Active parental consent in school-based research. *Evaluation Review, 32*(4), 335–362.

Evans, E. (2017). Learning from high school students' lived experiences of reading e-books and printed books. *Journal of Adolescent & Adult Literacy, 61*(3), 311–318.

Evans, M., Kelley, J., Sikora, J., & Treiman, D. (2010). Family scholarly culture and educational success: Books and schooling in 27 nations. *Research in Social Stratification and Mobility, 28*, 171–197.

Ewbank, A. D., & Kwon, J. Y. (2015). School library advocacy literature in the United States: An exploratory content analysis. *Library & Information Science Research, 37*(3), 236–243.

Farrant, B. M., & Zubrick, S. R. (2012). Early vocabulary development: The importance of joint attention and parent–child book reading. *First Language, 32*(3), 343–364.

Flowers, M. (2011). The movie is (sometimes) better than the book: Adaptations as literary analysis. *Young Adult Library Services, 9*(4), 21–23.

Fortunati, L., & Vincent, J. (2014). Sociological insights on the comparison of writing/reading on paper with writing/reading digitally. *Telematics and Informatics, 31*(1), 39–51.

Fox, M. (2013). What next in the read-aloud battle? Win or lose? *The Reading Teacher, 67*(1), 4–8.

Fraillon, J., Ainley, J., Schulz, W., Friedman, T., & Gebhardt, E. (2014). *Preparing for life in a digital age: The IEA International Computer and Information Literacy Study International Report.* Melbourne: Australian Council for Educational Research (ACER).

Fried, C. B. (2008). In-class laptop use and its effects on student learning. *Computers & Education, 50*(3), 906–914.

Gambrell, L. B. (1996). Creating classroom cultures that foster reading motivation. *Reading Teacher, 50*(1), 14–25

Garan, E. M., & DeVoogd, G. (2008). The benefits of sustained silent reading: Scientific research and common sense converge. *The Reading Teacher, 62*(4), 336–344.

Garces-Bacsal, R. M., Tupas, R., Kaur, S., Paculdar, A. M., & Baja, E. S. (2018). Reading for pleasure: Whose job is it to build lifelong readers in the classroom? *Literacy.* Retrieved from https://onlinelibrary.wiley.com/doi/full/10.1111/lit.12151

Giedd, J. N. (2012). The digital revolution and adolescent brain evolution. *Journal of Adolescent Health, 51*(2), 101–105.

Gordon, C. (2010). Meeting readers where they are. *School Library Journal, 56*(11), 32.

Gray, M., & Steinberg, L. (1999). Unpacking authoritative parenting: Reassessing a multidimensional construct. *Journal of Marriage and Family, 61*(3), 574–587.

Guthrie, J. T., & Davis, M. H. (2003). Motivating struggling readers in middle school through an engagement model of classroom practice. *Reading & Writing Quarterly, 19*(1), 59–85.

Hardy, L. (2011). *Position statement on children and young people's screen time as a health concern.* Sydney, Australia: Prevention Research Collaboration (PRC), University of Sydney.

Harkrader, M., & Moore, R. (1997). Literature preferences of fourth graders. *Reading Research and Instruction, 36*(4), 325–339.

Harrison, C. (2016). Are computers, smartphones, and the Internet a boon or a barrier for the weaker reader? *Journal of Adolescent & Adult Literacy, 60*(2), 221–225.

Haycock, K., & Stenström, C. (2016). Reviewing the research and evidence: Towards best practices for garnering support for school libraries. *School Libraries Worldwide, 22*(1), 127–142.

Hayes, N. (2015). Continuity and change in family engagement in home learning activities across the early years. PhD diss. Queensland University of Technology.

Heath, M. A., Sheen, D., Leavy, D., Young, E., & Money, K. (2005). Bibliotherapy: A resource to facilitate emotional healing and growth. *School Psychology International, 26*(5), 563–580.

Heller, R., & Greenleaf, C. (2007). *Literacy instruction in the content areas: Getting to the core of middle and high school improvement.* Washington, DC: Alliance for Excellent Education.

Hempel-Jorgensen, A., Cremin, T., Harris, D., & Chamberlain, L. (2018). Pedagogy for reading for pleasure in low socio-economic primary schools: Beyond "pedagogy of poverty"? *Literacy, 52*(2), 86–94.

Hiatt, B. (2017, August 21). Mobile devices drive student suspensions. *The West Australian.* Retrieved from https://thewest.com.au/news/wa/mobile-devices -drive-student-suspensions-ng-b88570984z

Hinz, B., & O'Connell, M. (2016). NAPLAN results don't tell the full story behind Australia's lack of education progress. *The Conversation.* Retrieved from http://theconversation.com/naplan-results-dont-tell-the-full-story-behind -australias-lack-of-education-progress-63444

Hopper, R. (2005). What are teenagers reading? Adolescent fiction reading habits and reading choices. *Literacy, 39*(3), 113–120.

Horrigan, J. B. (2016, September). *Libraries 2016.* Report for the Pew Research Center. Retrieved from http://www.pewinternet.org/2016/09/09/2016 /Libraries-2016/

House of Representatives. (2011). *School libraries and teacher librarians in 21st century Australia.* Canberra: Commonwealth of Australia.

Howard, V. (2009). Peer group influences on avid teen readers. *New Review of Children's Literature and Librarianship, 14*(2), 103–119.

Howard, V., & Jin, S. (2007). Teens and pleasure reading: A critical assessment from Nova Scotia. In M. Chelton & C. Cool (Eds.), *Youth information-seeking behavior II: Context, theories, models, and issues* (pp. 133–164). Lanham, MD: Scarecrow Press.

Hughes, H., Bozorgian, H., & Allan, C. (2014). School libraries, teacher-librarians and student outcomes: Presenting and using the evidence. *School Libraries Worldwide, 20*(1), 29–50.

Hughes-Hassell, S. (2008). Urban teenagers talk about leisure reading. *IASL Research Abstracts.* Retrieved from http://www.kzneducation.gov.za/portals /0/elits%20website%20homepage/iasl%202008/research%20forum /hughes-hassellrf.pdf

Hutton, J. S., Phelan, K., Horowitz-Kraus, T., Dudley, J., Altaye, M., DeWitt, T., & Holland, S. K. (2017). Story time turbocharger? Child engagement during shared reading and cerebellar activation and connectivity in preschool-age children listening to stories. *PloS one, 12*(5), e0177398.

Institute of Education Sciences. (2011). *The Nation's Report Card: Reading 2011.* Washington, DC: U.S. Department of Education.

Ipsos MORI (2003). *Young people's attitudes towards reading.* Croydon, UK: Nestle.

Jacobs, A. M., & Willems, R. M. (2018). The fictive brain: neurocognitive correlates of engagement in literature. *Review of General Psychology, 22*(2), 147–160. Retrieved from https://www.researchgate.net/publication/315075481_The _Fictive_Brain_Neurocognitive_Correlates_of_Engagement_in_Literature

Jeong, H. (2012). A comparison of the influence of electronic books and paper books on reading comprehension, eye fatigue, and perception. *The Electronic Library, 30*(3), 390–408.

Jetnikoff, A. (2005). Adaptation: A case in point about adapting films from books. *English in Australia, 143*, 88–94.

Jetnikoff, A. (2007). Square-eyed kids are not one eyed: Media education in Australia. *Screen Education, 48*, 99–108.

Johnson, G., & Buck, G. (2014). Electronic books versus paper books: Pre-service teacher preference for university study and recreational reading. *International Journal of Humanities Social Sciences and Education, 1*(8), 13–22.

Joo, S., & Cahill, M. (2017). The relationships between the expenditures and resources of public libraries and children's and young adults' use: An exploratory analysis of Institute of Museum and Library Services public library statistics data. *Journal of Librarianship and Information Science.* http:// journals.sagepub.com/doi/abs/10.1177/0961000617709057?journalCode =lisb

Kachel, D. (2015). The calamity of the disappearing school libraries. *The Conversation.* Retrieved from https://theconversation.com/the-calamity-of-the -disappearing-school-libraries-44498

Kalb, G., & Van Ours, J. C. (2014). Reading to young children: A head-start in life? *Economics of Education Review, 40*, 1–24.

Karrass, J., & Braungart-Rieker, J. M. (2005). Effects of shared parent–infant book reading on early language acquisition. *Journal of Applied Developmental Psychology, 26*(2), 133–148.

Karrass, J., VanDeventer, M. C., & Braungart-Rieker, J. (2003). Predicting shared parent–child book reading in infancy. *Journal of Family Psychology, 17*(1), 134–146.

Kell, M. (2009). Learning difficulties in literacy: Overcoming a construct of the literate student. In S. Gannon, M. Howie, & W. Sawyer (Eds.), *Charged with meaning. Reviewing English.* (3rd ed.). (pp. 151–160). Putney, Australia: Phoenix Education.

Kellett, M. (2009). Children as researchers: What we can learn from them about the impact of poverty on literacy opportunities? *International Journal of Inclusive Education, 13*(4), 395–408.

Keogh, R., & Pearson, J. (2017). The blind mind: No sensory visual imagery in aphantasia. *Cortex.* E-pub ahead of print. Retrieved from https://www.ncbi.nlm.nih.gov/pubmed/29175093

Keslair, F. (2017). How much will the literacy level of the working-age population change from now to 2022? Paris: Organisation for Economic Co-operation and Development (OECD).

Kidd, D., Ongis, M., & Castano, E. (2016). On literary fiction and its effects on theory of mind. *Scientific Study of Literature, 6*(1), 42–58.

King, D. L., Delfabbro, P. H., Potenza, M. N., Demetrovics, Z., Billieux, J., & Brand, M. (2018). Internet gaming disorder should qualify as a mental disorder. *Australian & New Zealand Journal of Psychiatry,* 0004867418771189.

Kirsch, I., de Jong, J., Lafontaine, D., McQueen, J., Mendelovits, J., & Monsuer, C. (2002). *Reading for change: Performance and engagement across countries.* Washington, DC: Organisation for Economic Co-operation and Development (OECD).

Klauda, S. L. (2009). The role of parents in adolescents' reading motivation and activity. *Educational Psychology Review, 21*(4), 325–363.

Knapp, N. F. (2003). In defense of Harry Potter: An apologia. *School Libraries Worldwide, 9,* 78–91.

Krashen, S. (2001). More smoke and mirrors: A critique of the National Reading Panel report on fluency. *Phi Delta Kappan, 83*(2), 119–123.

Krashen, S. D. (2004). *The power of reading.* Westport, CT: Libraries Unlimited.

Krashen, S. (2011). *Free voluntary reading.* Santa Barbara, CA: Libraries Unlimited.

Krashen, S. (2012). Direct instruction of academic vocabulary: What about real reading? *Reading Research Quarterly, 47*(3), 233–233.

Krashen, S., & McQuillan, J. (2007). The case for late intervention. *Educational Leadership, 65*(2), 68–73.

Lance, K. C., & Kachel, D. E. (2018). Why school librarians matter: What years of research tell us. *Phi Delta Kappan, 99*(7), 15–20.

Ledger, S., & Merga, M. K. (2018). Reading aloud: Children's attitudes toward being read to at home and at school. *Australian Journal of Teacher Education, 43*(3), 124–139.

Lee, J., Hong, J. S., Resko, S. M., & Tripodi, S. J. (2018). Face-to-face bullying, cyberbullying, and multiple forms of substance use among school-age adolescents in the USA. *School Mental Health, 10*(1), 12–25.

Lemola, S., Perkinson-Gloor, N., Brand, S., Dewald-Kaufmann, J. F., & Grob, A. (2015). Adolescents' electronic media use at night, sleep disturbance, and depressive symptoms in the smartphone age. *Journal of Youth and Adolescence, 44*(2), 405–418.

Lenkowsky, R. S. (1987). Bibliotherapy: A review and analysis of the literature. *The Journal of Special Education, 21*(2), 123–132.

Leonard, L., Mokwele, T., Siebrits, A., & Stoltenkamp, J. (2016). "Digital Natives" require basic digital literacy skills. The IAFOR International Conference on Technology in the Classroom. The International Academic Forum. Retrieved from https://repository.uwc.ac.za/bitstream/handle/10566/2372 /Leonard_Digital_2016.pdf?sequence=5&isAllowed=y

Li, G. (2010). Race, class, and schooling: Multicultural families doing the hard work of home literacy in America's inner city. *Reading & Writing Quarterly, 26*(2), 140–165.

Liu, Z. (2005). Reading behavior in the digital environment: Changes in reading behavior over the past ten years. *Journal of Documentation, 61*(6), 700–712.

Loera, G., Rueda, R., & Nakamoto, J. (2011). The association between parental involvement in reading and schooling and children's reading engagement in Latino families. *Literacy Research and Instruction, 50*(2), 133–155.

Loh, J. K. K. (2009). Teacher modelling: Its impact on an extensive reading program. *Reading in a Foreign Language, 21*(2), 93.

Lopes, M. A., Ferrioli, E., Nakano, E. Y., Litvoc, J., & Bottino, C. M. (2011). High prevalence of dementia in a community-based survey of older people from Brazil: Association with intellectual activity rather than education. *Journal of Alzheimer's Disease: JAD, 32*(2), 307–316.

Love, K., & Hamston, J. (2003). Teenage boys' leisure reading dispositions: Juggling male youth culture and family cultural capital. *Educational Review, 55*(2), 161–177.

Lupo, S., Jang, B. G., & McKenna, M. (2017). The relationship between reading achievement and attitudes toward print and digital texts in adolescent readers. *Literacy Research: Theory, Method, and Practice*, Early view. Retrieved from http://journals.sagepub.com/doi/abs/10.1177/2381336917719254

Mackey, M. (2014). Learning to choose. *Journal of Adolescent & Adult Literacy, 57*(7), 521–526.

Mackey, M., & Shane, M. (2013). Critical multimodal literacies: Synergistic options and opportunities. In K. Hall, T. Cremin, B. Comber, & L. C. Moll (Eds.), *International handbook of research on children's literacy, learning, and culture* (pp. 15–27). Chichester, UK: Wiley-Blackwell.

Mancini, A. L., & Pasqua, S. (2011). On the intergenerational transmission of time use patterns: Is a good example the best sermon? ZA Discussion Paper No. 6038, October 2011.

Mangen, A., Walgermo, B. R., & Brønnick, K. (2013). Reading linear texts on paper versus computer screen: Effects on reading comprehension. *International Journal of Educational Research, 58*, 61–68.

Mansor, A. N., Rasul, M. S., Rauf, R. A. A., & Koh, B. L. (2012). Developing and sustaining reading habit among teenagers. *The Asia-Pacific Education Researcher, 22*(4), 357–365. Retrieved from link.springer.com/article/10 .1007/s40299-012-0017-1

Manuel, J. (2012). Reading lives: Teenagers' reading practices and preferences. In J. Manuel & S. Brindley (Eds.), *Teenagers and reading: Literary heritages, cultural contexts and contemporary reading practices* (pp. 12–37). Kent Town, South Australia: Wakefield Press.

Manuel, J., & Robinson, D. (2003). Teenage boys, teenage girls and books: Reviewing some assumptions about gender and adolescents' reading practices. *English Teaching: Practice and Critique, 11*, 66–77.

Mar, R. A., Oatley, K., & Peterson, J. B. (2009). Exploring the link between reading fiction and empathy: Ruling out individual differences and examining outcomes. *Communications, 34*(4), 407–428.

Mares, M. L., Stephenson, L., Martins, N., & Nathanson, A. I. (2018). A house divided: Parental disparity and conflict over media rules predict children's outcomes. *Computers in Human Behavior, 81*, 177–188.

Marks, G., McMillan, J., & Hillman, K. (2001). *Tertiary entrance performance: The role of student background and school factors.* Camberwell: Australian Council for Educational Research.

Martin, T. (2003). Minimum and maximum entitlements: Literature at key stage 2. *Literacy, 37*(1), 14–17.

Martino, W. (2001). Boys and reading: Investigating the impact of masculinities on boys' reading preferences and involvement in literacy. *Australian Journal of Language and Literacy, 24*(1), 61–74.

Martino, W., & Kehler, M. (2007). Gender-based literacy reform: A question of challenging or recuperating gender binaries. *Canadian Journal of Education/Revue Canadienne de l'éducation, 30*(2), 406–431.

Martino, W., & Rezai-Rashti, G. (2013). "Gap talk" and the global rescaling of educational accountability in Canada. *Journal of Education Policy, 28*(5), 589–611.

Masters, G., & Forster, M. (1997). *Mapping literacy achievement: Results of the 1996 National School English Literacy Survey.* Camberwell, Australia: Department of Employment, Education, Training and Youth Affairs.

Mat Roni, S. & Merga, M.K. (2017). The influence of device access and gender on children's reading frequency. *Public Library Quarterly*. Retrieved from http://www.tandfonline.com/eprint/XABHBfp5Wb2hkJH99DdS/full

Mayher, J. S. (2012). English teacher education as literacy teacher education. *English Education, 44*, 180–187.

Maynard, S., Mackay, S., & Smyth, F. (2008). A survey of young people's reading in England: Borrowing and choosing books. *Journal of Librarianship and Information Science, 40*, 239–253.

McCormick, S. (1977). Should you read aloud to your children? *Language Arts, 54*(2), 139–163.

McCracken, R. A. (1971). Initiating sustained silent reading. *Journal of Reading, 14*(8), 521–583.

McGill-Franzen, A., Ward, N., & Cahill, M. (2016). Summers: Some are reading, some are not! It matters, *The Reading Teacher, 69*(6), 585–596.

McIntosh, S., & Vignoles, A. (2001). Measuring and assessing the impact of basic skills on labour market outcomes. *Oxford Economic Papers, 53*(3), 453–481.

McKool, S. (2007). *Factors that influence the decision to read: An investigation of fifth grade students' out-of-school reading habits.* Paper presented at the 3rd Annual National Reading Conference, Scottsdale, AZ.

McKool, S., & Gespass, S. (2009). Does Johnny's reading teacher love to read? How teachers' personal reading habits affect instructional practices. *Literacy Research and Instruction, 48,* 264–276.

McQuillan, J., & Au, J. (2001). The effect of print access on reading frequency. *Reading Psychology, 22*(3), 225–248.

Merga, M. K. (2013). Should silent reading feature in a secondary school English programme? West Australian students' perspectives on silent reading. *English in Education, 47*(3), 229–244.

Merga, M. K. (2014a). Exploring the role of parents in supporting recreational book reading beyond primary school. *English in Education, 48*(2), 149–163.

Merga, M. K. (2014b). Western Australian adolescents' reasons for infrequent engagement in recreational book reading. *Literacy Learning: The Middle Years, 22*(2), 60–66.

Merga, M. K. (2014c). Are Western Australian adolescents keen book readers? *Australian Journal of Language and Literacy, 37*(3), 161–170.

Merga, M. K. (2014d). Are teenagers really keen digital readers? Adolescent engagement in eBook reading and the relevance of paper books today. *English in Australia, 49*(1), 27–37.

Merga, M. K. (2014e). Peer group and friend influences on the social acceptability of adolescent book reading. *Journal of Adolescent and Adult Literacy, 57*(6), 472–482.

Merga, M. K. (2015a). Access to books in the home and adolescent engagement in recreational book reading: Considerations for secondary school educators. *English in Education, 49*(3), 197–214.

Merga, M. K. (2015b). "Bring your own device": Considering potential risks to student health. *Health Education Journal, 75*(4), 464–473.

Merga, M. K. (2015c). Are avid adolescent readers social networking about books? *New Review of Children's Literature and Librarianship, 21*(1), 1–16.

Merga, M. K. (2015d). "She knows what I like": Student-generated best-practice statements for encouraging recreational reading in adolescents. *Australian Journal of Education, 59*(1), 35–50.

Merga, M. K. (2015e). Do adolescents prefer electronic books to paper books? *Publications, 3,* 237–247.

Merga, M. K. (2015f). Supporting recreational book reading in adolescents. *The International Journal of the Book, 14*(1), 1–14.

Merga, M. K. (2016a). What would make them read more? Insights from Western Australian adolescent readers. *Asia Pacific Journal of Education, 36*(3), 409–424.

Merga, M. K. (2016b). "I don't know if she likes reading": Are teachers perceived to be keen readers, and how is this determined? *English in Education, 50*(3), 255–269.

Merga, M. K. (2017a). Interactive reading opportunities beyond the early years: What educators need to consider. *Australian Journal of Education, 61*(3), 328–343.

Merga, M. K. (2017b). What motivates avid readers to maintain a regular reading habit in adulthood? *Australian Journal of Language and Literacy, 40*(2), 146–156.

Merga, M. K. (2017c). What would make children read for pleasure more frequently? *English in Education, 51*(2), 207–223.

Merga, M. K. (2017d). Meeting the needs of avid book readers: Access, space, concentration support and barrier mitigation. *Journal of Library Administration, 57*(1), 49–68.

Merga, M. K. (2017e). Do males really prefer non-fiction, and why does it matter? *English in Australia, 52*(1), 27–37.

Merga, M. K. (2017f). Becoming a reader: Significant social influences on avid book readers. *School Library Research, 20*, 1–21. Retrieved from http://www.ala .org/aasl/sites/ala.org.aasl/files/content/aaslpubsandjournals/slr/vol20/SLR _BecomingaReader_V20.pdf

Merga, M. K. (2018). Silent reading and discussion of self-selected books in the contemporary classroom. *English in Australia, 53*(1), 70–82.

Merga, M. K., & Gardiner, V. (under review). The role of whole school literacy policies supporting reading engagement in Australian schools.

Merga, M. K., Gardner, P., Mat Roni, S., & Ledger, S. (2018). Five tips to help you make the most of reading to your children, *The Conversation*. Retrieved from https://theconversation.com/five-tips-to-help-you-make-the-most-of -reading-to-your-children-93659

Merga, M. K., & Ledger, S. (in press). Parents' views on reading aloud to their children: Beyond the early years. *Australian Journal of Language and Literacy*.

Merga, M. K., & Ledger, S. (2018). Teachers' attitudes toward and frequency of engagement in reading aloud in the primary classroom. *Literacy*. Retrieved from https://onlinelibrary.wiley.com/doi/full/10.1111/lit.12162

Merga, M. K., & Mat Roni, S. (2017a). The influence of access to eReaders, computers and mobile phones on children's book reading frequency. *Computers & Education, 109*, 187–196.

Merga, M.K., & Mat Roni, S. (2017b). Choosing strategies of children and the impact of age and gender on library use: Insights for librarians. *Journal of Library Administration, 57*, 607–630.

Merga, M. K., & Mat Roni, S. (2017c). Children prefer to read books on paper rather than screens. *The Conversation*. Retrieved from https://theconversation.com /children-prefer-to-read-books-on-paper-rather-than-screens-74171

Merga, M. K., & Mat Roni, S. (2018a). Characteristics, preferences and motivation of avid non-fiction readers. *Collection and Curation, 37*(2), 50–59.

Merga, M. K., & Mat Roni, S. (2018b). Empowering parents to encourage children to read beyond the early years. *The Reading Teacher*, Retrieved from https:// ila.onlinelibrary.wiley.com/doi/pdf/10.1002/trtr.1703

Merga, M. K., & Mat Roni, S. (2018c). Children's perceptions of the importance and value of reading. *Australian Journal of Education, 62*(2). Retrieved from https://doi.org/10.1177/0004944118779615

Merga, M. K., & Mat Roni, S. (in press). Parents as social influences encouraging book reading: Research directions for librarians' literacy advocacy. *Journal of Library Administration, 58*(7).

Merga, M. K., McRae, M., & Rutherford, L. (2017). Adolescents' attitudes toward talking about books: Implications for educators. *English in Education, 52*(1), 36–53.

Merga, M. K., & Moon, B. (2016). The impact of social influences on high school students' recreational reading. *The High School Journal, 99*(2), 122–140.

Merga, M. K., & Williams, R. (2016). The role of health educators in mitigating health risk from increasing screen time in schools and at home. *Asia-Pacific Journal of Health, Sport and Physical Education, 7*(2), 157–172.

Moje, E. B., Young, J. P., Readence, J. E., & Moore, D. W. (2000). Reinventing adolescent literacy for new times: Perennial and millennial issues. *Journal of Adolescent and Adult Literacy, 43*(5), 400–410.

Mokhtar, I. A., & Majid, S. (2006). An exploratory study of the collaborative relationship between teachers and librarians in Singapore primary and secondary schools. *Library and Information Science Research, 28*(2), 265–280.

Mol, S. E., & Bus, A. G. (2011). To read or not to read: A meta-analysis of print exposure from infancy to early adulthood. *Psychological Bulletin, 137*(2), 267.

Mol, S. E., & Neuman, S. B. (2014). Sharing information books with kindergartners: The role of parents' extra-textual talk and socioeconomic status. *Early Childhood Research Quarterly, 29*(4), 399–410.

Monaghan, J., & Hamman, B. (1998). Reading as social practice and cultural construction. *Indiana Journal of Hispanic Literatures, 13*, 131–140.

Montiel-Overall, P. (2005). A theoretical understanding of teacher and librarian collaboration (TLC). *School Libraries Worldwide, 11*(2), 24–48.

Montiel-Overall, P. (2008). Teacher and librarian collaboration: A qualitative study. *Library & Information Science Research, 30*(2), 145–155.

Montiel-Overall, P., & Hernández, A. C. (2012). The effect of professional development on teacher and librarian collaboration: Preliminary findings using a revised instrument, TLC-III. *School Library Research, 15*, 1–25.

Moore, D. W., Bean, T. W., Birdyshaw, D., & Rycik, J.A. (1999). Adolescent literacy: A position statement. *Journal of Adolescent and Adult Literacy, 43*(1), 97–112.

Moreillon, J. (2014). Preparing stakeholders for the School Librarian's instructional partnership role: Whose responsibility is it? In K. Kennedy & L. S. Green (Eds.), *Collaborative models for librarian and teacher partnerships* (pp. 67–81). Hershey, PA: Information Science Reference.

Morgan, A., Nutbrown, C., & Hannon, P. (2009). Fathers' involvement in young children's literacy development: Implications for family literacy programmes. *British Educational Research Journal, 35*(2), 167–185.

Morris, N., & Kaplan, I. (1994). Middle school parents are good partners for reading. *Journal of Adolescent & Adult Literacy, 38*(2), 130–131.

Morrow, L. M. (1982). Relationships between literature programs, library corner designs, and children's use of literature. *The Journal of Educational Research, 75*(6), 339–344.

Mullan, K. (2010). Families that read: A time-diary analysis of young people's and parents' reading. *Journal of Research in Reading, 33*(4): 414–430.

Murphy, P. K., Wilkinson, I. A., Soter, A. O., Hennessey, M. N., & Alexander, J. F. (2009). Examining the effects of classroom discussion on students' comprehension of text: A meta-analysis. *Journal of Educational Psychology, 101*(3), 740–764.

Nagy, W. E., Herman, P. A., & Anderson, R. C. (1985). Learning words from context. *Reading Research Quarterly, 20*(2), 233–253.

Nathanson, S., Pruslow, J., & Levitt, R. (2008). The reading habits and literacy attitudes of inservice and prospective teachers. *Journal of Teacher Education, 59*(4), 313–321.

Nation, K., & Snowling, M. J. (2004). Beyond phonological skills: Broader language skills contribute to the development of reading. *Journal of Research in Reading, 27*(4), 342–356.

National Assessment of Educational Progress (NAEP). (2016). What does the NAEP reading assessment measure? Retrieved from https://nces.ed.gov/nationsreportcard/reading/whatmeasure.aspx

National Endowment for the Arts (NEA). (2007). *To read or not to read: A question of national consequence.* Washington, DC: NEA.

National Reading Panel (NRP). (2000). *Report of the National Reading Panel.* Rockville, MD: NRP.

Neff, L. (2015). *The relationship between reading enjoyment, gender, socioeconomic status, and reading outcomes in PISA 2009.* (Dissertation for doctor of education). Retrieved from http://digitalcommons.georgefox.edu/edd/54 (Paper 54).

Neugebauer, M., Helbig, M., & Landmann, A. (2011). Unmasking the myth of the same-sex teacher advantage. *European Sociological Review, 27*(5), 669–689. Retrieved from http://esr.oxfordjournals.org/content/27/5/669.full.pdf+html

Neuman, S. B., & Knapczyk, J. J. (2018). Reaching families where they are: Examining an innovative book distribution program. *Urban Education.* Retrieved from http://journals.sagepub.com/eprint/hWhkIUpHuzUc5DTCcSj7/full

Neuman, S. B., & Moland, N. (2016). Book deserts: The consequences of income segregation on children's access to print. *Urban Education.* Retrieved from http://journals.sagepub.com/doi/abs/10.1177/0042085916654525

The New London Group. (1996). A pedagogy of multiliteracies: Designing social futures. *Harvard Educational Review, 66*(1), 60–93.

Nichols, S. (2002). Parents' construction of their children as gendered, literate subjects: A critical discourse analysis. *Journal of Early Childhood Literacy, 2*(2), 123–144.

Nieuwenhuizen, A. (2001). *Young Australians reading: From keen to reluctant readers.* Melbourne: Australian Centre for Youth Literature.

Nystrand, M. (2006). Research on the role of classroom discourse as it affects reading comprehension. *Research in the Teaching of English, 40*(4), 392–412.

Office for Standards in Education, Children's Services and Skills (Ofsted). (2012). *Moving English forward.* Manchester, UK: Ofsted.

Olle, S. (2016, October 3). Luke Beveridge has revealed how a children's book inspired his charges ahead of the 2016 season. *Fox Sports.* Retrieved from https://www.foxsports.com.au/afl/luke-beveridge-has-revealed-how-a-childrens-book-inspired-his-charges-ahead-of-the-2016-season/news-story/51fda152171dd0eb768d189ce787b531

Ophir, E. O., Nass, C., & Wagner, A. (2009). Cognitive control in media-multitaskers. *PNAS, 106,* 15583–15587.

Organisation for Economic Co-operation and Development (OECD). (2010). *PISA 2009 results: Executive summary.* Washington, DC: OECD Publishing.

Organisation for Economic Co-operation and Development (OECD). (2011a). *Are students who enjoy reading better readers?* Washington, DC: OECD Publishing.

Organization for Economic Co-operation and Development (OECD). (2011b). *Education at a glance.* Washington, DC: OECD Publishing.

Organisation for Economic Co-operation and Development (OECD). (2011c). *PISA in focus (Vol.8).* Washington, DC: OECD.

Organisation for Economic Co-operation and Development (OECD) (2011d). *Chart A6.5. What boys and girls read for enjoyment, OECD average.* Washington, DC: OECD Publishing.

Organisation for Economic Co-operation and Development (OECD). (2015a). *Trends shaping education 2015 spotlight 7.* Washington, DC: OECD.

Organisation for Economic Co-operation and Development (OECD). (2015b). *Students, computers and learning: Making the connection, PISA: Country note Australia.* Washington, DC: OECD.

Organisation for Economic Co-operation and Development (OECD). (2017). *PISA 2015 results (Volume III): Students' well-being.* Washington, DC: OECD Publishing.

Organisation for Economic Co-operation and Development (OECD) and Statistics Canada. (2000). *Literacy in the Information Age.* Paris: OECD Publishing.

O'Toole, L. (1982). Now read the movie. *Film Comment, 18*(6), 34–38.

Panero, M. E., Weisberg, D. S., Black, J., Goldstein, T. R., Barnes, J. L., Brownell, H., & Winner, E. (2017). No support for the claim that literary fiction uniquely and immediately improves theory of mind: A reply to Kidd and Castano's commentary on Panero et al. (2016). *Journal of Personality and Social Psychology, 113*(3), e5–e8.

Parsons, A. W., Parsons, S. A., Malloy, J. A., Marinak, B. A., Reutzel, D. R., Applegate, M. D., . . . & Gambrell, L. B. (2018). Upper elementary students' motivation to read fiction and nonfiction. *The Elementary School Journal, 118*(3), 505–523.

Partin, K., & Gillespie, C. (2002). The relationship between positive adolescent attitudes toward reading and home literary environment. *Reading Horizons, 43*(1), 61–84.

Penno, J. F., Wilkinson, I. A., & Moore, D. W. (2002). Vocabulary acquisition from teacher explanation and repeated listening to stories: Do they overcome the Matthew effect? *Journal of Educational Psychology, 94*(1), 23–33.

Perelman, L. (2018). *Towards a new NAPLAN: Testing to the teaching.* Retrieved from http://apo.org.au/system/files/139796/apo-nid139796-698251.pdf

Petri, A. (2017, March 16). Trump's budget makes perfect sense and will fix America, and I will tell you why. *The Washington Post.* Retrieved from https://www.washingtonpost.com/blogs/compost/wp/2017/03/16/trumps-budget-makes-perfect-sense-and-will-fix-america-and-i-will-tell-you-why/?utm_term=.4337773ec7d4

Petscher, Y. (2010). A meta-analysis of the relationship between student attitudes towards reading and achievement in reading. *Journal of Research in Reading, 33*(4), 335–355.

Pfost, M., Dörfler, T., & Artelt, C. (2013). Students' extracurricular reading behavior and the development of vocabulary and reading comprehension. *Learning and Individual Differences, 26*, 89–102.

Philippa McLean Consulting. (2012). *Australian Core Skills Framework (ACSF)*. Retrieved from https://docs.education.gov.au/system/files/doc/other/acsf_document.pdf

Phillips, G., & Paatsch, L. (2011). The invisible librarian: Why doesn't literacy mention libraries? *Practically Primary, 16*(3), 31–34.

Pihl, J., Carlsten, T. C., & van der Kooij, K. S. (2017). Why teacher and librarian partnerships in literacy education in the 21st century? In *Teacher and Librarian Partnerships in Literacy Education in the 21st Century* (pp. 1–22). Rotterdam: Sense Publishers.

Pitcher, S. M., Albright, L. K., DeLaney, C. J., Walker, N. T., Seunarinesingh, K., Mogge, S., . . . & Dunston, P. J. (2007). Assessing adolescents' motivation to read. *Journal of Adolescent & Adult Literacy, 50*(5), 378–396.

Polesel, J., Dulfer, N., & Turnbull, M. (2012). *The experience of education: The impacts of high stakes testing on school students and their families: Literature review*. Sydney, Australia: Whitlam Institute.

Polkinghorne, D. E. (2005). Language and meaning: Data collection in qualitative research. *Journal of Counseling Psychology, 52*(2), 137–145.

Raphael, T. E., & McMahon, S. I. (1994). Book club: An alternative framework for reading instruction. *The Reading Teacher, 48*(2), 102–116.

Raynaudo, G., & Peralta, O. (2018). Children learning a concept with a book and an e-book: A comparison with matched instruction. *European Journal of Psychology of Education*, 1–13.

Revelle, G., & Bowman, J. (2017, June). Parent–child dialogue with eBooks. In *Proceedings of the 2017 Conference on Interaction Design and Children* (pp. 346–351). Stanford, CA: Association for Computing Machinery.

Rideout, V., Foehr, U., & Roberts, D. (2010). *Generation M2: Media in the lives of 8- to 18-year-olds*. Menlo Park, CA: Henry J. Kaiser Family Foundation.

Rinehart, S., Gerlach, J., Wisell, D., & Welker, W. (1998). Would I like to read this book? Eighth graders' use of book cover clues to help choose recreational reading. *Reading Research and Instruction, 37*(4), 263–279.

Ross, C. S. (2009). Reader on top: Public libraries, pleasure reading, and models of reading. *Library Trends, 57*(4), 632–656.

Rutherford, L., Singleton, A., Derr, L. A., & Merga, M. K. (2018). Do digital devices enhance teenagers' recreational reading engagement? Issues for library policy from a recent study in two Australian states. *Public Library Quarterly, 37*(3), 296–305.

Ryan, R. M., & Deci, E. L. (2017). *Self-determination theory*. New York: Guilford Press.

Samuels, S. J., & Wu, Y. (2001). *How the amount of time spent on independent reading affects reading achievement: A response to the National Reading Panel*. Minneapolis: University of Minnesota Press.

Sana, F., Weston, T., & Cepeda, N. J. (2013). Laptop multitasking hinders classroom learning for both users and nearby peers. *Computers & Education*,
62, 24–31.

Sanacore, J. (1992). Reading aloud: A neglected strategy for older students. *View-
points*, 92–106. Retrieved from https://files.eric.ed.gov/fulltext/ED367971
.pdf

Sanacore, J., and Palumbo, A. (2009). Understanding the fourth-grade slump: Our
point of view. *The Educational Forum*, *73*(1), 67–74.

Scharber, C. (2009). Online book clubs: Bridges between old and new literacies
practices. *Journal of Adolescent & Adult Literacy*, *52*(5), 433–437.

Schiefele, U., Schaffner, E., Möller, J., & Wigfield, A. (2012). Dimensions of reading motivation and their relation to reading behavior and competence. *Reading Research Quarterly*, *47*(4), 427–463.

Scholastic. (2010). *2010 kids and family reading report*. Woodland Hills, CA:
Scholastic.

Scholastic. (2015). *Kids and family reading report, 5th edition*. Retrieved from
http://www.scholastic.com/readingreport

Scholastic. (2016a). *Kids and family reading report Australia*. Retrieved from http://
www.scholastic.com.au/readingreport

Scholastic. (2016b). *Kids and family reading report United Kingdom*. Retrieved
from http://www.scholastic.co.uk/readingreport

Scholes, L. (2010). Boys, masculinity and reading: Deconstructing the homogeniz-
ing of boys in primary school literacy classrooms. *International Journal of
Learning*, *17*(6), 437–450.

Scholes, L. (2015). Clandestine readers: Boys and girls going "undercover"
in school spaces. *British Journal of Sociology of Education*, *36*(3),
359–374.

School Curriculum and Standards Authority. (2015). Online Literacy and Numeracy Assessment. Retrieved from https://www.scsa.wa.edu.au/publications
/circulars/kto10-circulars/archive/2015/k-to-10-circular-edition-1-2015

Scieszka, J. (n.d.). Guys and reading. Retrieved from http://www.guysread.com
/about/

Scott, K. J., & Plourde, L. A. (2007). School libraries and increased student achievement: What's the big idea? *Education*, *127*(3), 419–430.

Segal, A., & Martin-Chang, S. (2018). The apple doesn't fall from the tree: Parents' reading-related knowledge and children's reading outcomes. *Reading
and Writing*, 1–17. Retrieved from https://link-springer-com.dbgw.lis.curtin
.edu.au/article/10.1007/s11145-018-9837-6

Shapiro, J. E. (1980). Primary children's attitudes toward reading in male and female
teachers' classrooms: An exploratory study. *Journal of Reading Behavior*,
12(3), 255–257.

Shin, F. H., & Krashen, S. D. (2008). *Summer reading*. Boston: Pearson Education.

Sims, C. (2012). School library circulation records: What do they reveal about boys'
reading preferences? Graduate Research Papers. Paper 24. Retrieved from
http://scholarworks.uni.edu/grp/24

Skelton, C. (2012). Men teachers and the "feminised" primary school: A review of
the literature. *Educational Review*, *64*(1), 1–19.

Small, R. V., Shanahan, K. A., & Stasak, M. (2010). The impact of New York's school libraries on student achievement and motivation: Phase III. *School Library Media Research, 13*, 1–35.

Smith, C. A., & Scuilli, S. (2011). "I can't believe we read this whole book!" How reading for their own purposes affected struggling teens. *English Journal, High School Edition*, 30–36.

Softlink. (2016a). The 2016 Softlink Australian and New Zealand School Library Survey participant summary. Retrieved from www.softlinkint.com/down loads/2016_SLS_Participant_Summary.pdf

Softlink. (2016b). The 2016 Softlink Australian and New Zealand School Library Survey report. Retrieved from https://www.softlinkint.com/downloads /Australian_and_New_Zealand_School_library_survey_report.pdf

Softlink. (2016c). Softlink Australian School Library Survey. A five-year review. Retrieved from https://www.softlinkint.com/downloads/ACCESS_2016 _Softlink_Australian_School_Library_Survey_A_five_year_review.pdf

Sokal, L., & Katz, H. (2008). Effects of technology and male teachers on boys' reading. *Australian Journal of Education, 52*(1), 81–94.

Sokal, L., Katz, H., Chaszewski, L., & Wojcik, C. (2007). Good-bye, Mr. Chips: Male teacher shortages and boys' reading achievement. *Sex roles, 56*(9–10), 651–659.

Spaull, N. (2017). Who makes it into PISA? Understanding the impact of PISA sample eligibility using Turkey as a case study (PISA 2003–PISA 2012). OECD Education Working Papers, No. 154. Paris: OECD Publishing.

Spear-Swerling, L., Brucker, P. O., & Alfano, M. P. (2010). Relationships between sixth-graders' reading comprehension and two different measures of print exposure. *Reading and Writing, 23*(1), 73–96.

Spichtig, A. N., Hiebert, E. H., Vorstius, C., Pascoe, J. P., David Pearson, P., & Radach, R. (2016). The decline of comprehension-based silent reading efficiency in the United States: A comparison of current data with performance in 1960. *Reading Research Quarterly, 51*(2), 239–259.

Spichtig, A., Pascoe, J., Ferrara, J., & Vorstius, C. (2017). A comparison of eye movement measures across reading efficiency quartile groups in elementary, middle, and high school students in the US. *Journal of Eye Movement Research, 10*(4), 5–17.

Standards and Testing Agency. (2018). Information for parents: 2018 national curriculum tests at the end of key stages 1 and 2. Retrieved from https://assets .publishing.service.gov.uk/government/uploads/system/uploads /attachment_data/file/694765/Information_for_parents_-_2018_national _curriculum_tests_at_the_end_of_key_stages_1_and_2.pdf

Stanovich, K. E. (1986). Matthew effects in reading: Some consequences of individual differences in the acquisition of literacy. *Reading Research Quarterly, 21*(4), 360–407.

Stanovich, K. E., West, R. F., Cunningham, A. E., Cipielewski, J., & Siddiqui, S. (1996). The role of inadequate print exposure as a determinate of reading comprehension problems. In C. Cornoldi & J. Oakhill (Eds.), *Reading comprehension difficulties: Processes and intervention* (pp. 15–32). Mahwah, NJ: Lawrence Erlbaum.

Steinberg, L. (2001). We know some things: Parent–adolescent relationships in retrospect and prospect. *Journal of Research on Adolescence, 11*(1), 1–19.

Strommen, L. T., & Mates, B. F. (2004). Learning to love reading: Interviews with older children and teens. *Journal of Adolescent & Adult Literacy, 48*(3), 188–200.

Sullivan, A., & Brown, M. (2013). *Social inequalities in cognitive scores at age 16: The role of reading.* London: Centre for Longitudinal Studies.

Swanson, E., Vaughn, S., Wanzek, J., Petscher, Y., Heckert, J., Cavanaugh, C., Kraft, G., & Tackett, K. (2011). A synthesis of read-aloud interventions on early reading outcomes among preschool through third graders at risk for reading difficulties. *Journal of Learning Disabilities, 44*(3), 258–275.

Taipale, S. (2014). The affordances of reading/writing on paper and digitally in Finland. *Telematics and Informatics, 31*(4), 532–542.

Tamura, N., Castles, A., & Nation, K. (2017). Orthographic learning, fast and slow: Lexical competition effects reveal the time course of word learning in developing readers. *Cognition, 163*, 93–102.

Taylor, B. M., Frye, B. J., & Maruyama, G. M. (1990). Time spent reading and reading growth. *American Educational Research Journal, 27*(2), 351–362.

Thomas, L. (2009). New challenges in school-based research. *Health Promotion Journal of Australia, 20*(1), 73–74.

Thompson, P. (2013). The digital natives as learners: Technology use patterns and approaches to learning. *Computers & Education, 65*, 12–33.

Thomson, S., De Bortoli, L., Nicholas, M., Hillman, K., & Buckley, S. (2011). *Challenges for Australian education: Results from PISA 2009.* Camberwell: Australian Council for Educational Research.

Tijms, J., Stoop, M. A., & Polleck, J. N. (2017). Bibliotherapeutic book club intervention to promote reading skills and social-emotional competencies in low SES community-based high schools: A randomised controlled trial. *Journal of Research in Reading.* Retrieved from http://onlinelibrary.wiley.com/doi/10.1111/1467-9817.12123/full

Torres, R., Johnson, V., & Imhonde, B. (2014). The impact of content type and availability on ebook reader adoption. *Journal of Computer Information Systems, 54*(4), 42–51.

Twenge, J. M., Martin, G. N., & Campbell, W. K. (2018). Decreases in psychological well-being among American adolescents after 2012 and links to screen time during the rise of smartphone technology. *Emotion.* E-pub ahead of print. Retrieved from https://pdfs.semanticscholar.org/8a74/241e6329e14b2 2f9586dec9261079cdc52cf.pdf

Uncapher, M. R., Lin, L., Rosen, L. D., Kirkorian, H. L., Baron, N. S., Bailey, K., . . . & Wagner, A. D. (2017). Media multitasking and cognitive, psychological, neural, and learning differences. *Pediatrics, 140*(Supplement 2), S62–S66.

Van den Bulck, J. (2003). Text messaging as a cause of sleep interruption in adolescents, evidence from a cross-sectional study. *Journal of Sleep Research, 12*(3), 263–263.

Vansteelandt, I., Mol, S. E., Caelen, D., Landuyt, I., & Mommaerts, M. (2017). Attitude profiles explain differences in pre-service teachers' reading behavior and competence beliefs. *Learning and Individual Differences, 54*, 109–115.

Varuzza, M., Sinatra, R., Eschenauer, R., & Blake, B. E. (2014). The relationship between English language arts teachers' use of instructional strategies and young adolescents' reading motivation, engagement, and preference. *Journal of Education and Learning, 3*(2), 108–119.

Vemuri, P., Lesnick, T. G., Przybelski, S. A., Machulda, M., Knopman, D. S., Mielke, M. M. & Jack, C. R. (2014). Association of lifetime intellectual enrichment with cognitive decline in the older population. *JAMA Neurology, 71*(8), 1017–1024.

Vemuri, P., & Mormino, E.C. (2013). Cognitively stimulating activities to keep dementia at bay. *Neurology, 81*(4), 308–309.

Verdaasdonk, D. (1991). Feature films based on literary works: Are they incentives to reading? On the lack of interference between seeing films and reading books. *Poetics, 20*, 405–420.

Verghese, J., Lipton, R. B., Katz, M. J., Hall, C. B., Derby, C. A., Kuslansky, G., & Buschke, H. (2003). Leisure activities and the risk of dementia in the elderly. *New England Journal of Medicine, 348*(25), 2508–2516.

Wagner, T. M., Benlian, A., & Hess, T. (2012). The role of product involvement in digital and physical reading: A comparative study of customer reviews of eBooks vs. printed books. *ECIS*, Paper 57. Retrieved from https://www.researchgate.net/publication/254404562_The_Role_of_Product_Involvement_in_Digital_and_Physical_Reading_-_A_comparative_Study_of_Customer_Reviews_of_eBooks_vs_Printed_Books

Walberg, H. J., & Tsai, S. L. (1984). Reading achievement and diminishing returns to time. *Journal of Educational Psychology, 76*(3), 442–451.

Wamba, N. G. (2010). Poverty and literacy: An introduction. *Reading & Writing Quarterly, 26*(3), 189–194.

Ward, A. F., Duke, K., Gneezy, A., & Bos, M. W. (2017). Brain drain: The mere presence of one's own smartphone reduces available cognitive capacity. *Journal of the Association for Consumer Research, 2*(2), 140–154.

Wasiuta, E. R. (2011). *A line in the sand: A fourth-grade teacher counters high-stakes testing by using read-alouds as the fulcrum around which students' perceptions of reading and writing are formed.* (Doctoral dissertation, Texas Tech University). Retrieved from Texas Tech Digital Library, https://ttu-ir.tdl.org/ttu-ir/handle/2346/45403

Watts, Z., & Gardner, P. (2013). Is systematic synthetic phonics enough? Examining the benefit of intensive teaching of high frequency words (HFW) in a year one class. *Education 3–13, 41*(1), 100–109.

Weinstein, A. M. (2010). Computer and video game addiction—A comparison between game users and non-game users. *The American Journal of Drug and Alcohol Abuse, 36*(5), 268–276.

Weldon, P. R. (2016). *Out of field teaching in Australian secondary schools.* Camberwell: Australian Council for Educational Research.

Wesseling, P. B. C., Christmann, C. A., & Lachmann, T. (2017). Shared book reading promotes not only language development, but also grapheme awareness in German kindergarten children. *Frontiers in Psychology, 8*, 1–13.

Westbrook, J., Sutherland, J., Oakhill, J., & Sullivan, S. (2018). "Just reading": The impact of a faster pace of reading narratives on the comprehension of poorer adolescent readers in English classrooms. *Literacy.* Retrieved from https://onlinelibrary.wiley.com/doi/full/10.1111/lit.12141

Wiessner, P. W. (2014). Embers of society: Firelight talk among the Ju/'hoansi Bushmen. *Proceedings of the National Academy of Sciences, 111*(39), 14027–14035.

Wigfield, A. (1997). Reading motivation: A domain-specific approach to motivation. *Educational Psychologist, 32*(2), 59–68.

Wigfield, A., & Eccles, J. S. (2000). Expectancy–value theory of achievement motivation. *Contemporary Educational Psychology, 25*(1), 68–81.

Wigfield, A., & Guthrie, J. T. (1997). Relations of children's motivation for reading to the amount and breadth of their reading. *Journal of Educational Psychology, 89*(3), 420–432.

Williams, L. M. (2008). Book selections of economically disadvantaged black elementary students. *The Journal of Educational Research, 102*(1), 51–64.

Wilson, R. S., Boyle, P. A., Yu, L., Barnes, L. L., Schneider, J. A., & Bennett, D. A. (2013). Life-span cognitive activity, neuropathologic burden, and cognitive aging. *Neurology, 81*(4), 314–321.

Wilson, R. S., De Leon, C. F. M., Barnes, L. L., Schneider, J. A., Bienias, J. L., Evans, D. A. & Bennett, D. A. (2002). Participation in cognitively stimulating activities and risk of incident Alzheimer disease. *Journal of the American Medical Association, 287*(6), 742–748.

Wollscheid, S. (2013). Parents' cultural resources, gender and young people's reading habits—Findings from a secondary analysis with time-survey data in two-parent families. *International Journal about Parents in Education, 7*(1), 69–83.

Worthy, J. (1996). Removing barriers to voluntary reading for reluctant readers: The role of school and classroom libraries. *Language Arts, 73*(7), 483–492.

Worthy, J., Moorman, M., & Turner, M. (1999). What Johnny likes to read is hard to find in school. *Reading Research Quarterly, 34*(1), 12–27.

Xie, Q. W., Chan, C. H., Ji, Q., & Chan, C. L. (2018). Psychosocial effects of parent–child book reading interventions: A meta-analysis. *Pediatrics, 141*(4), e20172675.

Zebroff, D., & Kaufman, D. (2016). Texting, reading, and other daily habits associated with adolescents' literacy levels. *Education and Information Technologies, 22*(5), 2197–2216. Retrieved from http://link.springer.com/article/10.1007/s10639-016-9544-3

Zhang, Y., Tardif, T., Shu, H., Li, H., Liu, H., McBride-Chang, C., . . . & Zhang, Z. (2013). Phonological skills and vocabulary knowledge mediate socioeconomic status effects in predicting reading outcomes for Chinese children. *Developmental Psychology, 49*(4), 665–672.

Index

An italicized *f* following a page number indicates a figure. An italicized *t* indicates a table.

Gillespie, C., 67
The Girl with All the Gifts (Carey), 103
Goodreads, 37, 85, 89, 117
graduating high school students, reading proficiency of, 5
graduation rates, 126
grapheme awareness, 69
Griffith, Andy, 53
Guthrie, J. T., 107

habit relationship to reading motivation, 17
Harrison, C., 84
Harry Potter (fictional character), 42
Harry Potter series: book and movie comparisons, 49; boys reading, 53; enjoyment of, 29; movies, impact of, 42, 47; reading perception changed by, 35–36
Hatchet (Paulsen), 103
health, screen time and, 78, 85
Heathcliff (fictional character), 45
hegemonic masculinity, 55
high school, 61, 110
high school English teachers, 106, 108
high-stakes testing, 9
The Hobbit (book and movie), 45
home culture, 54
home libraries, 67
home literacy environment, 19–20
homework, 7, 49, 50, 93–94, 95
Howard, V., 116
Hunger Games series, 35, 49, 53
hunter-gatherer societies, 14

identity relationship to reading motivation, 17
illiterate children, 134
imagination, 17, 45–46
in-class instruction, 43
independent reading, 30, 71–72, 74, 110, 118
information center, 125
instruction, changes in, 110–111
intellectual pursuits, 17
interactive reading experiences, 69–70, 72–73
interest as book selection guide, 91
International Literacy Association, 56
international literacy testing and benchmarking, 8
Internet, 77, 78, 79, 82
intrinsic motivation, 113

ISABR (International Study of Avid Book Readers), 2015: on adult book lovers, 65; influences on reading attitudes, 17, 18; on libraries, 124; on reading aloud, 69; on reading concentration struggles, 98
issues, strategies for dealing with, 15

Jackson, Peter, 45
James Bond books, 100
Jetnikoff, A., 48

Kachel, D. E., 126
Katniss Everdeen (fictional character), 42
Kiyosaki, Robert, 111
Klauda, S. L., 59
Knapczyk, J. J., 92–93
knowledge relationship to reading motivation, 17
Krashen, S., 113

Lance, K. C., 126
language, listening to, 68–69
language relationship to reading motivation, 17
languages other than English, 20
laptops, multitasking capacity of, 78
learning disabilities, 80
learning hub, library as, 125
learning issues, identification of, 9
Ledger, Susan, 71, 111
librarians, stereotype-busting, 123–124
librarian-teacher collaboration, 20, 125–126
libraries: access to, 93, 119, 123; collections, quality of, 123; environment of, 123–124; reading in, 124, 125; resources at, 122–123, 125–126; visiting, 122
literacy: benefit, 12; community, 122; curricula, consideration in, 15–16; devaluing of, 136; intergenerational transmission of, 64; opportunity and testing, 8–11, 105; whole-school approach to, 2
literacy achievement, 12, 74, 126
literacy advocacy, 87–88, 134, 136
literacy assessments, 7
literacy benefit, 3, 4–7, 67, 111
literacy development, 74, 105
literacy education, 2, 19
literacy improvement, 53
literacy in home, promoting, 19–20

About the Author

Margaret K. Merga, PhD, is a senior lecturer at Edith Cowan University in Western Australia. She is the author of more than 40 peer-reviewed journal articles primarily focusing on literacy and reading engagement. She has conducted six substantial research projects that explore the social influences on reading engagement from the early years to adulthood.